BABASAHEB

ADVANCE PRAISE FOR THE BOOK

'One may be led to believe that everything that could be said about Dr B.R. Ambedkar and everything that he said has been told and written, by him or others close to him or distant enough to gauge him with a keen yet objective eye. Well, one would be wrong. What the translation of this hidden treasure reveals is stunning and at once extraordinary. It is a deeply personal account of the author's relationship with one of the doyens of the twentieth century, a relationship of both the heart and the mind, and it affirms, if at all an affirmation was necessary, that Dr Ambedkar was not part of an army of men but, rather, a one-man army'—Anand Ranganathan, author and scientist

'It is a stark reminder of the kind of erasure that has happened with history in India that so few know of the incredible story of Savita Ambedkar. This book is a timely reminder also that in eulogizing the great men of India's past, we might still be forgetting to underline the role played by definitive women. Nadeem Khan has painstakingly done a meticulous job in bringing Savita Ambedkar's story, the way she wanted to tell it, to us. This book deserves to be on every bookshelf'—Hindol Sengupta, author and journalist

'For more than thirty years, this invaluable primary source on Babasaheb remained accessible only to Marathi readers. This excellent English translation now makes this treasure house available to the rest of the world. I hope the autobiography of Savita Ambedkar will add a new dimension to our understanding of the life and works of Dr B.R. Ambedkar' —K. Seetharama Rao, vice-chancellor, Dr B.R. Ambedkar Open University

'As an intimate, vivid, first-hand account of the last eight years of Ambedkar's life, this is an invaluable primary source, and Nadeem Khan has done us all a great service by translating it into English'—Ramachandra Guha, historian

'Nadeem Khan's translation is simply excellent. *Babasaheb* doesn't read as something that's been translated. It is some of the best translation work I've seen out of India, if not the best. Excellent job!'—Scott R. Stroud, Ambedkar scholar and professor

'We are familiar with the towering intellect of Dr Ambedkar, but this book by his partner, Savita Ambedkar, née Sharada Kabir, offers a fascinating insight into his physical condition and emotional life, especially in his final decade. As the book progresses, the iconic Babasaheb who surrounds us on tall pedestals in public spaces becomes more accessible, intimate and human. A range of emotions are contained here: love, loneliness, dedication, despondency, surrender, sacrifice, prayer, intrigue, bitterness, betrayal and flashes of connubial bliss. These emotions are intertwined with complex questions of caste, religion, society, history and justice. Both Ambedkarites and others will find this book absorbing'—Sugata Srinivasaraju, journalist, columnist and author

'A reviled and dauntingly suspicious person in the Ambedkarite community, Savita Ambedkar is nevertheless a household name. She expected the mantle of Ambedkar's leadership to be handed over to her as the great man's wife. Through this book, Savita inserts her rightful importance in the later life of Ambedkar as a faithful wife who served her great husband with all her might. A very good reminder that the hero of the oppressed was also ailing on account of his work and mental trauma caused by his political work. An intimate account of the lover and partner of a tender and soft-hearted Ambedkar. This book adds a very important perspective to Ambedkar's biography, seen and experienced by his companion. Ambedkar's romanticism and final years are a cue to history. This fine translation will absorb scholars, researchers and lay readers. A warm book'—Suraj Yengde, University of Oxford and Harvard University, and author of *Caste Matters*

'Mai has given an intimate eyewitness account of those critical years with Babasaheb when he was busy transforming the world. Without her, an extremely important segment of Babasaheb's life would have remained unrevealed. Nadeem Khan's wonderful translation of this exceptional book will carry the story of this extraordinary partnership to readers across the world. The translator cannot be thanked enough for this seminal work'—Yashvant Manohar, Ambedkar scholar, Marathi poet and novelist

BABASAHEB

My Life with Dr Ambedkar

SAVITA AMBEDKAR

Translated from the Marathi by NADEEM KHAN

VINTAGE

An imprint of Penguin Random House

VINTAGE

USA | Canada | UK | Ireland | Australia
New Zealand | India | South Africa | China

Vintage is part of the Penguin Random House group of companies
whose addresses can be found at global.penguinrandomhouse.com

Published by Penguin Random House India Pvt. Ltd
4th Floor, Capital Tower 1, MG Road,
Gurugram 122 002, Haryana, India

First published in Vintage by Penguin Random House India 2022

10 9 8 7 6 5 4 3 2 1

ISBN 9780670096695

Typeset in Adobe Garamond Pro by Manipal Technologies Limited, Manipal
Printed at Thomson Press India Ltd, New Delhi

www.penguin.co.in

Contents

Translator's Note

I had been vaguely aware that Dr B. R. Ambedkar's second wife was a physician and she had died around 2005 (she actually died in 2003). Thus, when I found out eighteen years after her passing away that she had left behind an autobiography, I felt almost ashamed at my ignorance about Marathi books. My bruised self-esteem was somewhat salved when I later found that at least half of my friends, otherwise well-informed people, were ignorant even of the existence of Dr Ambedkar's second wife. I received a bigger jolt when I read the publishing details page to find that *Dr Ambedkaranchya Sahavaasaat* was first published in 1990. I still haven't been able to figure out how this Marathi book has been around for thirty-one years without being translated into English! Dr Bhimrao Ambedkar was, after all, among the greatest opinion-makers of the twentieth century and one of the most consequential Indian leaders of his time. Many Indian universities run study programmes on his work as a lifelong opponent of caste discrimination and as one who oversaw, guided and actually sat down and drafted the Constitution; Columbia University in New York, USA, offers a course on his life; the Buddhist peoples of the world recognize him as an important thinker on Buddhism. How, then, could such an intimate source on his life have remained inaccessible to non-Marathi readers in India and abroad across three decades of its existence?

My response to this question was a question I asked myself: Why look a gift horse in the mouth? I found the mobile number of Vijayrao Surwade who was listed on the copyright page as the editor, compiler, researcher and writing assistant of the Marathi book and visited him at his residence in the town of Kalyan. An affable gentleman, Vijayrao lives in a cosy little flat and exudes supreme contentment in being inundated by books overflowing his shelves; with files and documents stacked in plastic shopping bags flooding all the space that lies below: tables, chairs, stools, divan and window ledge. Vijayrao has the reputation of holding the biggest personal collection of photographs, documents, letters, reference works and other memorabilia related to Dr Ambedkar in the entire country, which, by extension, should mean the entire world. Not that I had wanted to doubt it, but a single look at all that lay spread around the flat settled the issue for me.

During this first visit, Vijayrao gave me a brief history of his close relationship with Dr (Mrs) Savita Ambedkar (née Sharada Kabir), fondly addressed by her devotees as Maisaheb. He first met her in 1971 when he was a gawky eighteen-year-old studying at Siddharth College, Bombay, and Mai was the much-maligned widow of one of the greatest men of the century. She had been hounded by her detractors into spending fourteen years in the wilderness since the passing away of her illustrious husband in 1956, and had just returned to Bombay in the hope of reclaiming her rightful place in the hearts and minds of the people to whom she had committed her life. The sincerity, the energy and the utter selflessness with which young Vijayrao threw himself into Mai's service made him in due course the most important crutch for her to lean on. Her autobiography was the direct outcome of the bond that was created between mentor and disciple across almost two decades. Knowing her to be a treasure house of memories and experiences of historical importance, Vijayrao begged, beseeched and badgered her till she relented and agreed to write her autobiography—on the condition that she would only talk and he would do all the writing. This is how the peculiar designation of 'writing assistant' on the copyright page is explained.

Savita Ambedkar could not have found a person better equipped for the job of being her scribe. As an Ambedkar scholar, Vijayrao was not only aware of most of the salient events related to the great man's life and works, he also had racks full of photographs, letters, books, memoirs and other material with which her memory could be jogged.

The structure of the book carries all the telltale signs of this teaming up. It has no chapters but episodical units marking the sittings of the narrator and the scribe. The venerable old lady had the stories and her young acolyte had all the endorsements. The narrative pieces and the props supporting them—photographs, letters, speeches, remembrances—are so intricately intertwined that it actually became a game for me to guess what could have prompted what. Except for occasionally fusing some of the smaller units into a single piece and bringing a few closely related pieces together, I have retained this structure to allow the readers to play this game for themselves.

This manner of presentation also created its problems. Episodes kept popping up that didn't flow with the otherwise chronologically arranged exposition of events. Repetitions of incidents and assertions got to be too frequent for pleasurable reading. That put me in a dilemma as a translator. Ethics demanded that I gave to the reader the exact experience in English that I had gathered in the Marathi original. Also, considering that it was the wife of one of the greatest figures of his time talking, it would become an important reference work in academic and social circles. I thought of scholars who would want to search for meanings in the repetitions. But, on the other hand, they could be quite off-putting for general readers, who would most likely constitute the bulk of the audience for this book. Consultation with experienced authors helped me resolve the issue: I took the cosmetic surgeon's approach to the work and siphoned out as much of the flab as I could without damaging the essentials. The main part of the book is now slimmer by about 14,000 words. Those who are also interested in the flab may want to tap the publisher for the unexpurgated version.

The other problem I had was of the letters and speeches that were originally in English, but had been translated into Marathi for the book. It obviously wouldn't do for me to retranslate them from Marathi to English—at best, it would give the readers only a close paraphrase of the original. A related problem was of the handwritten letters that had been typed out for publication in the book. There was always the probability that the typist had read a word wrong or taken the well-intentioned initiative of correcting what were perceived as errors. That was where Vijayrao's gargantuan collection of Ambedkar-related documents came to my rescue. That was also when I realized that the mayhem of books and documents I had seen all over his residence had a method about it. Whenever I asked for the original of a document, Vijayrao would nod knowingly (or scratch his chin on a rare occasion), pull a plastic bag out of somewhere and fish out a photocopy of the original. It was good too that I checked them against the original documents. There were misreadings as also over-conscientious corrections by the typist. What you will find in this book is the exact reproduction—warts and all.

I have sourced almost every one of the quotations in this English translation to Vijay Surwade's wonderful personal collection. Wherever I have had the opportunity of double-checking them with my limited means, I have made mention of it. For all the others, Surwade's collection may be taken as the source by default.

However, for all of Surwade's resources and all my efforts at scouring through mine, I could not locate the original English versions of Dr Ambedkar's speeches delivered in Sri Lanka, Burma and Nepal that the author would have translated into Marathi for use in her book. The best I could do was to tally them against the descriptions of these events in Dhananjay Keer's celebrated biography *Dr Babasaheb Ambedkar: Life and Mission* and translate them back into English. I have acknowledged this in the Notes.

Now for the use of Sanskrit, Pali and Hindi terms. For a while I tried using the English translation but soon realized that it often didn't catch the nuances of the original. Also, it was depriving the translation of the native resonance that roots any writing to its culture. After researching what other translators have done, I resorted to taking a mixed approach, with the emphasis on using the native word. A glossary has been added to help those readers unfamiliar with these terms.

The fourth edition of *Dr Ambedkaranchya Sahavaasaat*, published in January 2020, carries as Appendix 1 four letters written by Dr Ambedkar to his fiancée Dr Sharada Kabir that were made available years after the first edition had gone to print in 1990. These four letters have been included in this English translation as Appendix 1. Three other letters written by Dr Savita Ambedkar to two of Dr Ambedkar's associates were also discovered later and included in the fourth edition. These three letters have also been included as Appendix 2 in this volume.

Along with the original Preface written by Dr Savita Ambedkar, the second and the fourth edition of 2020 also carry introductions by Vijay Surwade that contain interesting information. Excerpts from these introductions have been pieced together to serve as an epilogue for this English volume.

When the publishers got into their copy-editing, they decided that the author had blandished names in her Marathi book a little too fearlessly. After consulting with me, they have suppressed names at a few places to avoid the probability of having to face defamatory suits. They have, however, agreed to mark such suppressions with an asterisk (*).

The person I want to thank most is obviously Vijay Surwade, although, considering that he is a partner in this enterprise, it may sound like one hand thanking the other. I also thank Sathya Saran, the consulting editor for Penguin Random House India, who has been a personal friend across fifty years, for plodding through this translation and offering useful suggestions. I offer my deep gratitude to Professor Scott Stroud of the University of Texas at Austin, renowned Ambedkar scholar, for going through the document with a fine toothcomb and unearthing errors of many different kinds that I had committed. Two other persons to whom I consider myself deeply indebted are Professors Namdeorao Belsare and Prithvirajsing Rajput. Their mastery of English is great, but their Marathi belongs to an altogether different world from mine. Hour after hour, day after day, they sat comparing my translation with the Marathi original and ferreted out errors that would have caused me all kinds of embarrassment had they gone to print undetected. Thank you, gentlemen.

Foreword

The fact that Bhimrao Ambedkar is absolutely singular as a thinker does not negate the claim that he did not stand alone. He could not have scaled the heights he reached without the assistance of many others. Some of these supporting characters arrived through luck and fortune—K. A. Keluskar meeting a lonely young Bhim during his school days and introducing him to Sayajirao Gaikwad, or the brash young student in New York stumbling into John Dewey's classes as a respite from his heavy schedule of economics courses at Columbia University and initiating his lifelong interest in pragmatist philosophy. There is also the incredible, and often unnoticed, role that Bhimrao's first wife, Ramabai, played in facilitating his extended journeys to the West for his education, and in pushing forward his anti-caste activism back in India. So many individuals played important roles in Bhimrao's life and thought, and each deserves to be preserved and explored in the stories we tell about the anti-caste thinker. This volume tells the part of Babasaheb's story witnessed and affected by Bhimrao's devoted second wife, Savita Ambedkar. 'Maisaheb', as Babasaheb's companion was known, is one of the most important observers of Ambedkar's final years, the period that saw him complete his turn toward Buddhism and his reconstruction of the Buddha's legacy and doctrine. This was the period of increasingly frail health for Bhimrao, but it was also a time when his activities and speeches proselytizing for Buddhism as a social gospel reached their most feverish pitch. Savita's part in this grand tale of Bhimrao's life emerges from her story, a role that history often denied her while Bhimrao himself waged his wars against caste and injustice.

Of course, Savita was not without an agency or initiative of her own. As one reads through these recollections, one sees how active and assertive Savita was in her dealings with Bhimrao as well as in shielding him from many of the individuals who wanted something from Babasaheb. She was, in many ways, his protector and guardian. She thought and fought alongside him. But the traditions of the time kept her from taking a larger role in public affairs, and the habits of our times often leave her stories and contributions unnoticed. As this book reveals, Savita was thinking through Buddhism with her husband right as he was actively speaking for Dalit conversion to Buddhism. I had my own realization of this point standing next to Vijay Surwade on one of my first journeys to India in pursuit of Ambedkar's archives. As we thumbed through dusty journals from the 1950s, we often talked—or more aptly, I often listened raptly to his tales about Babasaheb's life. While looking at the handwritten notes about Buddhism in one slowly disintegrating journal, I pondered aloud about what Ambedkar—*Bhimrao*, I meant—was working through. I noted that the writing style was a bit off, as it lacked Bhimrao's artful extensions of one letter's final stroke merging into the next letter. Perhaps he was rushed, I ruminated. Surwade quickly set me straight, telling me that these notebooks on Buddhism and psychology were written by *Savita*, and not Bhimrao. It then struck me: as original as Bhimrao was, others were also thinking along *with* him or *alongside* him. Savita, the other *Dr* Ambedkar, was a medical professional who was also intensely interested in Buddhism. As Dr Bhimrao Ambedkar was deepening his vision of Buddhism, Dr Savita Ambedkar was also reading and thinking about what Buddhism could mean for society and for the removal of injustice. There was a synergy between the two individuals—

committed to Buddhism and to each other's development as they both were—that most observers often overlook.

Savita's observations and judgements in this book of her time with Bhimrao showcase her intellectual development, as well as her part in Bhimrao's intellectual development. She is thereby revealed as an integral part of the concluding chapters to Ambedkar's story from the late 1940s to his death in 1956. She was with him when they converted in the public ceremony in Nagpur in 1956, and she was there with him as he toured Nepal a few weeks before his death. She arranged earlier tours to international Buddhist conferences. He was never away from her company on travels and appearances in and outside of India. She oversaw Ambedkar's medical care, most likely extending his life and giving him the relief from pain that indirectly allowed us the privilege of contemplating the completed form of *The Buddha and His Dhamma*. Savita, as recounted in this book, also played a part in Bhimrao's deliberate shift from political action to religious advocacy *as* political action. As this wonderful book details, she was also there for the more quotidian parts of Bhimrao's life—including his short-lived (and failed) attempt to learn how to drive a car under her tutelage. Bhimrao largely directed his own life's journey, but—in more ways than one—Savita took charge of some of the driving.

Those interested in the history, biography and thought of Bhimrao Ambedkar are indebted to Savita Ambedkar for putting her experiences of this exciting time in Indian history into print. This book is sure to interest many individuals, all in different ways. Yet for some reason, this book, and Savita Ambedkar herself, have largely been left out of the Ambedkar, Buddhism and anti-caste research pursued in English. Nadeem Khan is to be thanked for taking the initiative to do what was necessary to right this wrong. His translation is incredible in its readability and in optimizing the transmission of Savita's message. Khan has rendered an enormous service to those of us in the West who want to survey all the pieces to the complex puzzle that was Ambedkar's life. As Khan states in his 'Translator's Note', this volume exists largely through the efforts of Vijay Surwade in interviewing Savita, in organizing and editing the materials her narrative provided, and in contextualizing them with archival material of his own. The resulting volume represents an invaluable constellation of details that demonstrate the importance of Savita to Bhimrao's final years, and also reveals her own significance as a thinker and activist. Norms and social pressures prevalent in her day have deprived us of works that Savita might have written in conversation with the texts and struggles we associate with Bhimrao's own efforts. Not much can be done about this past gender-based silencing. But Khan, in collaboration with Surwade, has done the next best thing: the two have made the ideas and ideals evident in Savita's experience and life more available to the world, and this is a great gain.

25 March 2022 Scott R. Stroud
Austin, Texas, USA

Preface

Dr Bhimrao Ambedkar is a magnificent dream of humanity that occurs once in many hundreds of years. It is said that the touch of a philosopher's stone turns iron into gold. That was what happened when I became Mrs Ambedkar—I came into contact with the philosopher's stone named Dr Ambedkar and my life turned into gold. In the latter half of his life, I gave company to this great, epoch-making man like his shadow till the time he passed away. I made body, speech and heart one and served him, worshipped him. My life got permanently bound to this great, epoch-defining man who was the glory of the world. Can a life be more fulfilling than this?

It has rightly been said that behind the success of every great man lies the contribution of his wife. Ramabai in the earlier half and I in the second half stand as evidence of this aphorism.

Being a great man's wife is an ordeal, and this I have learnt from personal experience. Others may not understand the kind of circumstances that a great man's wife has to confront by being told about them. Add to that the fact that our circumstances were so unusually different! I belonged to the so-called *savarna* class, the upper caste, and Dr Ambedkar belonged to the *mahar* community that was counted among the *ati-shudra*, the untouchables, by the Hindu religious institution. Since we came from extremely different strata of society, our social and domestic circumstances were extremely different too. That two persons coming from such different circumstances, growing up in such different environments and working in such different professions should have got married is a hugely surprising event. The reason why we did get married was that we both believed in the religion of equality and our ideal was Mahatma Gautam Buddha who gave to the world the message of peace and non-violence. As Saheb himself wrote to me in one of his letters, 'One soul saw the other soul, both recognized a common identity . . .' This was how our hearts met.

The second issue was the difference in age between the two of us and the third was Dr Ambedkar's ill health and the chronic ailments deeply embedded in him.

But neither our different social backgrounds, nor the difference in age nor again his ill health and his chronic illnesses came in the way of our marriage. The doctor in me was aroused to boundless sympathy, and I accepted Dr Ambedkar's proposal of marriage. When I first met Dr Ambedkar, his health was not good at all. His body had been hollowed out by chronic ailments, such as diabetes, rheumatism and blood pressure, and he was altogether lonely. My heart rose up at the sight of his physical health and his loneliness and filled up with great compassion. The doctor in me came to life and mandated that this man be provided proper medicines and a physician's help. It was this realization that made me instantly accept his proposal of marriage. The responsibility of the country's Constitution lay upon him; therefore, it was imperative that his health and treatment be looked after for the performance of his historical task. Now, when I think back to my acceptance of his proposal, I sincerely feel that I responded positively only because I was a doctor. What response I would have given if I had not been a doctor is impossible for me to say even now. But despite our most unusual circumstances, we accepted each other and treasured each other like something precious.

When Dr Ambedkar made his choice of me, I didn't have the vaguest idea of the kind of circumstances I would have to confront. I was his wife as well as his doctor, making it absolutely necessary for me to take care of his food, medicines, rest and everything else fastidiously. We got married on 15 April 1948, and discipline and sense arrived in Dr Ambedkar's daily routine. The handling of his daily schedule sometimes made it inevitable that some leaders and workers were denied the opportunity of meeting him. It was quite possible that some of them got upset, but I really had no choice except to suffer their resentment. It is unfortunate that these people did not carry sharp enough sensibilities. The Constitution of independent India was altogether the creation of Dr Ambedkar. He worked on it for sixteen to eighteen hours every day at a stretch. He would say, 'I am repaying my debt to the people of this soil.' When I got married to Dr Ambedkar, I had simply one thing in mind—complete surrender; walk every step with him like his shadow for the sake of the work he had undertaken and give him company in every sense of the word. I feel grateful that till his last moment I stayed with him like his shadow with body, mind and soul.

Dr Ambedkar was a pure, personified paragon of public life. We had nothing in our life that we could not lose.

After Dr Ambedkar's passing away, the Dalit leaders of those times did not want any obstructions from the members of the Ambedkar family. Accordingly, they created a rift between Yeshwant and me. They made him the president of the Bauddha Mahasabha and got him busy in touring and proselytization, and systematically spread poison in the Dalit community by conspiring to create suspicions against me related to Dr Ambedkar's death and keeping these suspicions alive. Their machinations are evidence of how low people can stoop to serve their own ends and to gain political power. This was how some self-seekers systematically performed the 'great deed' of creating a rift in the Dalit community and between us, mother and son. This plot was put into place to have me thrown out of the political stream that Dr Ambedkar had intended for me. From the domestic and political perspective, it was a terrible thing to happen because, in my opinion, it brought rack and ruin upon the community. These self-serving Dalit leaders wanted to raise a storm against me so as to separate me from the community. It was for furthering this despicable effort that they raised the demand of getting the cause of Dr Ambedkar's death probed. The government accordingly investigated the matter and on 26 November, the then home minister of India, Pandit Govind Ballabh Pant, declared in the House that Dr Ambedkar had died of natural causes. But the ardour of these leaders who were being driven by political impulses and ambitions of leadership was not to be cooled. It is not difficult to understand why these leaders threw absurd accusations at me so as to have me tossed out of the community: after the passing away of Dr Ambedkar, the entire and universally acceptable leadership of the community would have automatically fallen upon me. Nobody can deny that the negative propaganda let loose by these Dalit leaders destroyed my image among the Dalit people. But by doing so, these people not only humiliated me, but also insulted their great, noble benefactor—Dr Ambedkar.

For the all-round progress of the Dalits, Dr Ambedkar gave his followers the great message—educate. Through his efforts, he got an entire generation educated during his lifetime. But have the educated become educated and knowledgeable in the real sense of the term? Did the followers of Ambedkar understand Dr Ambedkar's definition of education? I have to say with deep regret that my answers are in the negative.

By the word 'educate', Dr Ambedkar had not meant merely the acquisition of degrees, but education in all respects, wisdom and perception included. Dr Ambedkar's community acquired degrees, all right, but they didn't acquire wisdom and perception. How else can one make sense out of this: a bunch of persons, driven by the lust for political power, mislead people about me and nobody either speaks out or investigates the matter with an open mind? If this community that calls itself educated had been educated in the sense in which Ambedkar meant it, this would never have happened. The satisfying thing is that with the passing of time, wise and perceptive researchers as also the followers of Ambedkar are stepping out in large numbers.

'Bury caste discrimination' is the slogan that Dr Ambedkar dinned into the ears of his followers. Dr Ambedkar himself was an active social revolutionary, which was why he married me and gave impetus to national unity. What lesson, however, have these educated people who call themselves Ambedkar's followers learnt from the grand ideal he created by establishing equality through marrying me? The question, therefore, that strikes me is: Have those who call themselves Ambedkarites understood Ambedkar?

I became an MBBS in 1937 from Grant Medical College, Bombay. During those times, forget a Dalit woman, a woman belonging to even the savarna community becoming a doctor was a rarity. The doctor's profession is a sacred, service-oriented one. It is not a business, it is service. The doctor's duty is to bring to the patient freedom from ailments and give the patient the gift of life. The accusation raised against me began from the point of claiming that I was not even a doctor. By wilfully creating doubts about Dr Ambedkar's death, objections and despicable accusations were raised against me. The accusations that were thrown against me do not limit themselves to me, but indirectly reach out against the entire medical profession. Since, therefore, it had become a matter of the integrity of the entire medical world, a number of renowned doctors and my colleagues in the profession suggested that I should file a defamation suit in the court, but I did no such thing.

I have no intention of filing a suit at this later date either, because I do not want to cause a split in the community. Secondly, it does not suit my nature that the name of a great person like Dr Ambedkar should be taken to court on account of the accusations raised by some foolish Dalit leaders. The third thing is that as the wife of a great man, I have a reputation to protect. I have maintained my prestige as an Ambedkar with all my zeal and shall continue to do so with equal fervour. So, why give importance to inconsequential people and why get into confrontations with them?

This autobiography is the baring of my heart. The purpose hasn't merely been to present my side, but it has also been to capture in words the Dr Ambedkar that I got to experience through living with him and the ordeal of walking through fire after he passed away. Actually, the insistent demand for writing this kind of a book has been coming to me from all strata for the previous twenty-five to thirty years, but I had steadily been ignoring it. But it was necessary, even at such a late point of time, to place before society whatever happened and in whatever manner it happened. Therefore, I have recorded the truth and only the truth with complete honesty. I do not need to bother about how it stands in terms of literary merit.

For the writing of this biography, I enjoyed in every possible way the advantage of two eager, loyal, sincere and kind persons. My associate Devchand Ambade (Tathagat Prakashan) helped me enormously in the publishing of this book. His assistance to me was priceless. In the same way, my close colleague Vijay Surwade was the second passion-driven young man to urge me on. As a perspicacious student, Vijay is forever absorbed in researching and gathering artefacts and pictures related to Dr Ambedkar's life. He made available to me Dr Ambedkar's letters, press-cuttings, photographs, reference books and other rare and original material from his own substantial personal collection. Even for preparing handwritten and printed copies, researching and editing them and for searching for printed material, he has worked extremely hard. I received invaluable help from these two gentlemen, without whose help this book would not have been possible. I remain indebted to these two for helping me every time I needed help.

Sharada Printing Press (Ulhasnagar) and Kiran Quality Press (Kalyan) did attractive and clean printing of this book while the artist Shivaji Parulekar imaginatively designed the beautiful cover page in colour. Subhash Pawar (Kalyan) laid out the inner pictures with great creativity. I consider it my duty to acknowledge my gratefulness to them.

I believe that the readers will welcome this book and arrive at their realistic judgement on every episode with sagaciousness.

24 March 1990
Mumbai

Savita Ambedkar

My Role of Yashodhara

When I entered Dr Ambedkar's life, he was suffering from diabetes, neuritis, rheumatism, high blood pressure and several other ailments. Along with that, he had had his first heart attack in 1953. He somehow came out of it, but his health had turned so fragile that walking with support was a far cry, even getting up and sitting had become impossible. But despite this situation, I humbly record that if I had not encouraged him for the religious conversion ceremony at Nagpur, that great historical event would never have happened.

Since we had always been inclined towards Buddhism during our nine years of living together, we had had no time to focus on the other things in the world. He had made no impositions on me. A principle with him was, whatever one does, one should do after careful thinking. That was why we accepted Buddhism.

Didn't Tathagat Gautam Buddha offer his wife Yashodhara the same counsel?

'*Attahi attaano naatho*' [One's refuge is within oneself].

Isn't then my role in Dr Ambedkar's life like that of Yashodhara, in a sense?

The Man I Married

The prime sculptor of the Constitution of free India, the first law minister of the Republic of India, the Booker T. Washington of India, the Bodhisattva who initiated the *dhammachakra* of Buddhism, the great espouser of human freedom, the warrior who fought for the dignity of man, a modern Manu, one among the five greatest intellectuals of the world, eminent savant of law, the liberator of India's destitute, the monarch of the downtrodden, the great humanitarian of the world, the defender of democracy, the skilled parliamentarian and great constitutionalist, a gem in Nehru's council of ministers, a revolutionary messiah, a social reformer, a Bharat Ratna, the pride of the world—the moment any of these glorifying terms comes to mind, there's just one image that flashes in the mind's eye: that of Dr Babasaheb alias Bhimrao Ramji Ambedkar. The moment one recalls Dr Ambedkar's name, one simultaneously recalls the serpentine list of the greatest degrees acquired from international universities of the greatest repute. Within a short span of six years he acquired an MA, PhD, DSc, LlD, DLitt, Bar-at-Law and a host of other degrees in the top grade and established a singular record. Through his deeds and his extreme sacrifices, Dr Ambedkar has given the eulogies above a different dimension.

Dr Ambedkar ploughed in all his learning, all his strength; nay, his entire life for the upliftment of the depressed classes and to bring about equality in this country. No surprise, therefore, that Dr Ambedkar occupies a seat among world leaders of the highest order. The sacred and historical work he has done for the freedom of humankind makes him a jewel worthy of reverence not in India alone, but in the entire world. The religion of Tathagat Gautam Buddha that originated in India spread to all corners of the world, but it had more or less disappeared in the land of the Buddha's birth and scene of action. Dr Ambedkar rejuvenated Buddhism in India and revived the Buddha's philosophy in his motherland. By embracing Buddhism that rests on the three principles of equality, freedom and brotherhood, and by giving the *deeksha*[1] of Buddhism publicly to millions of his followers, Dr Ambedkar became a Bodhisattva[2] himself.

Dr Ambedkar was one of the towering personalities of this century. All through his life he used his voice and his pen to inflict grievous wounds on the caste system mandated by the Manu Smriti.[3] He was the person to awaken a sense of identity and self-respect among the depressed classes of India. Dr Ambedkar's historical work has no match not merely in India but in the history of the world. Equally, Dr Ambedkar's name shall undoubtedly remain coupled to the history of modern India forever.

I have always felt blessed to have had the singular good fortune of becoming the wife of this great man of the epoch, whom millions of people address respectfully and with deep gratitude as Babasaheb. The godsend of being his life-mate made my existence meaningful. I became one with Doctor Saheb's life. I did all that I could within my limits to help him with every one of his activities. I stayed with him like his shadow, gave him medical care for so many of his chronic maladies, fed him his favourite foods, served him with heart and soul, and this has been my greatest privilege and the most glorious aspect of my life. After Dr Ambedkar's acceptance of me, I became the 'maisaheb' of millions of people, I became the recipient of the love and affection of the greatest person of his era. What bigger benefaction could I have asked for than this? It was exclusively because of him that I got to be not merely acquainted with but also became the recipient of the esteem of those great persons.

Dr Ambedkar was one of the greats of the twentieth century and the life of a great person is like the fathomless ocean. What space do I occupy in the life of this boundless ocean called Dr Ambedkar? Whenever this question comes to mind, I think of the bubbles that rise momentarily to the surface of the ocean. I believe that looking at the totality of Dr Ambedkar's life, my place is that of that bubble that appears on the surface of the ocean. Even so, it is my conviction that my proximity to that fathomless ocean gave my life its value and a special meaning. An ocean is, after all, an ocean. It recognizes no confines, and it cannot be compared in any way with anyone. It is destiny alone that grants the privilege of becoming a bubble of this fathomless ocean. I received this privilege, even if for a short time, and that has been my greatest fortune. What tale can one tell of a bubble in the presence of an ocean? That is the reason why I have not delved much into the details and the events marking my life. I have tried to present here, authentically and with sincerity, those golden moments that I was privileged to spend as a bubble on that ocean. But before I shed light on the memories of the loving companionship that I enjoyed with Doctor Saheb, it will be in the fitness of things to talk in passing about the prominent events related to my family background. I have no doubt that it is important not merely from the point of view of history but also for the sake of chronological propriety, to refer to the important events of my life, even if briefly and sketchily, before I first met Dr Ambedkar.

My Family Background

Our family belonged to the *saraswat* Brahmin community and went by the surname of Kabir. Our ancestors were natives of Ratnagiri district. By an amazing coincidence, Dr Ambedkar's ancestors were natives of Ratnagiri too. Both my father and my mother came from the Rajapur taluka of Ratnagiri district. My father's village in the taluka was Dorle. My father had left the Konkan belt years ago and shifted to Pune on account of his job. As a result, our family had more or less lost contact with Konkan. At that time my father was working as a superintendent in the pharmacy section of the health department of the Bombay Province of those times. My father's name was Krishnarao Vinayakrao Kabir, while my mother was Janakibai.

A large number of saraswat families had taken up jobs in Mumbai and settled there. So, although we lived in Pune, many of our relatives had settled in Mumbai. It was natural, therefore, that we visited Mumbai at the drop of a hat. Mumbai was not alien to us; on the contrary, it was our home away from home. We had no close relatives living either in Pune or in Konkan; almost all our relatives had settled in Mumbai. As a result, for all our ailments and for all my mother's confinements, our father found it convenient to take us to Mumbai. All my mother's deliveries, therefore, happened in Mumbai. I was delivered there too. My parents named me Sharada.

School Education

With my father working in Pune, I obviously spent my childhood there; my schooling also happened in this city, regarded as the mother city of education. During that period, we lived in the Rastapeth locality. After I finished my primary education, my father got me admission in the renowned Huzoorbagh School. After I passed my matriculation [SSC] from Huzoorbagh School in the first division, my father got me admission in the science stream at Parshuram College. I passed the first year in the first rank, after which I was admitted to the inter-science course at Fergusson College. In the meanwhile, my father had shifted his household from Rastapeth to Somwarpeth. From the perspective of further studies, the inter-science course is considered to be as important as it is difficult. To ensure that I got all the time I needed without any kind of hindrance, my father got me admission in the women's hostel of the college. The matron of this hostel was a lady called Mrs Kirtane. She was a widow who later married the well-known socialist leader and distinguished thinker Nanasàheb Gore. Since it was a widow-marriage, it became the subject of great curiosity during those times. Before they got married, Nanasàheb Gore would come visiting our matron and the two would set off for a ride, causing great amusement and curiosity among us hostel girls.

I had always been extremely smart and intelligent. I had all the time I needed for my studies, and I utilized it to the hilt by ploughing it all into my studies. The outcome was the expected one: I stood first in all of Fergusson College in the inter-science examination of that year. The question that now began being discussed in my house was whether I should go for a BSc or for medicine.

My Admission in Grant Medical College

I feel very proud as I write that all of us siblings were extremely obedient. It was a custom among us to behave as our parents wanted us to; to never go against their wishes. As soon as my father voiced his desire that I should become a doctor, I happily gave my assent. Accordingly, he got me admission in Grant Medical College in Mumbai. Since my parents lived in Pune, I had to move into the women's hostel of the college. While I was pursuing my medical education, my father retired and shifted the family from Pune to Mumbai and established home in a building called 'Matruchhaaya' on the then Portuguese Church Road [now Rao Bahadur S. K. Bole Marg] in Dadar East.

Although my parents had now begun to live in Mumbai, they told me to continue staying in the hostel, so that I would have sufficient time and solitude to pursue my medical studies. They would, of course, come to meet me with great regularity. They would unfailingly bring with them foodstuffs specially prepared for me. My father took particular care to ensure that I didn't face any kind of difficulty or suffer from any kind of shortage. He took immense care of me. From my side, I too was determined to fulfil my father's desire and studied very hard to become a doctor. If I missed the people at home, I would find a convenient time and go over to Dadar, spend some time with them and come back. Hence, college, hostel and rare visits home were the limits of my existence. It was just I and my studies—no concern with anything or anybody else. I didn't take a whiff of anything else around and I didn't care for it either.

I was driven by one single obsession—I absolutely had to become a doctor. My strategy for studying was that I would write down notes for all the subjects and absorb and memorize the material on the basis of those notes and references. I still have in my collection a number of notebooks in which I had made those notes.

The Mani Bhavan Coincidence

The hostel of Grant Medical College in which I lived was located right in front of Mani Bhavan. Readers, of course, know that whenever Gandhiji was in Mumbai, he lived at Mani Bhavan. Readers are likely to be aware that it was in this Mani Bhavan that the first meeting between the two great men, Gandhi and Ambedkar, took place on 14 August 1931. Well, actually, instead of calling it a meeting, I suspect that it would be more appropriate to call it the first crossing of swords between two great warriors. Quite obviously, I, who lived in the hostel opposite, had not the slightest knowledge of this Gandhi–Ambedkar meet. It was much later, after we were married, that Doctor Saheb would tell me stories of incidents, about the movement and about his own life. As we sat in our bungalow in Delhi, he would often get into the flow and narrate to me the bitter and sweet events that he had experienced. It was during one such flow of conversation that he described to me his first meeting with Gandhiji. This was how it went:

When Dr Ambedkar went with a few of his select associates to meet Gandhiji at Mani Bhavan, Gandhiji, as was his wont, quite ignored Dr Ambedkar. A restlessness began to grow among Dr Ambedkar's associates. The situation was moving towards a point where they feared Dr Ambedkar would leave in a huff. It was ultimately Gandhiji himself who broke that dreary silence and forestalled the development of an ugly scene. A conversation began between the two great men on the caste system prevailing in Hindu society and what the Indian National Congress had been doing to abolish untouchability.

Dr Ambedkar made a point-wise and well-corroborated presentation, but Gandhiji came out in support of the *chatur-varna* [the caste system],[4] triggering a spirited clash between the two on the subject. In an effort to cut Dr Ambedkar down to size, Gandhiji said, 'Doctor, I have been thinking on the subject of untouchability since before you were born. It's I who have woven the subject of eliminating untouchability into the Congress programme with a lot of effort. The question of the abolition of untouchability is closer to my heart and far more important than the Hindu–Muslim question. That's the reason why twenty lakhs of rupees have already been spent on it till date.'

Dr Ambedkar immediately retorted, 'It's true that you've been doing this work since before I was born. There are plenty among us who use this argument of seniority of age. How can I ever deny the fact that you are senior to me in age? It is also true that it is on your insistence that the Congress has approved this programme of eliminating untouchability. But the Congress has done nothing special at all beyond granting a formal approval. You say that the Congress has spent twenty lakh rupees for the untouchables, so I have got to accept it. But I can tell you in no uncertain terms that all your money has gone down the drain. If such a large amount of money had landed in the hands of somebody like me, I would have put it to use with dedication and propriety and would have given a big momentum to progress among the untouchables.'

It was in this meeting that Dr Ambedkar admonished Gandhiji to his face by saying, 'Mr Gandhi, we shall make our own path on the strength of our self-reliance and self-confidence. We have no trust even in a Mahatma like you, therefore we are not going to depend on you. History bears evidence of the fact that Mahatmas are like passing illusions. Their bustle kicks up a lot of dust and smoke, but they cannot raise the level of a society.'

This was how Dr Ambedkar launched a frontal attack on Gandhiji's Mahatmahood. Mani Bhavan stands witness to this historic first meeting between Gandhiji and Ambedkar.

The interesting thing here is that Gandhiji used to think that Dr Ambedkar was a Brahmin. He had arrived at a very convenient understanding that Dr Ambedkar was a highly qualified young Brahmin man who was fighting for the rights of the untouchables. All this history I obviously got to hear from the mouth of Dr Ambedkar himself after we were married.

I Became a Doctor

I began studying very hard from the day I joined Grant Medical College. Clearing every year with high grades, I passed the MBBS finals in 1937. I felt ecstatic at having fulfilled my father's wish. The others in the family and my relatives were thrilled too. The very idea of a woman becoming a doctor was revolutionary for those times, hence my becoming one was a matter of great pride and joy. My name was registered in the Medical Council. My registration number was 2845.

Once I received my degree, discussion began in my house on whether I should practise medicine independently or work in a government hospital. Finally, it was decided unanimously that instead of getting into a job or private practice, I should go for postgraduate studies. My father felt particularly that I should do my MD (Doctor of Medicine). Accordingly, I registered myself for the MD programme and got into my studies.

My Ill Health

I had immersed myself in my studies with new vigour and enthusiasm. I have already mentioned that I was a very bright student, and I had my own style of studying. Accordingly, I had finished my studies with great tenacity and doggedness. I had written my papers in the exams quite well too. There was a gap of a few days between the written exams and the practicals. But as bad luck would have it, I fell seriously ill just before the practical exams and had to remain confined to my bed for a long time. Consequently, I could not take my practical exams and my MD exams remained half-done. The anguish of this misfortune made my health even worse, and I had to remain confined to my bed for many months. My health plummeted alarmingly and made me awfully weak. The doctors treating me advised complete rest.

The illness and the mental anguish hit me so hard that I could not recover fully in spite of all the medicines and the rest. Once the machinery of my body went awry, it never recovered its earlier status. Even after I had recovered from my illness, health complaints continued to haunt me. The outcome was that despite being very keen to do my MD, I could not carry forward my education. Typhoid, dehydration, boils and health issues just came chasing each other, and my physical and mental health both took a serious knock.

An Unexpected Benefit of My Illness

I had become sick and tired of having to stay confined at home for months together. Doing nothing except lying around was boring me to distraction. Time refused to move. It was to fill time with something that I began reading extensively. I got into the rhythm of reading whatever came to hand. To start with, I read whatever I could lay my hands on; there was no particular area in which I was specifically interested. But as I read on, I found my reading slipping into a direction and a discipline. Moving away from stories and novels, I began reading more thought-provoking books. Without my realizing it, my interests had moved to the intellectual, religious, political and biographical kind of books instead of stories and novels. After having studied all religions and all the other books that were available to me, I began comparing ideas and forming my own opinions on them.

At that time I also began getting impressed by the philosophy of the Buddha and started gluttonously consuming whatever books I could get on Buddhism. The Buddha got a firm grip on my mind from those days onwards. Some people are likely to think that my attraction towards Buddhism perhaps began when I started living with Dr Ambedkar, but this is not true. This, however, is certain that Dr Ambedkar's companionship brought about a huge increase in my store of knowledge; I began to form very definite opinions on the Buddha's philosophy; even beyond that, it was only on account of Doctor Saheb that I could publicly embrace Buddhism. I declare with gratitude that it was only on account of Doctor Saheb that the latent attraction that rested inside me for the Buddha's philosophy found outward expression and was converted into concrete action.

This is a good place for me to let out a secret to which no one has been privy except those who were exceptionally close to Doctor Saheb: both Doctor Saheb and I had embraced Buddhism in Delhi before we went to the World Buddhist Conference in Rangoon in 1951. From the very beginning of our marriage in 1948, we began working together in the cause of Buddhism. One can get a good idea of our joint involvement with Buddhism from the note that Doctor Saheb sent to his associate on 6 February 1955: 'We have both been engaged very deeply in our Buddhist work.' Be that as it may, the history and details of all these events will come at the chronologically appropriate place in this narrative. What I want to record here is that although the philosophy of the Buddha had already influenced me before Saheb entered my life, the credit for my becoming totally absorbed in Buddhism has to go to Doctor Saheb, and this I record with all humility and gratitude.

Thus, although my illness deprived me of the MD degree, the philosophy of the Buddha showed me an altogether new direction and by putting my mind through its paces, prepared the background for the religious revolution that Dr Ambedkar wrought later in life.

Practice with Dr Malvankar

Although I had taken to intensive and extensive reading while I was confined, how much, after all, can a person read? Even reading can turn wearisome! Time began moving heavily, and I told my father that it would be nice if I could work part-time in a clinic somewhere. Instead of simply lying around, I would gain useful medical experience and pass the time too. Dr Madhavrao Malvankar was a senior and experienced consultant who had his clinic on Hughes Road in Mumbai. He had the reputation of being a skilled physiotherapist and a renowned medical consultant.

We enjoyed a close and intimate family relationship with Dr Malvankar. Particularly, physiotherapy was my favourite subject, and all forms of physiotherapeutic treatment methods were available in Dr Malvankar's consulting room. Hence, we decided that I should begin practising with Dr Malvankar, and I began working as a junior doctor there. We had known of Dr Malvankar's expertise and his fame through hearsay, but when I began observing him at work, as a junior doctor in his group, I understood that he was indeed a divine physician. Many of the most eminent people of those times, princes of royal households, as also many people from the political and social arena visited him for medical consultation and treatment.

He was particularly proficient in curing all kinds of ailments with just physiotherapeutic treatment, without resorting to surgery. I realized I could learn a great deal from working under such an accomplished doctor. Being senior to us in age and experience, he occupied the position of our preceptor. Even Dr Ambedkar, when writing letters to me, would refer to him as 'guruji'. Since I had always been interested in physiotherapy, I began to learn a lot of things related to treatment strategies in physiotherapy from practical, hands-on experience. Once I involved myself in work, the lassitude that had arrived because of my illness disappeared and time began passing well too.

My Job in Gujarat

Meanwhile, I received a letter from a big hospital in Gujarat appointing me as chief medical officer. When I consulted my family members and my doctor colleagues on whether I should accept the appointment to this high position, they all advised me to go for it. The fact was that I was not at all inclined to abandon Mumbai and to live there alone, but with everybody insisting that I should take it up, I made up my mind and sent them my acceptance letter. I packed all the things I would need for my stay there, and as had been decided, left for Gujarat with my father. My father settled me down, put everything in place and returned to Mumbai. The unfamiliar place, the unknown people quite bewildered me, but within a few days I got used to the atmosphere and to my responsibilities. The work was so intense that I would hardly realize how time slipped away. I was the chief medical officer of an approximately 200-bed women's hospital; alongside, I was also the head of the department of physiotherapy of the general hospital. It was the experience I had gained in physiotherapy that earned me the complete charge of the department of physiotherapy. On account of my work and my discipline, I soon acquired recognition and appreciation as an efficient and skilled doctor.

Since I was appointed to a Class I post, I was naturally given all kinds of facilities and comforts: a motorcar, a bungalow, domestic help, a driver and so on. I had become one with my work. One feels a kind of satisfaction in curing people of their afflictions; one gets the contentment of doing social service along with one's job. This was how days rolled by. My father would come and visit me occasionally and stay with me for a day or two.

Things went on quite smoothly for a while, but after some time my health problems re-emerged. I would be well for a couple of days and unwell for the next four. As the chief medical officer, I naturally carried a lot of responsibilities. My work brought unbearable strain upon me, which left me completely exhausted. My constitution, which was delicate to begin with, began to plummet because of this unbearable strain. Also, I had nobody with me who could look after me and take care of my needs. My father came and stayed with me for a few days, but that didn't make any difference to my health. The weather there was not agreeable either. As a result of all this, I finally put in my resignation papers and returned to Mumbai with my father.

While all these things were happening in my life, it is important to cast a glance at the events that had been occurring in my family. My mother had passed away while I was still studying medicine. Consequently, the responsibility of the household and of bringing us up had fallen on my father. Under these adverse circumstances, my father fulfilled his responsibilities and gave us siblings the best possible nurturing. He never let us feel the absence of our mother.

We were five sisters and three brothers, adding up to a total of eight siblings. The eldest was our sister, Indira, the next was our brother, Murlidhar, I was the third; the fourth was brother Bhalchandra, the fifth was sister Sudha, Kamal was the sixth, the seventh was Vijaya and our youngest brother was Vasant. From among our eight siblings, my elder brother, my elder sister (who was also an MBBS) and the brother after me (Bhalchandra) are not alive today. I feel extremely proud as I write that out of us eight siblings, six of us (including me) had inter-caste marriages. This large number of inter-caste marriages clearly shows that (keeping in mind the social situation of those times that strongly believed in caste distinction), in spite of belonging to the saraswat Brahmin caste, we were an extremely progressive family. The reason for this is that our father never made any impositions on us. Quite obviously, all of us siblings were well-educated and we lived by forward-looking, liberal principles. None of us ever did anything that would make our father feel small or that would not agree with his principles. We never betrayed the confidence that our father had placed in us.

After I left Gujarat and returned to Mumbai after giving up my job, I was still poorly disposed health-wise. Thus, the question of taking up a job didn't arise. I didn't have the desire for it either. But then, after having taken enough medicines and sufficient rest, I began wearying of merely sitting at home. I therefore resumed working with Dr Malvankar as a junior doctor. This was how my routine in Mumbai began all over again. Merely lying around in bed at home had begun to tangle my hair, and I had also started loathing having to braid my long hair; accordingly, I went and got myself a bob-cut. These, then, were my circumstances before I met Dr Ambedkar in 1947 for the first time.

My First Meeting with Dr Ambedkar

A lot of people have been curious about how, where and when I entered Dr Ambedkar's life. Likewise, a number of them have spun their own absurd yarns in this matter according to their predilections. Obviously, I don't need to care about these preposterous imaginations that others have allowed to run free.

It can be seen everywhere in India that not only the followers, but also the opponents of a great man can never be satisfied without weaving circles of miracles, legends and hare-brained rumours around his life. History can reveal to us any number of examples of the lives of extraordinarily great men being festooned with all kinds of rumours, good and bad, according to whether they want to deify them or demonize them. If this is the state of affairs among the upper castes in this country, the community that is regarded as educated and advanced, it's best not to imagine the state of the community that has been incapacitated by thousands of years of slavery, against whom religion has shut the doors of education, which has lived life ostracized by the rest of society.

In this community of untouchables emasculated by thousands of years of slavery and darkness, Dr Ambedkar didn't merely flash like lightning shining through pitch-black clouds, he carried on blazing away forever like the sun. How, then, could the life of an epoch-making person like Dr Ambedkar escape the predation of the public rumour mill?

Among the many rumours pasted to Dr Ambedkar's life, a few of those doing the rounds relate to where, how and when he and I met each other. When I hear of some of the more miracle-ridden stories on this matter, I really don't know whether to laugh or to cry. Sometimes I feel amused and sometimes I am wonderstruck. How such rumours and tales of imagination get attached to the lives of great men is a huge conundrum. Particularly, how the tellers imagine them and how the listeners are willing to believe them is impossible for me to understand. Also, the tellers of these stories do it with such confidence and with such spicing up that one would believe it all happened before their eyes.

I know that extreme curiosity exists in the minds of everyone regarding my first meeting with Dr Ambedkar. Therefore, without stretching their patience any further, I throw light here on our first meeting.

Dr Rao and Dr Ambedkar

A Mysorean gentleman by the name of Dr Rao lived in the Parle suburb of Mumbai. This scholar was an economist and he had gone abroad for his higher education. The Rao family was highly educated and extremely cultured. Their family and ours enjoyed considerable intimacy, as a result of which we often visited each other. Dr Rao's daughters were also very suave, highly educated girls; consequently, I became great friends with them and would naturally visit their house quite often.

By sheer coincidence, Dr Rao and Dr Ambedkar were close friends too, which meant that Dr Ambedkar was a frequent visitor to the Rao house. As Dr Ambedkar had been inducted into the Viceroy's Executive Council as labour minister in 1942, he was living in Delhi. Whenever he came touring to Mumbai, he would make it a point to squeeze out the time to visit his dear friend. And once the duo of Dr Ambedkar and Dr Rao settled down to chat, the discussion would invariably turn seriously intellectual. As they nibbled on snacks, the two scholars would hold deep, no-holds-barred discussions on a wide variety of subjects; on rare occasions they would even get into arguments. On a few such occasions I had the good fortune of listening to these exchanges. Till the time I actually met Dr Ambedkar at Dr Rao's house, I had no knowledge of his frequent visits there. I would go there only to meet my friends.

I was on one such casual visit to Dr Rao's house when Dr Ambedkar arrived there. This event happened during the early days of 1947. Till that point I didn't know much about him. I had, of course, heard his name, and I knew that he was a minister in the Viceroy's Executive Council. I had never had any reason to know anything more about him. During my life as a student, I had focused single-mindedly on my studies. Later, when I began working, my attitude had been to stay confined to my work.

Since I was right there when Dr Ambedkar arrived, Dr Rao introduced me to him as a basic formality. He told him that I was his daughters' friend, I had done my MBBS, I was working as a junior doctor with the eminent Dr Malvankar and so forth.

While introducing Dr Ambedkar to me, Dr Rao said that Dr Ambedkar had risen up through extremely difficult circumstances and had acquired degrees from foreign universities. He talked about Dr Ambedkar's work on social reform, his priceless writings, his erudition, his library and so on. I was obviously delighted at being introduced to such a great person. I was overawed by Dr Ambedkar's scholarship and his deeply impressive and illustrious personality. At this very first meeting, I knew that Dr Ambedkar was no ordinary person; I was in the presence of a very great man.

Dr Ambedkar possessed an impressive personality. His grand forehead, his bright, piercing eyes, his sharp look, his ultra-modern, tip-top attire, the lustre that rested upon his visage—the very first sight of him gave assurance of an utterly exceptional personality.

Whoever saw him for the first time would immediately understand why foreigners referred to him as a German prince. His awesome personality combined with his enormous scholarship left an indelible impression upon the observer.

After the introduction, Dr Ambedkar inquired about me with great affection. He was deeply concerned about women's progress. Since it was a rather rare thing during those days for a woman to become a doctor, he congratulated me. Alongside, he expressed his desire of seeing women joining steps with men in every field with zest and vigour. As the conversation proceeded, I heard some wonderful things from Dr Ambedkar, a vast number of which I had never known.

We also talked about Buddhism during this very meeting. His knowledge of Buddhism left me literally goggle-eyed with wonder. Every word he uttered dripped with colossal knowledge and immense learning. When he put forward his points, he did so by supporting them with evidence, context and examples. His arguments were so well-grounded and so unassailable that even his opponents could do little other than nod their heads. One could clearly see that along with a vast amount of reading, there were hours of contemplation and sharp reasoning behind every word he uttered.

We did meet a few times after this first meeting, every time by coincidence and every time in Dr Rao's house at Parle. Each time we met, we had formal conversations on a wide variety of issues. I learnt a lot of new things during these conversations and kept increasing my treasure of knowledge. Each time I felt blessed and delighted and proud to have begun to know such a great man.

Dr Ambedkar's Ill Health

On 15 August 1947, India became independent and the names of the ministers of the first cabinet formed under Nehru's leadership were announced. Dr Ambedkar's name was among them as the first law minister of independent India. On 29 August 1947, the Constituent

Assembly formed a drafting committee and appointed Dr Ambedkar as its chairman [sic].[5] He was also nominated as a member of the flag committee. Thus it was that all these responsibilities were placed upon Dr Ambedkar's shoulders at the same time.

Dr Ambedkar's health would remain quite uncertain. When he came to visit Dr Rao, he would always voice some complaints about his health. This discussion on his health had happened a couple of times in my presence too. Since I was a doctor, I naturally asked him about his health, and he informed me too about his ailments. It was very important that his state of health should be investigated and appropriate medication begun.

One day I was busy as usual at Dr Malvankar's consulting room at Hughes Road when an extremely impressive-looking gentleman dressed in Western clothes suddenly entered the room. That gentleman was Dr Ambedkar. I was surprised to see him and extremely glad too. I introduced him to Dr Malvankar and to my other colleagues. Everybody was delighted at having such an eminent person coming to the consulting chamber. After the formal introduction, he said that Dr Rao of Parle had recommended that he should take Dr Malvankar's treatment. Dr Malvankar had earlier treated Dr Rao's wife and helped her get well. Mrs Rao had been suffering from convulsions for a long time, and she had taken treatment from eminent doctors in Mumbai and elsewhere without any success. Somebody had then advised her to consult Dr Malvankar. She had accordingly taken Dr Malvankar's ministrations and recovered permanently from what had seemed an intractable affliction. On the basis of this personal experience, it appears, Dr Rao had recommended that Dr Ambedkar too should get himself treated by Dr Malvankar. For that matter, I was a doctor too and had coincidently met Dr Ambedkar. It would not have been unusual or novel if he had felt that he should get himself treated at the place where I was working.

When he came to our consulting room, he was in an extremely poor state of health. Dr Ambedkar related to Dr Malvankar the complete history of his ailments. Dr Malvankar too asked him several questions and gathered all the information he could on the state of his health. We then took Dr Ambedkar to the investigation chamber and subjected him to a detailed and thorough examination. The investigation revealed that Dr Ambedkar had been suffering severely for many long years from chronic ailments such as diabetes, high blood pressure, neuritis and rheumatism. Diabetes had virtually hollowed out his body. Similarly, rheumatism would keep him writhing in pain through many a night. Despite having taken several treatments, he had shown little sign of recovery. In view of the overall status of his physical health, it was imperative that his treatment should start immediately.

History of Dr Ambedkar's Ailments

Dr Ambedkar was forever concerned about the upliftment of the poor and destitute. He had to fight his battles simultaneously on multiple fronts. Despite the huge turmoil that engulfed him, he never allowed a break in his reading, thinking and thought-provoking writing. He forged his movement for establishing equality under the most adverse of circumstances. While working for his supreme mission of establishing equality and procuring the legitimate rights of the downtrodden, Dr Ambedkar never cared for his health; the deleterious consequence on his health was inevitable: the arrival of painful maladies such as high blood pressure, diabetes and rheumatism that afflicted him all his life.

If researchers were to examine Dr Ambedkar's letters from 1922 onwards, they would find repeated mention of his health in most of them. Dr Ambedkar's associates and friends were well aware of the delicate state of his health, and they would regularly make solicitous inquiries about it.

Dr Ambedkar and I met for the first time in the early half of 1947 and our marriage took place on Thursday, 15 April 1948.

I believe it proper that a look be taken at the state of his health until the time I met him or even till the time we got married.

I am sure that it will be more instructive to form an estimate of the state of his health not from my words or anybody else's, but by searching through Dr Ambedkar's own correspondence. So that proper cognizance may be taken of his health through his letters, I am deliberately giving the references in the original form and in the language in which they were written. The meaning and the import therein will, therefore, be more effectively expressed and will gather authenticity alongside. An examination of the upward-downward swings will reveal that these fluctuations began from 1922 onwards. That is the reason why I am presenting below a review of his health status from 1922 onwards till the date of our marriage, i.e., 15 April 1948.

A Record of Dr Ambedkar's Ill Health in His Own Words

Maharaja Sayajirao of Baroda had sent Dr Ambedkar to England on a scholarship for higher education. Even during his student days, he had felt the need for a newspaper for bringing about awakening among the masses. With financial help from Rajarshi Shahu Maharaj of Kolhapur, Dr Ambedkar started the periodical *Mook Nayak* and thus took on the leadership of his *mook samaaj*, his community of untouchables. During those days, a gentleman from the *chamar* community named Sitarampant Shivtarkar, a teacher by profession, looked after the management of *Mook Nayak*. He also doubled as Dr Ambedkar's secretary. Later, after 1936, he joined the Congress, and was finally thrown out of the movement permanently. Here is Dr Ambedkar's letter to Shivtarkar of 24 August 1922, written from C/o. Henry Kings & Co., Pall Mall [translated from Marathi]:

> '. . . It's been a long time since I received your letter. I couldn't respond because my health has lately become very unwell. I hope you will forgive me . . .'

Dattoba Santram Pawar, a person belonging to the chamar community, who was working in the court of Kolhapur, was a friend of Dr Ambedkar. It was this Dattoba who had first introduced Dr Ambedkar to Shahu Maharaj. In 1935, Dr Ambedkar voiced his thoughts on religious conversion. Dattoba Pawar was not in agreement with this conversion. Later, Pawar joined the Congress. Differences of opinion having thus arisen between Dr Ambedkar and Pawar on conversion and other political issues, their friendship did not survive and merely formal relations remained. There seems to have been quite a lot of correspondence between the two. Here is a letter from Dr Ambedkar to Dattoba Pawar written on 7 February 1927, from Damodar Hall, Mumbai:

> '. . . You must be wondering at my silence. But I have been so ill since I returned from Panhala that I could not work. I am just getting better and the first thing I am doing is to reply to the heaps of letters that have reached me in the matter of my nomination to the Council . . .'

Bhaurao Gaikwad of Nashik had taken an enthusiastic and active part in Dr Ambedkar's movement since the Mahad satyagraha of 1927. He was counted among the closest associates of Dr Ambedkar. Doctor Saheb wrote countless letters to Bhaurao discussing the movement, offering guidance, and talking about a large number of personal matters. Here is Dr Ambedkar's letter[6] to Bhaurao Gaikwad in December 1930 from Damodar Hall, Parel, Mumbai–12:

> '. . . You must have been surprised at my silence. But there was no way but to be silent. My health as you know has been going down and the pressure of work has been increasing. The study of the Chowdar Tank suit was the last straw that has broken the camel's back. I went to Mahad in a broken condition on [the] 11th and was extremely disappointed when I heard that the case has to be postponed on account of [the] illness of the Pleader of

the opposite party. All this has told on me and I am again prostrate with my fainting fits . . .'

This is Dr Ambedkar's letter[7] to Bhaurao Gaikwad on 24 May 1930, again from Damodar Hall [translated from Marathi]:

'. . . My associates have gone out of town for a change of air. Therefore, not one of them can come for your meeting. I myself have been lying alone rotting in Mumbai. Having to take daily injections makes it impossible for me to stir out . . .'

The British government had appointed the Simon Commission to conduct an in-depth study of the political situation in India and make recommendations. The commission, accordingly, toured India and submitted its report to the British government. As per the commission's recommendation, the British government invited the top leaders of the various parties in India to discuss the demands of the people of India. Along with other leaders, Dr Ambedkar and Rao Bahadur R. Srinivasan of Madras had been invited as representatives of the untouchables to participate in the round table conference. Dr Ambedkar went to London to participate in the conference.

Dr Ambedkar's letter to Govindrao Adrekar of 29 October 1930, written from 8, Chesterfield Gardens, Mayfair, London [translated from Marathi]:

'. . . I reached safely on the 18th. There's no improvement in my health worth talking about. But there is no cause for worry . . .'

Dr Ambedkar's letter of 6 January 1931, to Shivtarkar from 42, Clifton Gardens, Maida Vale, London [translated from Marathi]:

'. . . My health has gone really bad. I have begun to feel that it is not merely proper, but imperative to look for some remedy.

Hence I have decided to go to Germany for treatment after the Conference gets over. The Conference will get over at the end of the month.'

Dr Ambedkar's letter of 10 September 1931, written to Shivtarkar from 3rd, Bernard Street, Russell, London sq. [translated from Marathi]:

'. . . I fell terribly ill from last Thursday onwards. Fever, influenza, dysentery and vomiting have suddenly gained strength. It was absolute mayhem for two days, to the extent that it felt that my life was at stake. I have been slightly better since last Monday. But my strength has dissipated exceedingly . . . Please enquire and let me know what has happened regarding the Mahad appeal. Please don't let my people at home know about my ill-health.'

Doctor Saheb writes[8] to Bhaurao Gaikwad on 23 September 1931, from London:

'. . . I was very glad to receive your letter of the 4th. I should have written to you long before without waiting to hear from you. But you know in what poor state of health I left and I had to conserve all my energy for writing to the Janata . . .'

The round table conference appointed the franchise committee under the chairmanship of Lord Lothian for recommending the conditions under which the people of India should be given voting rights. Dr Ambedkar was nominated as a member of this committee. The English members of the committee and Dr Ambedkar travelled by the same ship from London to India. The first sitting of the committee was to happen in the first week of February at Delhi. That meant that Dr Ambedkar had to leave for Delhi immediately after reaching Mumbai. The committee was touring across India to collect information on where the people's inclination lay. When the committee was stationed in Simla, Doctor Saheb wrote to Shivtarkar on 15 April 1932 [translated from Marathi]:

> '. . . The Hindu members of the Committee are vigorously opposing the untouchability question; to the extent that we are not even talking to each other. Because of this, I am writing a separate report for expressing my independent opinion. I shall place it before the Committee for discussion. I feel quite enfeebled because of all these squabbles.'

Dr Ambedkar writes to Shivtarkar again from Simla on 23 April [translated from Marathi]:

> '. . . because of being struck quite badly by dysentery, my health has gone down considerably.'

Doctor Saheb had to return to England for the second round table conference in 1932. While he was still travelling, he wrote a letter from the ship (Port Said) to Shivtarkar on 2 June 1932 [translated from Marathi]:

> '. . . Nothing unusual has happened since we left. My health had gone very bad . . .'

Doctor Saheb writes to Shivtarkar from London on 14 June 1932 [translated from Marathi]:

> '. . . My work here is over. There is nothing much left to do. But in the opinion of some people from our party who are here, it is important for me to stay on here, so I have considered staying on for a few more days. But instead of staying on in London, I shall go to Dresden in Germany and stay in a sanatorium there, which

> means that I shall be able to go over to London as soon as the need arises. I have decided upon this course of action because of my uncertain health . . .'

Doctor Saheb writes to Dattoba Pawar of Kolhapur on 15 June 1932, from London:

> '. . . Just to say that I am leaving London for Germany. As my health is very bad, I propose to stay in a sanitorium [sic] . . .'

As written in the letter above, for the purpose of being treated for his ill health, Doctor Saheb stayed in Dr Moller's sanatorium in Dresden, Germany, for a few days. He wrote a letter to Shivtarkar from there on 12 July 1932 [translated from Marathi]:

> '. . . My health is much better. I propose to leave this house next Wednesday because it is quite expensive . . . I shall reach Mumbai on August 16 . . .'

After having arrived in Mumbai, Doctor Saheb was again called over to London. He writes from there to Shivtarkar on 19 May 1933 [translated from Marathi]:

> 'I reached here on the 6th. My health is all right. Don't worry . . .'

Dr Ambedkar was known all over the world for his love of books. His personal collection of books is second to none. Even when he couldn't afford them, he would starve so that he could increase his stock of knowledge. For the sake of providing a secure and well-ordered refuge for his 'treasure of knowledge', he got a house constructed as per exact specifications under his personal supervision in Hindu Colony, Dadar (Mumbai). In this [house called] 'Rajgraha', this apotheosis of wisdom would sit night and day in his contemplation of knowledge. It was in this building that he planned his movement for the achievement of equality. Rajgraha enjoys a privileged place in the life of Dr Ambedkar.

Dr Ambedkar's letter from Rajgraha, Mumbai, on 15 April 1934, to Dattoba Pawar:

> '. . . There has been no communication from you since you left. I hope you are better. I came from Bordi on the 1st but I fell ill. I am going back tomorrow . . .'

Dr Ambedkar's letter to Dattoba Pawar from Mumbai on 3 May 1935:

> 'My illness has grown worse and I propose to come to Kolhapur on the morning of the 11th May 1935 . . .'

The Jat-Pat-Todak Mandal of Lahore had invited Dr Ambedkar to preside over their annual conference. Despite being unwell, he had prepared his presidential address with a lot of labour. But making the excuse that the statements and the inferences in the address were very provocative and incendiary, the Mandal first postponed and then cancelled the conference. The Mandal requested Doctor Saheb to soften the inferences and statements, but Dr Ambedkar refused to modify his incisive and solid opinion. Doctor Saheb later had the same address published in book form in 1937 with the title *Annihilation of Caste*. A substantial correspondence took place between Har Bhagwan of the Jat-Pat-Todak Mandal and Doctor Saheb. Doctor Saheb writes[9] to him on 27 April 1936:

> '. . . All the grace has by now run out and I shall not consent to preside even if your Committee agreed to accept my address as it is in toto. I thank you for your appreciation of the pains I have taken in the preparation of the address. I certainly have profited by the labour if

[no] one else does. My only regret is that I was put to such hard labour at a time when my health was not equal to the strain it has caused . . .'

This address of Doctor Saheb that was not delivered is extremely thought-provoking and important. Every sentence of this address reveals his immense scholarship, his profound reading and contemplation. Despite not being in good health, he prepared this research paper with a lot of labour.

Doctor Saheb writes[10] to Bhaurao Gaikwad on 25 August 1936:

'. . . I have received your letter of the 22nd in which you say that you have written earlier a detailed letter. I have not received any such letter. I can't understand what you and Rankhambe have been doing. My health has completely failed and doctors have been advising me to go out of India and rest. I may go abroad any time . . .'

He writes[11] to Bhau again on 13 October:

'. . . I have your letter of the 9th. I am very bad from the point of view of health. I have no energy left and I feel exhausted after very little exertion. I wish you spared me the trouble of going about . . .'

D. G. Jadhav was one among the close associates of Doctor Saheb. Particularly in matters related to the People's Education Society, i.e., in matters related to education, he participated in a big way. Even when Doctor Saheb was alive, he had been given the authority of the chairman. It was Jadhav who took over as chairman after the Doctor's passing away.

Dr Ambedkar writes to Jadhav from Delhi on 14 October 1940:

'. . . I arrived in Delhi last Saturday. I expected a complete breakdown, so tired and exhausted I was. But I am happy to say that nothing of the kind has happened . . .'

The Doctor wrote again to Jadhav on 14 June 1940:

> '. . . I have been working very hard. My health has gone down. I had a complete collapse for the last few days. My doctor Kritts Babu gave me some tonic. I am feeling better. He also asked me to resume my evening meal as he feels that abandonment of my evening meal has had a bad effect on my health. I have started taking a small evening meal. I am feeling better . . .'

Doctor Saheb tells Jadhav in the letter of 3 March 1945, that he wrote from Delhi:

> '. . . As to my health, you should not worry. I am not unmindful of my health. But I can't put health above work . . .'

If we study Dr Ambedkar's social movements, we will notice that from the earliest days he received help from people who were not untouchables. Kamalakant Chitre's name will have to be included in that list. Chitre was the general secretary of the Independent Labour Party that Doctor Saheb had established in 1936. The Doctor established the People's Education Society in 1946 and started Siddharth College. During those days, since he was in the Viceroy's Executive Council, he lived in Delhi. Naturally, the entire responsibility of Siddharth College rested on Chitre, Donde and other prominent people. Chitre worked at the Mumbai Municipal Corporation. After finishing his day at the corporation, he would go straight to the Siddharth College office and sit there till late into the night looking after the office work at the college, and that too pro bono. Chitre carried the burden of Doctor Saheb's work in the educational field with great integrity, honesty and efficiency. Later, after work at the college had increased, Doctor Saheb got Chitre to resign his job at the corporation and take over as the first registrar of the People's Education Society.

Writing to Chitre on 13 August 1947 from Delhi, Doctor Saheb says:

> '. . . But owing to my illness which has not [abated?], I had no peace of mind. Today I decided not to postpone the reply any longer so I am up and doing it . . .
>
> 'I am anxious to come to Bombay to see what our doctors have to say. Very probably, I shall come towards the end of next week . . .'

He again writes to Chitre on 31 August:

> '. . . I take [it] that everything about the college is all right.
>
> 'My health is on the down-grade. For the last fifteen days I have not had a wink of sleep, the nights have [become] a nightmare to me. The neurotic pain always comes at midnight and continues throughout. I am taking insulin as well as homeopathic medicine. Neither seems to give me relief. I must now learn to endure what appears beyond cure.
>
> 'Dharap used to suffer from similar diabetic and neurotic pains. I wonder if he had found any remedy. Surba must be knowing. Will you enquire from him? . . .'

Writing from Delhi on 2 November 1947 to Revaram Kawade, his associate from Vidarbha, he says:

> '. . . I have received your letter of 11th October just this minute. As you know I have been very ill even now. I am more or less confined to the [sic] bed doing only the work which I must do . . .'

Doctor Saheb informs D. G. Jadhav from Delhi on 28 November 1947:

> '. . . I am distinctly better though I have not enough strength to walk about . . .'

The chart of Dr Ambedkar's health swings between 1922 and 1947 becomes quite clear from a study of the letters given above. It can be seen with corroboration that this swing began from 1922. The other thing that needs to be remembered here is that all of Doctor Saheb's letters are not available to us. Countless letters would have got destroyed by time, some may still not have been located, some might have been destroyed either on account of ignorance or intentionally. There can be no doubt, however, that the above references will give the reader a clear enough idea of the background and the state of his physical health at the time that I entered his life.

In the same manner, other than the letters, if the prefaces of the many priceless books that Doctor Saheb has written were to be studied, several references that he has made to his ill health could be located. It will also be found that Doctor Saheb has remarked on his ill health even in the conferences and meetings he held from time to time and in his public addresses. Yet again, references to Saheb's ill health and concern expressed about it can also be found in the memoirs—either written or spoken—of his associates and other people who spent time with him.

Causes of Dr Ambedkar's Ill Health

Before we get into discussing all that happened after my meeting with Doctor Saheb, let us look at some of the main reasons that caused his health to become so bad. Why did his health suffer so many fluctuations right from the very beginning? He had to carry forward his movement through extremely adverse circumstances, that is true, but what were those difficult episodes that he had to confront? What impact did these episodes continue to have on his mind and on his health? Most people are aware of the life-sketch of Dr Ambedkar, but even if I am to be faulted for repetition, I believe it necessary to briefly go through the important events in Doctor Saheb's public, family and personal life to locate the important reasons.

Doctor Saheb had to suffer grievous wounds of the terrible custom of untouchability from his earliest childhood. They left a very deep impact on the child's mind. Untouchability stood against him at every step. He spent his childhood and his student days in extremely pernicious circumstances and right from a very young age onwards, his mind was constantly assaulted.

When he was barely five years old, Bhimrao suffered the deprivation of his mother's love. Since barbers didn't offer their services to an untouchable, his sisters were required to meet the need of clipping his hair at home. He did not have the right to sit with the rest of his classmates, because of which he would sit in a corner outside the classroom. Once, when he was caught drinking water from a public well, he was thrashed like an animal by the upper caste people. These so-called upper caste people who considered themselves 'savarna' believed that the mere touch of an untouchable would render their wells impure. He had to suffer many more such bitter experiences from his earliest childhood onwards.

The Masoor Incident

After retiring from the army, Saheb's father, Subhedar Ramji, was living in Goregaon, taluka Khatav, on account of the job he had taken up there. One day the foursome of Bhimrao, his brother Anand and two of their nephews set off by train from Satara to Goregaon to meet him. When they alighted at the Masoor railway station, they found that Ramjirao had not arrived to pick them up because he had not received their letter. Even when all the passengers had left, these boys were still hanging around at the railway station. The station master looked at their natty clothes and made affectionate inquiries, believing, of course, that they belonged to a well-to-do, upper caste family. But as soon as he got to know that they were untouchables, he sprang away as if a lizard had suddenly fallen upon him. Finally, after much beseeching, he showed the good grace of hiring a bullock cart for carrying them. Thus began their journey from Masoor to Goregaon.

As they rattled on in their journey and had covered a considerable distance, in the course of conversation the cartman realized that the boys sitting in his cart were untouchables. That did it for him. Within moments he assumed the form of an irate god and pushed the boys out of his cart. It had turned frightfully dark by then, with not the smallest trace of light anywhere. The boys were petrified with fear. But instead of feeling pity for the poor boys, the cartman kept raging and spitting expletives at them for having defiled his cart.

After endless pleading, when the boys promised to give him twice his fare, the cartman finally agreed to take them ahead. His condition, however, was that the boys would drive the cart and he would walk behind. The boys were agonizing with thirst, but nobody was willing to give water to a bunch of untouchables. It was summer, the thirsty boys begged and pleaded, but they couldn't turn a single heart to pity. It was on the following day that the boys reached their destination half dead.

There were many such episodes that Doctor Saheb had to suffer during his childhood. Whenever he narrated this heart-rending episode, Doctor Saheb would become overwrought. His voice would quaver, and tears would run down his cheeks. On every step of the way, Bhima was made to suffer the hot, branding scars of humiliation and disgrace administered by the inhuman behaviour of these so-called upper caste 'savarna' Hindus. The brutality of the Goregaon episode awakened in him the realization in practical terms of what it meant to be an untouchable. This event scoured Doctor Saheb's heart so deeply that he never ever forgot it. He would always say, 'This incident holds an important part in my life. I would have been barely nine years of age then, but the mark that this episode has left can never be wiped out.'

The Baroda Episode

Despite having acquired degrees from world-renowned universities, all that Doctor Saheb received in return was scorn and dishonour. He joined the Baroda job in the last week of January 1913. Although he occupied a high position in the Secretariat, the fact that he was an untouchable resulted in not only senior and junior officers, but even the peon class refusing to cooperate with him. To avoid getting defiled by his touch, even the peons used to toss files at him from a distance. He was not allowed to drink water from the earthen pitcher that was kept in the office for public use.

Being an untouchable meant that nobody was willing to give him a place to live in. With the consent of the manager in a Parsee hotel, he assumed a Parsee name and began living there with the stipulation that he would pay a rent of a rupee and a half every day. On the eleventh day, however, a dozen or so extremely agitated Parsees armed with sticks arrived at the door of his first-floor room and began raining questions on him. They flung abuses at him and bad-mouthed him for having polluted the hotel. They threatened him with dire consequences if he did not vacate the hotel by that very evening and left frothing and fuming. He then tried to get himself living space with a friend who had been born a Brahmin but had later converted to Christianity. But even there his untouchability became an obstacle; although the friend had become a Christian, the concept of untouchability had seeped far too deep into his bones to be easily flushed out.

After leaving the Parsee hotel and meeting with disappointment at his friend's house, he was confronted with the difficult question of where to find shelter. He was scared that the incensed Parsee goons would assault him for having polluted the hotel, kill him, perhaps.

Since there was a lot of time for the next train to Mumbai, he went and sat in a public park, trembling with fear and worry. Besides, he was also afraid of hovering close to the railway station for fear of that Parsee gang. Feeling helpless and deeply depressed, he sat under a tree and wept incontinently. He left Baroda for Mumbai in a disconsolate state of mind.

A point that doesn't settle well in the mind is this: it was the Maharaja of Baroda, Sayajirao Gaikwad, who had given Dr Ambedkar a scholarship and sent him abroad for higher studies. He was the one who had given him his appointment in his state. Why then, despite being the maharaja of the state, could Sayajirao not arrange a government house for him to stay in? This point not only hurts, it also astounds.

Dr Ambedkar made a written application to Sayajirao and even talked to him personally about his circumstances, yet it is a matter of deep regret that the maharaja could not make any staying arrangement for him. The only conclusion that one can draw from this episode is that Sayajirao found himself helpless and inadequate against the regressive forces. The concept of untouchability was too deeply rooted.

Father's Death

On 2 February 1913, Dr Ambedkar suffered a terrible blow, and that was the death of his father, Subhedar Ramjirao. The one single person who had stood firmly behind him as a pillar of strength had gone. Along with all other deprivations, this anxiety of domestic responsibility had also come and landed on his head.

Bitter Experiences at Sydenham

After abandoning Baroda and returning to Mumbai, Doctor Ambedkar joined Sydenham College as a professor of economics.

Although within a very short time he acquired a reputation as an erudite professor, the stigma of untouchability refused to let go of him. He was not allowed to touch the pitcher of water and the glasses kept for the use of the teaching staff.

Bitter Experiences at the High Court

After having acquired his Bar-at-Law from the renowned English law school Gray's Inn, Doctor Saheb began practising in July 1923 as a lawyer at the Bombay High Court. But even there, the stigma of being an untouchable prevented him from getting sufficient response. Touchable solicitors would not allow him to come close to them as he was a mahar barrister; nor would he get touchable clients. As a result, Barrister Ambedkar was compelled to accept whatever cases he could manage to get in the suburban and/or district courts.

The Bitter Experience on Mahad Road

Once, the river along Mahad Road was in flood and the untouchables' colony was on the other side of the river. The flood didn't subside for two days. The colony on this side of the river belonged to the touchable community. Because Dr Ambedkar had got stuck on this side of the river, he could not cross over to the untouchables' colony on the yonder side. He had to go hungry for those two days because no touchable was willing to serve food to an untouchable.

The Bitter Experiences of the Start Committee

In 1929, the Government of Bombay had appointed a committee under the chairmanship of B.H. Start to study the educational, economic and social status of untouchable and adivasi communities and to make recommendations for their upliftment. Dr Ambedkar was a member of this committee. Although he was a member of a government-appointed committee, the headmaster of a school did not allow him to enter a classroom only because he was an untouchable.

The second episode is of Chalisgaon. The committee made a tour of the East Khandesh district. When Dr Ambedkar arrived in Chalisgaon on 23 October 1929, the untouchables requested him to visit their colony. This colony was at a certain distance from the station, but how would the touchable tonga drivers allow an untouchable to climb into their tonga? It was after a lot of entreaty and the promise of paying a hiked-up fare that a Muslim tonga driver was persuaded; but since he refused to drive the tonga, an untouchable man was hired for the job. This person, however, was a novice; the horse got startled and the tonga overturned. Dr Ambedkar was thrown out and he fell on the stone steps nearby and fractured his right leg. He had to move around for many days with his leg in a plaster.

The Mahad Satyagraha and the Burning of *Manu Smriti*

Having encountered bitter experiences at every step of the way, Dr Ambedkar rose up in rebellion and resolved to take up the fight against inequality as his life-mission. He rolled up his sleeves to restructure society on the triad of equality, independence and fraternity, and jumped into the arena of social work.

The social reformer Rao Bahadur Sitaram Keshav had presented a bill for the provision of independent entrances to water facilities, schools, courts, inns, etc., in the Bombay Assembly and had it passed. With the intention of putting this resolution into effect, Dr Ambedkar marched with thousands of his followers to the lake at Mahad and got into the lake and drank water from it with his cupped hands. His followers imitated their leader and thus underscored their right as human beings. That historic day was 20 March 1927. The touchable Hindus flared up. Believing that their lake had been defiled, they began attacking the untouchables returning from the campaign. Countless untouchables were injured, leading to the filing of court cases. Doctor Saheb had to bring the situation under control and fight the cases in the court too.

Later, a second conference was held in Mahad under the chairmanship of Dr Ambedkar in which he took another revolutionary step: he got a resolution passed for burning the *Manu Smriti*, the Code of Manu, that lay at the root of inequality. On 25 December, under the leadership of Dr Ambedkar, the book *Manu Smriti* was publicly set on fire at the hands of Gangadhar Nilkanth Sahasrabuddhe, a Brahmin associate of Dr Ambedkar.

The burning of *Manu Smriti* was a slap in the face of the keepers of the Hindu religion across India. The fanatics among the Hindu religious orthodoxy were jolted, the *peeths* [schools of religious learning] of Hindu religion were rocked, resulting in sharp and provocative protests all across the country. The entire Hindu community had risen up in arms against Dr Ambedkar; but this personification of courage never faltered and confronted the situation with great intrepidity. But for all that, he was put under immense mental strain.

The Kalaram Temple Satyagraha

On 2 March 1930, Dr Ambedkar blew the battle horn at Nashik for entry into the Kalaram temple. The satyagrahis sat in front of the temple doors and prevented entry of the upper caste Hindus into the temple. The upper caste Hindus arrived at an agreement that they would pull Lord Rama's chariot together with the untouchables. But the agreement was never implemented. Confusion reigned among the satyagrahis, and they began running this way and that. Countless satyagrahis were injured, including Dr Ambedkar. The Nashik satyagraha went on for five years during which hordes of satyagrahis were arrested. But wherever Doctor Saheb was, he would always keep a sharp eye on the satyagraha and offer guidance.

Working on Multiple Fronts

While Dr Ambedkar's entire life was an incessant struggle, the period between 1930 and 1936 was particularly turbulent. Although the Mahad satyagraha had taken place in 1927, the litigations emerging from it carried on. During this period, Doctor Saheb had to pay attention to many things. Personally attending to the work related to the satyagraha cases running in the Mahad court; giving witness; gathering other witnesses; organizing satyagrahas and guiding the satyagrahis and the Satyagraha Committee of the Kalaram temple entry satyagraha at Nashik either personally or through leaflets; creating public awareness through organizing satyagraha-related meetings and through releasing statements and letters; attending the sittings of and participating in the work of the Bombay Assembly of which he was a member; running a legal practice for the sake of his own wherewithal; looking after the management of the newspaper *Bahishkrut Bharat* (Ostracized India) and writing for it; sending statements, applications and appeals to the government—for performing all these activities he was required to constantly travel between Mumbai, Mahad and Nashik. It cannot be doubted, therefore, that the deleterious effects that all these activities were bound to have on his health went on happening in their natural course. But what needs to be noticed is that whenever duties had to be performed, he never cared for personal health.

Round Table Conference

The British government organized a round table conference under the chairmanship of Prime Minister Ramsay MacDonald to discuss the recommendations of the Simon Commission regarding the political demands and rights of the people of India. The prominent leaders of India were sent invitations to participate in the conference. Rao Bahadur R. Srinivasan of Madras and Dr Ambedkar were invited to participate in the conference as representatives of the untouchables. By presenting before the conference the pitiable state of the untouchables of India in an extremely systematic and impressive manner, for the first time ever, Dr Ambedkar hung at the doorstep of the world the miseries of the untouchables. He presented with supporting evidence the manner in which the untouchables of India were being crushed under the stone-grinder of an inhumane custom.

The Poona Pact

Dr Ambedkar made a forceful and evidence-based presentation before the round table conference on how the Hindus, the Muslims and the government itself made capital out of the untouchability question and exploited it for their own convenience and how it was detrimental to the cause of the untouchables themselves.

The members of the Minorities Committee (among whom Dr Ambedkar and Aga Khan were prominent members) had got the draft of their demands approved unanimously, and thus the work of the Minorities Committee, which was appointed to find a solution to the minorities question, had come to an end.

This committee had demanded separate electorates for all the minority communities: Muslims, Indian Christians, Anglo-Indians, Europeans and the untouchables. But amazingly, Gandhiji, who gave approval to the granting of separate constituencies to all the other minorities, vigorously opposed the granting of a constituency to the untouchables, in spite of the fact that they were a minority community too. No general agreement could be arrived at on this question. Finally, Prime Minister MacDonald suggested that the members of the Minorities Committee should sign a joint statement declaring that after the conference was over, they would accept the arbitration of the prime minister on this matter and would be bound by whatever decision he took. Accordingly, along with Gandhiji, all the members signed the statement. It is very important to keep in mind here that Dr Ambedkar did not sign this statement.

On 17 August 1932, the British government publicly announced the result of its arbitration that granted for all the minorities, including the untouchables, their independent constituencies.

Gandhiji did not have any opposition to the granting of constituencies to the other minorities. For the one single reason that only the untouchables (who were not only a minority but were also extremely backward) should not be granted an independent constituency, he went on a fast until death in the Yerawada jail. Gandhiji, who had gone to attend the round table conference to discuss the entire country, came back with the single plea that the untouchables should not be granted an independent constituency. This was not merely a surprising, but also an extremely unfortunate episode.

Since it became a life-and-death question for Gandhiji, the entire country was naturally thrown into turmoil. Tension and worry spread everywhere. While it was Gandhiji who was doing the fasting, really speaking it was Dr Ambedkar's life that was in bigger danger. He began receiving threatening telegrams, letters and telephone calls from every corner of the country. Some opponents went to the extent of sending their threats written in blood. Instead of saying that an anti-Ambedkar atmosphere spread across the country, it would be more appropriate to say that an anti-Ambedkar atmosphere was deliberately created across the country. Leaders all over the country began running to and fro to arrange discussions. The eyes of every one of them, of course, were fixed on Dr Ambedkar, who himself was fighting for the legitimate rights of his Dalit brethren. He, of course, confronted this calamity with great courage, but after all that, he still had to bear the extreme mental tension that had sprung up on account of these circumstances. A compromise was finally arrived at, and the Poona Pact was signed by the leaders and the representatives of the touchables and the untouchables on 24 September 1932.

Ramabai's Passing Away

Dr Ambedkar was struck by another calamity in the year 1935: on 27 May, his wife Ramabai passed away after a prolonged illness. Along with the responsibilities of social work, therefore, he now had to carry the load of domestic responsibility too. Ramabai's untimely death left Dr Ambedkar grievously impacted. He was so busy working night and day fighting for the rights of the untouchables and for social equality that he could never find enough time to devote to his family. Actually, even before he had submerged himself in the movement, he had spent a large portion of his student days abroad acquiring higher degrees. Ramabai had been bedridden for many months with tuberculosis. Dr Ambedkar got several expert doctors to treat her, but she never recovered. This tragic incident left a deep impact on Dr Ambedkar. He started living a solitary life. Even before Ramabai died, he had lost four children—three boys and a girl. With his wife too dying in 1935, Dr Ambedkar never enjoyed domestic well-being and happiness. From 1935 onwards, he lived a solitary life. Till the time I entered his life, he did not have a single person with whom he enjoyed any degree of intimacy. In Delhi too he was a loner.

Response to His Announcement of Conversion of Religion

The announcement of the change of religion was the outcome of the satyagraha at the Chowdar Lake in Mahad, the satyagraha for entry into the Kalaram temple in Nashik and the bitter experiences gained during these struggles. Dr Ambedkar organized a conference at Yevle [sic], district Nashik, on 13 October 1935, to discuss the topic of change of religion by the untouchables. Speaking at this historic conference as its chairman, he made the revolutionary announcement, 'Although I was born an untouchable Hindu, I shall not die a Hindu.' This historic announcement of change of religion provoked a lot of sharp and sour responses from across the country. There was a virtual maelstrom of telegrams and letters threatening him with death. The announcement shook the religious institutions of Hinduism. The high priests of Hinduism rose up in a frenzy of anger.

Mahatma Gandhi himself stood against this announcement of religious conversion. Obviously, the Harijans (untouchables) who had joined the Congress camp also began opposing the announcement. The Congress had made some special arrangements for some leaders among the untouchables demanding their rights. Two among these important leaders were M.C. Raja of Madras and Ganesh Gavai from Vidarbha. In other words, along with facing bitter opposition from the upper caste Hindus, Dr Ambedkar also had to face opposition from untouchable leaders such as Raja, Gavai, Kajrolkar, P. Balu and others.

Dr Ambedkar in the Bombay Assembly

As per the Act of 1935, general elections were held in 1937 for all the provincial legislative assemblies in India. In that election, fourteen candidates (including Dr Ambedkar) of the Independent Labour Party established by Dr Ambedkar were elected to the Bombay Legislative Assembly. The doctor tabled several bills directed at public welfare. He participated in the debates in a major way and when presenting his case, he used well-reasoned arguments to counter the arguments presented by his opponents. He prepared his addresses in the Assembly with great care and labour. The Assembly remained in existence from 1937 to 1939, when it was suspended sine die when the World War began. Investigation will reveal that during his three years in the Assembly, Dr Ambedkar could not attend several sessions due to ill health.

In the Viceroy's Executive Council

When the names of the ministers in the Viceroy's Executive Council were announced on 2 July 1942, Dr Ambedkar's name was among them. As labour minister in the Council, he worked with great enthusiasm and got several laws passed particularly dealing with workmen and women. The establishment of employment exchange offices was the result of his foresight.

The Blow Struck by the Cripps Mission

A three-member delegation of Stafford Cripps, Lord Pethick-Lawrence, the then Secretary of State for India, and A. V. Alexander was sent to India in 1946.[12] This delegation interviewed several political leaders in the Raj Bhavan.[13] Dr Ambedkar was invited on 5 April for the interview. Dr Ambedkar's political status had turned quite pitiable by then. Because of adverse results in the elections, the very existence of his political party, the Scheduled Castes Federation (SCF), had fallen into doubt. However, as the sole representative of the SCF, he presented his side systematically and with supporting evidence. Alongside, he also submitted an independent representation regarding the legitimate rights of the untouchables. Both during the interview and in the written representation, he mentioned several demands such as an independent constituency for the untouchables, sufficient representation in the central and provincial legislatures, reservation in government jobs, educational scholarships and concessions, etc. He also insisted that the essence of these demands should be included in the Constitution.

The Cripps delegation later published its conclusion as a State Paper in May. Much to his shock, Dr Ambedkar's demands had been altogether ignored in the document. It looked as if all his efforts made on behalf of the untouchables had been washed away.

In the meanwhile, Lord Wavell, the viceroy of India, asked his Executive Council to submit its resignation because it had been decided to establish a government of the Indian political parties that had emerged victorious in the general elections. The post of the labour minister that Dr Ambedkar occupied, therefore, would automatically move out of his hands. Dr Ambedkar departed from Delhi in a very gloomy state.

With the sole exception of Jagjivanram, not a single untouchable leader had been included in the Interim Ministry of the Viceroy formed in August. As a matter of fact, when Dr Ambedkar sent a telegram demanding that the untouchables should get as many seats as possible in the Executive Council, Jagjivanram had supported it fully and assured his cooperation. The SCF had requested the Dalit leaders that if adequate representation was not given to the untouchables, they should not accept any position.

With the untouchables not being given sufficient representation, it appeared that all the work that Dr Ambedkar had done all through his life for the rights of the untouchables had gone to waste. He would sit worrying night and day in an extremely depressed state.

These shocking events followed in quick succession, delivering painful knocks to Dr Ambedkar one after another. But it wouldn't do for him to stop trying. It was imperative for him to present the miseries of his Dalit brethren before the British government and create a mechanism for procuring their rights and their security. The last option, therefore, was to go to London and see if he could do something. He therefore travelled to London in October and met a number of leaders, but no ray of hope appeared. Finally, he decided that he should meet Churchill himself, but even there he was unsuccessful. The meeting with Churchill just didn't happen.

The impact on Dr Ambedkar of all the episodes recounted above was so deleterious that his health collapsed rapidly. He never regained it. With regard to this, he told me this himself, 'When I went to England then, a few of my acquaintances asked me why I looked so dispirited. I replied to them that after the Cripps Mission had left India, when I read their report, I felt as if someone had pushed me from the top of a very high cliff into a deep abyss.'

A person's resistance is much stronger during the time of youth; illnesses and setbacks are not felt much, and recovery is faster too. But as a person ages, his bodily resistance becomes feebler. Dr Ambedkar's entire life was one of humongous struggle. He endured mental jolts and physical distresses all through his life. Therefore, the state to which his mind and body would have been reduced after he crossed fifty can only be imagined. He was already in a state of considerable debility when the Cripps Mission gave him the final knockout punch.

Constituent Assembly

For the sake of the rights of the untouchables and for their security, it was important that Dr Ambedkar should be in the Constituent Assembly. There were no members of the SCF in the Bombay Legislature. It was with the help and efforts of Jogendranath Mandal that the representatives of the Dalit class of the Bengal Assembly recommended Dr Ambedkar's name, and with the support of the Muslim League, Dr Ambedkar was elected to the Constituent Assembly. Dr Rajendra Prasad was the president of the Constituent Assembly. Dr Ambedkar was later appointed the chairman of the Drafting Committee. I have presented detailed discussions on this issue at the appropriate place. Narayanrao Kajrolkar takes credit for Dr Ambedkar's election to the Constituent Assembly, and that's an outright lie, which I shall discuss at an appropriate place in this book. There were in all seven members of this Drafting Committee, out of whom one resigned, and his place was never filled. Out of the remaining six, one left for America. Again, out of the five remaining, one passed away and that seat remained unfilled too. One of the remaining four was always occupied with the work of the royal court he was working for. Two of them lived far away from Delhi and were often unwell. The outcome was that Dr Ambedkar had to take on additional responsibility. Even under these difficult circumstances, he saw the work through with efficiency.

While performing this historically significant job of the Constitution, Dr Ambedkar never bothered either about his health or about taking rest. He would get so totally involved that he would work eighteen to twenty hours at a stretch. In this regard, Dr Rajendra Prasad, the president of the Constituent Assembly, has expressed his gratitude in his valedictory address.

The further slump in his health from August 1947 onward can be seen from the letters that he has written to his colleagues. His letter of 31 August 1947, written to Kamalakant Chitre, gives an idea of the rapidity with which his health was slipping. Doctor Saheb writes to him:

> 'For the last fifteen days I have not had a wink of sleep, the nights have [become] a nightmare to me. The neurotic pain always comes at midnight and continues throughout. I am taking insulin as well as homeopathic medicine. Neither seems to give me relief. I must now learn to endure what appears beyond cure.'

I entered Dr Ambedkar's life only after his work on the Constitution had begun. Even so, I have given a brief and hurried account of all of Dr Ambedkar's campaigns as also the main events that bruised him until the end of 1947. Even after I had entered his life, he had to continue enduring a number of terrible assaults. The Hindu Code Bill, the defeat in the 1952 elections, the defeat in the 1954 Bhandara by-election, the internal split in the Scheduled Castes Federation, the atmosphere created by the conversion of religion, the bitter experiences with his associates, the court case filed by the contractor with regard to the extension work done on Rajgraha, the atrocities that continued upon the untouchables even after Independence, the concern about the upliftment of the untouchables living in the villages, the humongous reading and writing that continued in spite of his failing health, all of these things continued to leave their injurious mark on his health. I have discussed each one of these events in detail at its appropriate place.

Remedial Treatment on Dr Ambedkar

After my first meeting with Dr Ambedkar, he arrived one day at Dr Malvankar's consulting room where I was working. Dr Malvankar's examination of him has already been mentioned above. Let's look into the history of what happened after that. A thorough investigation of the state of his health revealed that along with a daily injection of insulin he would have to exercise regularly and observe a dietary regimen. It would be imperative for him to consume a specific kind of food. We wrote down for him a detailed list of information and instructions. Handing over this list of prescriptions and diet-related information to Dr Ambedkar, I told him, 'Doctor Saheb, please begin consuming what has been listed here and observe a proper dietary regimen.'

'How am I ever going to manage this?' he asked.

'If your people at home cannot manage this,' I responded, 'you will have to keep a nurse.'

Since I had got to know him quite well by then, out of a sense of affection I said to him, 'If you wish, I can come and stay with you for a few days and train your wife about all this.'

He turned a little sombre when he heard this and just smiled a rather regretful kind of smile. I couldn't fathom that smile. Could I have hurt his feelings? But I hadn't said anything that could have hurt him! I kept wondering what could have happened.

Later, every time he came to Mumbai, he would visit our consulting room without fail and talk about his health. The medicines prescribed by Dr Malvankar began to bring some improvement in his health. Very soon, Dr Malvankar graduated from being his medical consultant to becoming a fast friend. He would often call Dr Malvankar from Delhi, inform him about his health and take his opinion on his treatment. He would always stay in touch with Dr Malvankar either through letters or through the telephone. Dr Malvankar too would interact with his illustrious patient with a lot of affection. Often he would push aside his work at hand and give priority to Dr Ambedkar. If the need arose, Dr Ambedkar would even call him over to Delhi. On his part, Dr Malvankar would set off for Delhi immediately. It hardly needs telling that it was a great honour for us doctors to be treating a great person like Dr Ambedkar, the architect of the Constitution, the law minister of India.

The Lonely Dr Ambedkar

Whenever Dr Ambedkar came to Mumbai, he would invariably visit our consulting room as well as Dr Rao's home. Thus it was that I would always meet him at one of these two places. On one such occasion, I was telling him about his food and the observance of diet when he cut me short and said a little helplessly, 'All that is fine, doctor, but I don't have a woman living with me at home. I live absolutely alone, so who am I going to tell all this stuff about diet and all?'

I turned contemplative when I heard this. I felt a deep sense of sympathy for him. The doctor in me was shaken awake at that moment, and I began to think. Here is a man desperately in need of medical help. If he can be immediately provided with medical advice, guidance, a proper diet and regular treatment, his lifespan will certainly increase. With the intention of keeping faith with humanitarianism and medical ethics, I decided that I should do something about it. In the flow of excitement, I took a moment's pause and said, 'Doctor Saheb, I am pained to hear of your domestic situation. Your health is in a delicate state, and it is absolutely necessary to treat it. Along with the treatment, it is equally important to observe dietary discipline. If it helps, I am quite willing to live with you for two or three months and take care of you. That is to say, once you get into the routine and get habituated to it, there won't be any obstacles to your continuing further with your treatment.'

To which he responded, 'How is that possible?'

I said, 'You are a minister. You would have a large bungalow, secretaries, servants and all. Your bungalow would have a large number of rooms; I can stay in one of them.'

'You staying in my bungalow!' he said. 'How is that possible?'

'Well, all right,' I responded, 'instead of living in your bungalow, I'll stay in your guest house.'

To which he responded instantly, 'You see, doctor, I am alone. Absolutely alone. Listen,' he went on, 'I am an absolutely lonesome, solitary man. What will people say when they see that a young and beautiful doctor is looking after me? I can understand your concern, but what you say is absolutely impossible.'

In one of our earlier meetings, when I had been talking to him about the need for taking medicines regularly and a proper diet, he had smiled wanly. Now I understood the reason behind that melancholic smile. I also understood how lonely he was. Even today, when I think of Dr Ambedkar's loneliness, I realize the amount of distress and loneliness he really endured. He never allowed his loneliness or his afflictions to become impediments to his campaigns or to the acquisition of his goals. When Ramabai passed away in 1935, his son Yeshwant and his nephew Mukund were very young. Within a few days his sister-in-law (Mukund's mother) died too. As a result, the responsibility of bringing up two young boys fell upon him. There was no lady member left at home and there were no close relatives either. In 1942 he had to move to Delhi as a minister in the Viceroy's Executive Council where he lived a solitary life in a grand bungalow while Yeshwant and Mukund lived in Rajgraha. He has even made mention of this in a letter he wrote to Barrister Samarth.

His associates were scattered everywhere, most of them living in Mumbai. Besides, however intimate the friends and associates, they too had their own families and occupations. Meetings, conferences, sittings, tours, discussions, these were the occasions when he came in contact with them. The rest of the time he had to live alone. Who did he have who could devote himself to serving him full-time and with affection? He really had no option but to lie in bed twisting and turning in pain night after night.

There were millions who would offer their lives at one word from Doctor Saheb, but in his personal and domestic life, he was absolutely lonely. On the strength of his enormous scholarship and his history-making work, Dr Ambedkar had reached a very high stature in life. The result was that there was an invisible but enormous abyss of intellectual calibre and concerns that separated him from his associates and followers. Naturally, it was impossible that any of them could interfere in or participate in his personal and domestic life.

Dr Ambedkar's Marriage Proposal

Dr Ambedkar was a person of heroic stature. That we got to know each other and began meeting each other was a matter of great pride and privilege for me. During each of these meetings, his culture, his erudition and his humility would leave a deep impression on my young mind. I carried boundless respect for him, and it was out of this extreme veneration for him and out of appreciation of his physical and domestic circumstances that I used to interact with him with a feeling of affection. If someone had ever suggested to me at that time that I would marry him in the future, I would certainly have regarded that person as a rank lunatic. My equation with him was that of a doctor and a patient; there was nothing in my heart except respect, sympathy and the sincere desire that he should live on for the good of the nation and should therefore be given the best possible medical attention and treatment.

It was on a day in December, when he had come to Mumbai, that he walked into our consulting room. Dr Malvankar gave him a physical examination and prescribed a line of treatment. As he was leaving, he came up to me and said, 'Come, I'll drop you to your house at Dadar. I am heading towards Rajgraha.' There was nothing at all new in this. So often before this event we would sit and chat, and occasionally even go out for a spin. My family was obviously completely in the know about all this. But all our chats and spins were as between a doctor and a patient.

Every time we met, we would talk on various subjects. If we went out for a spin, we would often have snacks and tea together. People who knew Doctor Saheb would often look at me with startled eyes. No doubt they were wondering who this young woman was, loafing around with the great man. I don't know what he would have told his acquaintances about me, but in my heart, I always held him in great esteem.

As I began to know Dr Ambedkar better, I got to know more and more about him. I began seeing from close quarters his attainments and his historic work, and I was stunned. That day he told me, 'Look, doctor, my people and my colleagues have been insisting that I should get married, but it is very difficult for me to find someone to my liking, of adequate qualities and suitable to my state. But for the sake of millions of my people, I have to live on; and for living on, it is only right that I should consider the request of my people with seriousness.'

I stayed silent for a moment and then replied, 'You certainly must have someone who can take care of you.'

Doctor Saheb then went on, 'I begin my search for the right person with you.'

I was flustered at hearing this and just didn't know what to say, so I stayed silent.

As per his schedule, Dr Ambedkar left for Delhi, and I once again got busy with my work. I even forgot all that he had said to me, but he obviously didn't. I realized that on 25 January when I received a thick envelope, which, going by the stamp that it carried, had come from Delhi. I guessed that it was from Dr Ambedkar, and on opening the envelope I found that my guess was right. Obviously, I had no reason to be surprised by it because I assumed that with his treatment in progress, he was seeking advice on some health and treatment issues. But what can one really know about things? After some courtesy talk, he came to the point: 'I am beginning my search for a wife with you, that is, of course, if you are agreeable to it. Think about it and let me know.' He wrote further, 'Considering the difference in age between you and me, and also considering the state of my health, if you turn down my proposal, I shall not be offended at all.'

I became very serious on reading the letter. I just didn't know what to do. I had never even dreamt that Dr Ambedkar could be nursing these kinds of feelings for me. Despite the fact that I was completely blown away by him, despite holding him in extreme respect, I certainly hadn't carried the desire to become his wife.

All through the day I pondered over Dr Ambedkar's letter and his marriage proposal. There was a storm of confusion raging inside me. All through the night I wondered what my decision should be. How was one to turn down such an important personage? How to say yes either? Whose opinion should I take? Many such questions were cropping up in my mind. After thinking over it all night, I decided that since Dr Malvankar and Dr Ambedkar enjoyed such excellent relations, and since he was my senior and a widely experienced person, I should seek his advice. The next day I went to Dr Malvankar's and started work, but I could neither concentrate on work nor could I collect the pluck to go and talk to him. Finally, gathering all my courage in my hands and steeling my heart, I went over to Dr Malvankar and gave him the letter. He read the letter, thought for a moment and then said, 'Dr Ambedkar has made this proposal. He has not imposed himself upon you. Therefore, think on all aspects with a cool head and take your own decision.'

I returned home in an extremely confused state of mind. I was just not able to decide. I took my elder brother into confidence and asked him what decision I should take. He said, 'Ah! That means you are going to become the law *ministerin*[14] of India! Don't think of turning it down! Move forward!' Another of my brothers began teasing me. 'Look,' he said, 'Dr Ambedkar's followers love Dr Ambedkar more than they love their own lives. If they ever get to know that this "*doctorin bai*" is turning down their Babasaheb's proposal, you will be at risk. If you say no, they are very likely to kill you! So, get back to him with an instant yes. Do that, otherwise there is no saving you.'

I was young and inexperienced. In comparison with Dr Ambedkar, I didn't count for anything at all. His personality, his work, his sacrifice, his scholarship, they were all mightier than the Himalayas. Placed against his lofty personality, I was an utterly shrunken phenomenon. How was one to turn down a great person like Dr Ambedkar? My brothers got after me to send him my acceptance. After an entire day of thinking and an entire night too, I made up my mind, in whatever state of bewilderment: all right! Acceptance! The reason was that I was myself a doctor, and I knew very well the state into which his health had slipped. The doctor inside me was prodding me to go and serve him medically. The government had placed upon his shoulders the historic responsibility of drafting the Constitution of free India, and therefore it was utterly imperative that his health should be well looked after, and he should be given appropriate treatment.

Once having decided, I wrote a letter to Dr Ambedkar and conveyed to him my acceptance of his proposal. The reason behind my acceptance was only one: Doctor Saheb's health must be improved, whatever the circumstances. Only then would he be able to perform the historic act of writing down the Constitution of the country in the best possible manner.

After I had sent my acceptance, my brother Balu and I happened to go out for some work. While I was travelling in the local, I casually looked around and noticed the phrase 'Jai Bhim' written in large letters on most of the coaches. The coaches of the trains going to other cities had 'Jai Bhim' painted on them. A gathering of people was also shouting the slogan 'Jai Bhim'. I asked my brother, 'Balu, what's happening here? And who is this Jai Bhim? And who are these slogan-shouting people?'

Balu laughed and said, 'Bhim is your person, and the slogan-shouting people are his infatuated, loyal followers.'

That was the first time I understood the loyalty of these people. That was also when I learnt how these poor, miserable, Dalit followers of Doctor Saheb were so focused and driven. He was the one single leader and guide of millions of the poorest and the most dispossessed people in the country. In a way he was their uncrowned king. He obviously didn't appreciate being addressed as a king, but it won't do to ignore the fact that he very definitely was their king.

I had now accepted the responsibility of the raja of millions of the destitute. After having dispatched my consent, I did some contemplating and realized that I had dragged a great but quite a difficult responsibility over my head. I also began to worry about how I would manage. Would I be able to live up to this great, difficult and hazardous responsibility? Could I have made a grievous error by saying yes? Would I be able to measure up to the expectations of such a great person? What would be the outcome of my decision? What reactions would I have to face from society? Many such questions were creating mayhem inside my head. But finally I calmed my thoughts and decided that as I had already given my consent, there was no backing out. The responsibility had been accepted. I would now move heaven and earth, I would absorb all the pain I had to, but I would most certainly fulfil it with efficiency. I made a firm resolve that I would become one with Doctor Saheb's life and dissolve myself in him.

Dr Ambedkar's Opinions on Marriage

It was quite natural that the doctor should be utterly delighted with my assent to his proposal; after all, it was he who had taken the initiative, and I had satisfied his expectations. I had responded to him around the first week of January 1948. Call it a reply if you will or call it a reciprocation, in the last week of January, Doctor Saheb sent a gold chain for me. In the centre of the chain was a pendant with an anchor etched on it. Since the chain had been put into a small, sealed receptacle, it was impossible that the person who brought it to me had any idea what lay inside. The person who brought this receptacle to me was Shankaranand Shastri. That gold chain was a token of Dr Ambedkar's acceptance of me. That only firmed up my decision to march ahead. It was now final that I would not withdraw under any circumstance.

After the gold chain had reached me, I sent two letters to Doctor Saheb: one on 5 February and the other on 6 February. He responded from Delhi to my letters on 12 February with a letter that ran into twenty-five pages. During those days he was very busy with his work on the Constitution. He would work for eighteen to twenty hours every day. That was why the letters he wrote to me then were written at midnight. The letter of 12 February contained information on his work on the Constituent Assembly, his sentiments behind sending me the gold chain and the medal, and his opinion on what marriage meant to him. Since his thoughts are so educative, I am giving below relevant excerpts from the letter. I have no doubt that the readers will find them educative too. Doctor Saheb wrote:

> 'The last two letters of yours have dashed upon me in quick succession. One is dated the 5th and the next 6th inst. I have been extremely busy in the drafting of the new Constitution, which has been trusted to a Committee of which I am the Chairman. I have promised the President of the Constituent Assembly to hand over to him the final draft on the 15th Feb., i.e. three days from today. I am determined not to ask for more time and as the date of the presentation is approaching near, I am working day and night to keep to the time-table. That is one reason why I was not able to reply to each of your letters as it came.

'. . . The chain is a new one. I have three or four, I thought I could spare one. I selected a chain because I feel it could easily be converted into a necklace, which, so far as I know, women are very fond of. The pendant—what you call medal—was not a part of the chain. The pendant is a rare, old, unique piece which I had purchased maybe 20 years ago when I was a student in London. I purchased it for a watch belt, which it was then the fashion to wear. When the fashion changed, I ceased wearing it. It was lying with me. I send it to you because of the anchor which is engraved on it. It stands for deep love and attachment. I felt I could not select a better symbol and token of my feelings for you. That is why I sent it along with the chain. I have been wondering what made you say that the idea behind it was to tie it into your neck and to treat you as a dog. Only a person holding [the opinion] that I was devoid of all culture could have thought of saying so. I must say that it hurt me very much. I know I come from the lowest strata of society. But I don't think I have met anybody so far who has found me wanting in culture. I have been the greatest champion of the elevation and emancipation of women and in my own community I have done my best to raise the status of women and I am very proud of it . . .

'. . . Marriage can be founded on love, which can be described in no other terms except the longing to belong . . .

'. . . My view is that marriage is an everlasting union. It is indestructible . . .

'. . . At this stage of my life my aim is to reach the end of my existence . . . in peace and honour. It would be well if happiness was added to it. A loving wife can do that. If there is none, the loss would be of happiness only. I would at least have peace and honour. By your adverse reaction you would be doing me neither wrong nor loss. I shall be where I was, therefore avoid all sentiments . . .'

Our correspondence carried on steadily from then onwards. Every one of his letters inundated me with a torrent of love and affection.

Our Personal Correspondence

The correspondence between Dr Ambedkar and me is enough to justify a full volume. It is altogether personal, and therefore also confidential. But on the other hand, there are several letters that throw light on some unpublished aspects of Doctor Saheb's life. A lot of things are reflected in these letters: the principles by which Doctor Saheb lived his life, his philosophy, his goals and policies, the meaning he made of rumours, the traditional principles as he understood them, his intellect, and so on. All these things give his letters extraordinary importance and worth.

A number of people had been insisting for many years that I should ignore the constraints of formality and get the entire personal correspondence published just as it is. My well-wishers and friends said that the publication of these letters would throw authoritative light on several known and unknown matters. Even beyond that, my position and role in Dr Ambedkar's life would become clearer. A movement having started of studying Dr Ambedkar's life and his campaigns, a large number of scholars, researchers and commentators from India and abroad are investigating various aspects of Dr Ambedkar on the basis of available resources. I too, therefore, appreciate the need and the necessity of publishing the letters exactly as they are. But since some of the matter there is of a personal nature, I do carry doubts as to whether they should be published or not.

When it is a matter of publishing letters of a personal nature, issues like procedure, decorum and other proprieties that need be observed in the public space have to be considered. Even though I am a doctor, I am alive to the fact that letters are genuine and extremely important resources. Now, in the context of this autobiography, it has become not only necessary but imperative to use relevant excerpts from some of the letters. In the interest of providing context to events, for the sake of continuity and to bring in legitimacy, I am using a few excerpts in this book. But if a demand arrives at a later time from scholars and the public at large, I shall certainly publish a compilation of our entire correspondence as historical documents. Meanwhile, readers and scholars may find satisfaction in the excerpts of letters I have used here from the perspective of this autobiography and to lend support to historical events.

I have deliberately not presented here the letters that I wrote to the doctor, the reason being that he has given point-wise responses to whatever I had written to him; therefore, what I wrote to him has automatically got reflected in his responses. It can be observed everywhere that he held such clear positions and opinions that there would be no equivocation anywhere. He would state his position and opinions uninhibitedly, uncaring of the company in which he was. He would never accept anything just because it had been said by some great person or because it was popularly accepted. He would accept only that which he had tested against the touchstone of his own intellect or experience. His values and his philosophy of life are of course sharply visible in his letters; what is also visible is the extreme concern he had for me and the love and affection in which he held me.

I have always been fond of reading, particularly history, religion and politics. As a result, I would get immense joy in holding discussions on various topics with Dr Ambedkar. When I began living with Dr Ambedkar, the range of my reading spread in all directions. I learnt several new things from him. In the course of our conversations, a lot of personal experiences would also crop up, making the exercise quite exciting and animated. When debating or conversing with Doctor Saheb, I would not be found wanting in any way, which would bring from him the appreciative response, 'Sharu, you have great literary sense. If you take it to heart, you can create good literature. After all this talent, why did you get into the medical profession?'

My response to him was, 'There was no reason for the question to arise as to why I went into the medical profession. The custom and the inclination among us siblings was to do whatever our parents wanted us to do, never to turn them down. My father had wanted that I should become a doctor, and that was it! That was good enough for me. As per my father's wishes, I and another sister of mine became doctors.'

Dr Ambedkar's perceptive followers and discerning researchers will experience the revelation of distinctive aspects of his personality. I hope, therefore, that the discerning among Doctor Saheb's followers, analysts, researchers, professors and knowledgeable readers will make an informed and just assessment of all the rumours and misunderstandings that are rife relating to my marriage with Dr Ambedkar and the role I have played in his life and rely on truth alone.

Happenings Related to Our Marriage

I informed Dr Malvankar that I had sent my acceptance of his marriage proposal to Dr Ambedkar. He was very happy. After receiving my acceptance letter, Dr Ambedkar wrote to Dr Malvankar too on this matter. The sequence of events related to our marriage that happened between February and April becomes evident on reading the letters that Dr Ambedkar wrote to his associates, friends and to me.

The reply that Doctor Saheb sent to Dr Malvankar on 16 February 1948 is nothing short of a commendation. Dr Ambedkar writes to Dr Malvankar:

> 'Your two letters have reached me. Your first letter giving me a short history of Dr Kabir did not surprize [sic] me in the least. She deserves all the high praise you have bestowed upon her. I have no hesitation in saying that she is a woman of high intellectual

attainments and (although my knowledge of her is very meagre) of high character and virtue. She is worth the money you say she earns per month. I wish I had her sharp intellect . . .'

There was incessant correspondence between Dr Ambedkar and me. He responded to my letter of 16 February 1948, on the 19th, in which he wrote:

Dearest Sharu,

I received your letter of the 16th this afternoon. The joy with which I read it was indeed boundless—infinite, as we say. I said that you were [the] first to be a casualty. But you were quite right in saying that I had concealed my feelings, though more successfully. For I too was a casualty from the very beginning. I wonder if there is a similar case of love at first sight from both sides. I am sure we shall be two bodies animated by one soul. Nothing but death shall put us asunder. I am sorry my letter made you weep. Tears are good. They wash off all impurities and make the heart clean. If you have wept believe me I too have wept probably for a different reason—namely the realization of a dream—of finding a woman possessed both of virtue and intellect to be my wife—and the joy [that] has come in its wake. Let us make a determination to make each other happy. I am glad Guruji has blessed our decision . . .

One must learn to control even love. I am afraid you have become a victim of it. I know you can't bear separation any longer. I too am tired of the loneliness. I long to have you near me. But pray give me some little time. I assure you, I will not try your patience . . . Please do not be disgruntled. When we have to live together [for] the rest of our lives a little time lost before we join cannot be a matter of grievance.

. . . But I was very much grieved to learn that you had not taken food for three days. What on earth you did this for. [sic]

> I thought Sharu was a wise girl. I hope you will not do this again. You are my treasure and I do not want you to suffer either in body or in mind . . .
>
> How strange and mysterious are the ways of destiny!! Who could have thought that I and you would be husband and wife. Born in different strata, lived in different circles, trodden different paths, here we are meeting as patient and nurse and then led to the altar. Destiny has been kind to me in establishing this contact.
>
> . . . Another mysterious thing is the pet name you have given me. It was the very name by which I was called by my fellow students when I was studying in the Elphinstone High School. I am wondering what suggested it to you? [sic] You are welcome to use it . . .
>
> With fondest and deep love,
> From – Raja.

Imagine the kind of intense love Doctor Saheb bore for me and how concerned he was for me. Sentence after sentence oozes with his love and affection for me. While writing to him, I had spontaneously addressed him as 'Raja' because he was the raja—the king—of millions of the dispossessed and the downtrodden, and I too had accepted him as 'my Raja' in my heart. That was why I would address him as Raja in my letters. He too always signed off as Raja.

Once Dr Ambedkar and I had decided to marry each other, we informed Dr Malvankar about this decision. He gave us his good wishes and his blessings. Since Dr Malvankar was senior to me in all respects and was also in the seat of my teacher in my medical profession, Dr Ambedkar would respectfully refer to him as 'Guruji' in his letters.

Many references can be found in the letters he wrote to his associates of our decision to get married. Doctor Saheb wrote from Delhi to his close associate Kamalakant Chitre on 20 February 1948:

'. . . My health has suddenly gone down and I am facing a relapse. There has been a reversion to the old state as it existed before. I phoned Dr Malvankar. I have passed four nights without a minute of sleep with most excruciating pain in both the legs. My servants have to keep awake and nurse me the whole night. I have been examined by two most eminent doctors who say that if my condition does not improve immediately, the trouble in the legs [will become] chronic and incurable. This has naturally unnerved me. I am now thinking of your suggestion of having someone to look after my health more sympathetically than I was prepared to do before. I have decided to marry Dr Kabir, she is the best match I can find. I thought of informing you what was happening. Right or wrong, the decision is made. I would, however, welcome any observations you may have to make. In the meantime, I would like you to keep this a top secret, not to be disclosed to anybody except Jadhav, who wished it and I also believe helped to bring it about at the Bombay end . . .'

On 21 February, Doctor Saheb writes to Jadhav from Delhi on the topic of our marriage:

'. . . You will be glad to learn that myself and Dr Kabir have decided to get married. I like to inform you of this because you know you have played a very great part in bringing it about.

'I am sure, my choice has fallen on the right person and that she is just the person equipped both by intellect as well as virtue to suit my needs. I have done it to avoid the general and persistent criticism that I am not doing everything I am told to do to preserve my health. This is a new chapter in my life and I hope it will end well. I would like you to keep this a close secret for the moment . . .'

Along with informing Kamalakant Chitre, Dr Malvankar, Daulat Jadhav, Bhaurao Gaikwad and others, he also informed Dr Nair of the *Free Press Journal* about our decision to get married. Dr Ambedkar enjoyed a close relationship with Dr Nair and the main reason for this intimacy was Dr Nair's strong inclination towards Buddhism. The Buddha temple on the premises of Nair Hospital in Bombay Central is evidence of Dr Nair's attraction for Buddhism. Whenever Dr Ambedkar had felt the need for some relaxation while in Mumbai, Nair's bungalow at Juhu would always be available to him. I could not procure the letter that Dr Ambedkar wrote to Dr Nair. I remember that information related to this letter had appeared in an interview of the biographer Dhananjay Keer published in a Marathi newspaper a few years ago [1985]. It was the last interview that Keer had given and was published after his death to pay homage to him. In the interview, Keer referred to that letter written to Dr Nair and mentioned that he himself had read that letter. Keer talked about the contents of the letter (of giving me credit and expressing his gratitude) in that interview.

I had written a letter to Doctor Saheb in Marathi, which he received on the evening of 19 February. He had sent me a letter that very afternoon, which I have given above. After reading my Marathi letter, he replied to me on that very day, the contents of which are given below:

> My dear Sharu,
>
> I have posted today a letter addressed to you. This evening I got a letter written in Marathi. I am intensely grieved to learn that my first letter made you so disconsolate. You are imagining that you hurt me by your first letter and unless I write to say that I have forgiven you, you will not be happy. To know that you have given up food from the 16th has made me feel miserable, terribly miserable. I had no intention to cause such unhappiness to you.
>
> . . . What can I do to atone for this wrong and to console you. I treasure your letters. When I am alone at night and most often

awake, I read them over and over again. You might be doing the same about my letters though I know they do not have the same soft and sweet aroma which yours have. I therefore hesitate to ask you to destroy this particular letter. It will help you to forget its harsh and harsher tones. As for me, you will believe me once for all—that I have no such feelings of anger or punishment as you think I have. Would I not forgive my Sharu 100 such indiscretions? I shall not be happy until you write to me that you have overcome the sense of having done wrong to me and that you are now your original self.

Having decided to have you I have not the slightest desire to keep you [away] longer than it is absolutely necessary. . . Our marriage should be legal in your own interest. I shall never agree to place you in a false position. The Hindu Marriage Law is being amended and as amended, it will permit inter-caste marriages among Hindus. The Bill is already before the Central Legislature. In fact, I as the Law Minister of the Government of India I [sic] am in charge of it. The Legislative programme of the Government of India is so crowded that it is doubtful if it could be passed before the end of this year. I am dead certain that you will not agree to wait till then. The only way that remains is to get married under the Civil Marriage Act. The procedure under this Act is as follows:

i. The bride or the bridegroom lodge an application declaring their intention to marry with the Registrar of Marriages.
ii. No marriage can be performed until fourteen days have elapsed from the date of the lodging of the application.
iii. Within this period of 14 days any person may file an application stating that he has an objection to the parties marrying.
iv. If any such application under (iii) is received, the matter goes to the High Court for decision.

v. If the High Court rejects the objection the parties can proceed to solemnize the marriage.

This is an expeditious way. If there is no objection, parties can be married within [sic] 14 days of the date of their application. I don't think that there is anybody who will come forward to put in an objection. Certainly none on my side. Is there likely to be anybody on your side? Of course, objection on the ground of caste will not be allowed. It must be an objection on some other ground.

My plan was this. When I come to Bombay in the first week of March, we will file the application. I will, thereafter come back to Delhi and return in the first week of April when we get married. This may carry us to about the 15th of April. Is that too much of a delay for you? There is no way of cutting it short. I hope you will buck up to bear this much separation. Let me know.

I was very agreeably surprized [sic] to have your letter written in Marathi. It pleased me very much. I love the English language. Indeed even Englishmen have admired my English prose. But, even I have to confess that your style of English writing is much superior to mine. I can never imitate or reproduce the homely touches you give to your thoughts by some very original phrasing, which has a charm all its own. Your letters send me to sleep, so soothing they are. If you hereafter adopt your mother tongue in one sense I will indeed be sorry. In another sense, I welcome your new departure. For your Marathi is as good as your English. I therefore don't mind your writing in Marathi provided you do not give up English altogether . . .

I have not the slightest objection to your proposal to address me in the singular. The old Hindu traditional mode of address, the husband to address his wife in the singular and wife to address the husband in the dual is a relic of the past which has placed the wife on a lower footing than the husband. It ought to be abandoned at least in private.

> When you wrote in Marathi you probably expected that I should reply in Marathi. At one time, I had a mastery over the Marathi language. No one even now [can] claim to have read so much classical Marathi literature as I have done. I was the editor of a weekly paper in Marathi for well nigh twenty years—and my writings, if they were collected together, would fill in at least three fat volumes. I have lost touch with the Marathi language and feel no confidence that I could write in it something which could have the charm, the simplicity and the grace which you seem to be able to produce. I am therefore very hesitant to sit down and reply to you in Marathi. I will, however, venture to do it but on one condition—namely that you promise not to laugh at my mistakes.
>
> With fondest love from
> Raja
>
> You dubbed my last letter as an essay, a very legitimate comment I must say. But [you] dare not call this an essay, can you?

Although he admits in the above letter that my style of writing English is better than his, I believe that it was simply the magnanimity of his enormous heart. Dr Ambedkar has written in one of his letters and he would always say to me too that 'your intelligence and my labour' would produce wonderful things.

I sent him a letter in Marathi. Doctor Saheb responded to it on 21 February. Beginning his letter with [Marathi translated into English]: 'Loving and respectful salutation from her Raja to Sharu', he writes on [in Marathi]:

> The letter written by Sharu reached her Raja 2/3 days ago. Sharu's Raja has responded to it in English. It's quite certain that Sharu would expect the reply to be in Marathi, hence Sharu's Raja is writing this Marathi letter.

Raja's Sharu, Sharu's Raja is incalculably regretful that some harsh words in Sharu's Raja's letter caused her pain—she stopped eating, stopped sleeping. Sharu's Raja had not the slightest idea that his letter would leave such a terrible impact. Does she believe that Sharu's Raja could hurt his beloved Sharu intentionally? Sharu's Raja is most certainly not such a hard-hearted and indifferent person. There's a saying in Marathi which means 'First bitter, then sweet', which Raja's Sharu surely remembers. When Sharu becomes Raja's and Raja becomes Sharu's, no distance should arrive and no misunderstandings should happen between them during their journey through this mortal world; it was merely with this intention that Sharu's Raja placed before Sharu some questions that are unpleasant but deserving of thought. Sharu's Raja's intention was pure when he did this. Keeping this in mind, Sharu's Raja expects and believes that Raja's Sharu will allay her grief and forgive her Raja.

Sharu's Raja is fully aware that Sharu shall not tolerate even the slightest agony of separation. Sharu's Raja has reassured Sharu in his previous letter that the extent of the separation shall be pared off to the minimum possible . . .

Sharu, in her letter, has taunted that it is Sharu's Raja's resolve that Sharu should not cross the threshold without being lawfully bonded, Sharu's Raja is not afraid of the world. It's 25 years now that he has been fighting against all of Hindustan. Nobody had the courage to stick his chest out before Gandhi, but Sharu's Raja was not afraid of assaulting him with harsh words and he went on triumphing in this battle and people's respect for him increased too; Raja's Sharu will have to admit this. It has to be said with regret that Sharu has not sufficiently reflected on how this triumph was achieved and why the respect increased. If she had done so, Raja's Sharu would have herself realized that her taunt was misplaced.

The key to my success lies in my pure and virtuous conduct. Since Raja's Sharu has not experienced this, she may perhaps find it difficult to endorse what I say, but Sharu's Raja is certain that experience will lead her to accept the truth of this statement. My role in my conflict with the world was of justice and ethics. Some freedom-loving people say that one must do what one feels and not be afraid of popular indictment. I cannot accept the principle that one should not be afraid of public indictment. One should not be afraid of public indictment while working for the advancement of truth, morality and good conduct, this I accept. Sharu's Raja does not feel that there is any issue of truth, morality and good conduct involved in getting intimate without the observance of proper rituals; hence the insistence that we wait till the rituals are done with. There is no doubt that Raja's Sharu will accept this position and this line of thought.

Sharu says that Raja is her divinity; but it is equally true that Sharu is Raja's divinity too and Raja sees no need to present Sharu with any evidence for this. Sharu is Raja's devotee and Raja is Sharu's devotee. Sharu knows of no divinity except Raja and Raja knows of no divinity except Sharu. In appearance and in bodily needs, they look like separate bodies; but both Raja's Sharu and Sharu's Raja firmly believe that there is a single soul that resides in them. The coming together of Sharu and her Raja is not an animal coincidence but a divine coincidence. If it hadn't been divine coincidence, how could Sharu, living in faraway Gujarat, and her Raja, floundering in the whirlpool of politics, have met? But it may also be said that this is a soul-coincidence. One soul saw the other soul, both recognized a common identity and embraced each other. Will this embrace ever loosen? Raja is certain that nothing except death can break this embrace. It's a big desire with Raja that both should die at the same time. Who will look after Raja after Sharu is gone? Hence it looks that Raja should die earlier. But from the other perspective, Raja's mind has no peace when he thinks of what will happen to Sharu after Raja passes away. Having been swept away by public service, Raja has not gathered any wealth. Sharu's Raja has not been able to do anything beyond working for the slaking of hunger. Sharu's Raja has no pension. If Sharu's Raja had been in good health, there wouldn't have been any problem; but doubts spring up on account of his ill-health, and when the thought comes of what will happen to Sharu, the heart becomes agitated. Sharu's Raja believes that Lord Buddha will find some way out of all this.

A Registered Parcel is being sent along with this letter. It carries (1) the image of Ashoka's Pillar. This image will be printed on the cover page of the Constitution volume that we have prepared. I have selected this. Sharu will like it and will feel that Raja too has a love for beauty. (2) There are three pictures from the *Illustrated Weekly* that show women's clothing from various regions. I thought that if ever Sharu feels like buying some sleeping dress [sic], these pictures will help her to decide how they should be. In Raja's opinion, the Marwari dress looks very beautiful. Its scalloping and flare look very attractive. If the folds are reduced, that would be the end of it. These are only Raja's opinions, Sharu should decide for herself, she is free. If Raja's choice is approved, five or six sleeping dresses should be made . . .

As mentioned in the earlier letter, Raja does not know Marathi as well as Sharu does; it's English that's his mother tongue. This effort has been made only for satisfying Sharu. But as Gyaneshvar has said:

Jaisa swabhaav mai-baapaacha | Apatya boley jaree bobadi bhaashaa
Tari adhik tayaachaa Santosh aathi ||

[If children imitate the conduct of their parents, even with a lisp, the satisfaction derived is great.]

Tari nyoon tey purate | Adhik tey sarate | karooni ghyaavey he tumatey vinavit asey

[Even if something is in a small quantity, it lasts. Something available in abundance finishes off quickly. Hence you are requested to find satisfaction in smallness.]

It is with this faith that this child-like babble has been written.

That's all there is for today.

Good wishes and hugs to Sharu from Raja.

Sharu's Raja.
21/2/48

Possessing no wealth, no pension, illness-ridden, he would feel very agitated about what would happen to his Sharu. Since his passing away, I have been experiencing how well-placed his apprehensions were.

The national emblem adopted by India is the lions atop the Ashoka Pillar. The above letter gives evidence that this emblem was chosen by Dr Ambedkar. The selection of the national flag and the national emblem along with drafting the Constitution—these are but a few of his services to the nation.

He would pay personal attention to everything related to me. Particularly in the matter of clothes, the choice would always be his. That was why he had expressed his wish that I should get sleeping dresses made as per the different designs that had been printed in the *Illustrated Weekly*. He obviously never imposed his wishes on me, but his desire and his choice would be so appropriate that I would always find them acceptable. Needless to say, I did get five or six Marwari-style sleeping dresses stitched as he had written in the letter.

Love-Deprived Dr Ambedkar

Dr Ambedkar's mother had passed away when he was barely five, so he had no memory of receiving his mother's love. After his mother passed away, his father's sister, Meerabai, took care of him. Ramjirao later took a second wife, but a stepmother is after all a stepmother; what love could he have got from her? Dr Ambedkar never got along with her. In February 1913, Subhedar Ramjirao himself passed away in Mumbai. With the passing away of his father, his one single support disappeared. He was left bereft of a father's love too.

Even while he was a student, he was married in April 1906 to Ramabai, who was the daughter of Bhiku Walangkar, a relative of Gopalbaba Walangkar. But domestic bliss he was not to experience, because after his father's death in 1913, the responsibility of his family, as also of his own education, fell upon him. He worked for some time in the Baroda government. Later, from July 1913 to June 1917 he had to live in England and America while pursuing his higher education. As per the agreement with the Baroda government, he began work there in 1917. Bitter experiences there brought him to Mumbai. From 1920 to 1923, he again went to England and Germany to finish his MSc, DSc and Bar-at-Law degrees. From 1924 onwards he submerged himself in public service. The Chowdar Lake satyagraha at Mahad, the Kalaram temple entry satyagraha, Nashik, the three Round Table Conferences, the Poona Pact and plenty of other things happened in succession. Living such a busy life, how much time could he have spent at home? After the time spent at his legal practice, reading, writing, meetings, conferences, tours, how much time could he have spent in the company of his wife? Ramabai was illiterate, while the doctor himself was a giant of a scholar, and that made Ramabai behave bashfully. The group photo (included in this book) of Dr Ambedkar's family shows Ramabai sitting shrunk into herself, and that tells its story. One can feel an invisible distance between husband and wife—arising probably out of the disparity in their educational attainments. A second point is that Dr Ambedkar spent most of his time in his office at Damodar Hall, Parel, and visited home once in two or four days whenever he had the time.

Ramabai became increasingly feeble on account of her worries for Dr Ambedkar and the austerities she practised. She then fell prey to tuberculosis and passed away in 1935. This was how Dr Ambedkar was deprived of his wife's love too.

He remained deprived of children's love and children's joy. Yeshwant was born in December 1912; he would always be unwell. Yeshwant's ill health was a constant source of worry for Dr Ambedkar. There were four other children after Yeshwant: three boys and a girl, but not one of them survived. Particularly, his youngest son Rajratna, who passed away in 1926, was his father's darling. After his passing away, Dr Ambedkar wrote a letter to his friend Dattoba in which he wrote, 'My last boy was a wonderful boy the like of whom I have seldom seen. With his passing away life to me is a garden full of weeds.' With Rajratna's death, Dr Ambedkar lost interest in his domestic life. He would rarely return home after that.

He never experienced a daughter's love. That left just Yeshwant, but he too would always be ill. Either because of his illness or because of some other adverse circumstances, Yeshwant didn't learn much. The doctor had a keen desire to send him to Columbia University in America, but that desire remained unfulfilled.

Dr Ambedkar was also denied the love of siblings. His elder brother died in November 1927, and his sister passed away within a few years of that. He was left with no close relatives at all. Having thus been perpetually denied a mother's love, a father's love, a wife's love, children's love, siblings' love and the love of other close relatives, he grew up with a deep yearning for love. But for all that, he never let the shortcomings of his personal life interfere with his commitment to the upliftment of Dalits. His work inevitably left its mark on the state of his health. It was his ill health that eventually led to our meeting; it turned out to be a life-changing meeting and my entire life became meaningful.

Despite the insistence of his associates, he had never thought of a second marriage. It was on account of his ill health that he was compelled to think more seriously about a second marriage, and that was when I met him. Since he had been denied love all his life, the dam burst for him, and he inundated me with a torrent of love and extreme affection. I responded to him in equal measure.

Like a pure, clear spring under a rock, that was how it was with Dr Ambedkar. His face was rather stern; his overall personality reflected a combination of seriousness and an impressive lustre arising out of an extremely studious nature. But how clear and gentle his mind and heart were can be seen in every one of his letters.

I had written a letter to him on 13 March 1948, to which he replied on 15 March:

> Dear Sharu,
>
> I got your second letter of the 13th just this afternoon. I expected your first letter of the 11th to come to my hand along with the second. But it did not. Evidently, it is lost in the post. I am sorry to have missed it . . . I believe it is Tolstoy's life that has been the cause of your mental disturbance and depression. You seem to think that I had some secret motive in asking you to read the same. I do not wish to say that it is your nature to suspect everything I do which is capable [of] many readings. Or it may be that coming as you do from a world different from mine, you do not like to trust. I cannot hope to cure you of this. But I hope our association will teach you in course of time that you had no ground for distrust.
>
> I had no particular motive in recommending you to read Tolstoy's life. Certainly, it was not my purpose that you should play the part of the Countess and [I] of the Count and do whatever they did just to dramatize their life as our own. Such a thing would be foolish and if Sharu had the slightest idea of the intelligence and character of her [Raja], she would not have attributed such a motive to him. My idea in asking you to read Tolstoy had [no] such foundation. I am very fond of literature, particularly biography.

Every man's and woman's life is short—and the channel in which it runs is always very narrow. Consequently the experience of every individual is always very limited. A limited experience gives a narrow range of sympathies. Such a person is often a misfit in life. For in one's life one is bound to meet persons who have led a different sort of life and have different experiences to recount—and unless one is aware of experiences undergone by other people there is no ennoblement—and enrichment in the values of life. Tolstoy is not my hero. In fact no author is my hero. I am very selective. I choose what is worth choosing from any author worthy of perusal—and assimilate into myself and build my own personality which if you will allow one to say is not an imitation of anybody howsoever high. It is my own original self. If I asked you to read Tolstoy it is not because he is my model. I asked you to do so only because I thought that you would like to know his experiences of married life. After you had finished reading his life, I was going to ask you to read the life of Disraeli. Tolstoy's life is at one end and Disraeli's is at the other end. In Disraeli's life you would have found how married life can be perfect bliss. I did not ask you to read Disraeli first because it consists of six fat volumes. There is, therefore, no catch & no game in my having asked you to read Tolstoy.

There was, if any, one motive which I do not mind disclosing [to] you. Scientists are good in their laboraties [sic]. But the laboratory is not the whole world. The world we live in is quite different from the laboraties [sic]. Scientists appear to be such poor specimens of humanity outside their laboraties [sic]. It is because they have no general knowledge of humanity and this is so because they never read general literature. I have a feeling that you too have the faults of the scientists and it is because I don't want you to look [a] fool when you appear in society that I want you to inform your mind, enlarge the scope of your ability for intelligent conversation that I want you to read general literature.

Do you doubt the necessity of your being educated along the lines I suggest? Do you doubt my motive in asking you to read Tolstoy?

. . . At this age I cannot be as active as a man of 20/25. My disease has made me more inactive that [sic] I would otherwise be. Since you seem to abhor sex, my condition is an advantage to you. I cannot however say that I am altogether devoid of [the] sexual urge. However, you can rest assured I will not force myself on you against your wishes. I am a gentleman and if a woman against whom I have rights of a husband [does not like it], I can practice self-control and continance [sic], which I have been used it [sic] for the last 15 years . . . But having given my word to take you as my wife, I will not paw, sniff and snot [sic] as an angry cat does when it is annoyed. I am determined to make you happy no matter what . . .

. . . I am sorry for the depression that overcame you. I hope this letter will lift it up.

With fondest love,
From Raja
15.3.48

Along with our correspondence, there would also be telephonic conversations on an almost daily basis. His trunk calls would arrive mostly at night. We had talked on the 16th. One cannot talk for very long or in any detail over the telephone. Even after our conversation, he wrote to me on the 16th at midnight. It will be appropriate to give important excerpts of that letter here:

[Translated from Marathi]

Dear Sharu,

It is 12 o'clock of [sic] the night and I am feeling sleepy too. I had not wanted to sit down for writing a letter at this hour, but listening to your twaddle has made it necessary, so I sit here making day of night . . .

It looks like you have a suspicious nature. I had just asked you to read a book and the end of its plot was not sweet, and there! Suspicion arrived! There was some secret motive at the root of my asking you to read the book. So, the persistent demand of telling you what that motive was! It appears that your character is to some extent like that of Tolstoy's wife. She too was a suspicious person like you. She was so full of suspicion that she turned hysterical and jumped into a well and then she started screaming, 'Pull me out!' I have begun to fear; will you harass me like Tolstoy's wife harassed her husband? I am afraid as I write this sentence too—who knows, you may abandon food and water and sit crying! And decide for yourself that something bad is going to come out of all this! The conclusion that can be drawn from all this is that Sharu has no faith in her Raja. It is unfortunate that Sharu has still not begun to believe that Raja will never harm her and Raja loves her boundlessly. I do not know what to do about it. As Tukaram has said, 'Devaavar Bhaav thevonee' [letting god carry the burden], Raja has decided to do just that.

[English from here onwards]

I have received only one letter so far. What has happened to the rest I don't know. This is my third letter against one of yours. I hope to receive one more tomorrow and I trust it will be a sweet one, without any doubts and difficulties.

I have purchased one wristwatch for you. It is a most beautiful article. Its price is Rs. 780/-. The gold band to replace the leather band has been ordered from Calcutta. It is sure to cost more than Rs. 350/-. I am sure you will like it.

. . . The event as arranged will take place here in Delhi. Similarly, there is no truth in the report, which has appeared in the

Bombay press, that I am resigning from Govt. I want to stay for some time, if [for] no other reason at least to give my dear Sharu to share in the pride and the joy of the office of her husband, which does not come to every lady.

I am much better. The intensity of [the] pain in my legs has lessened. I am, however, feeling very weak.

With fondest love,
From Raja

Wedding Date Fixed

The letter that Doctor Saheb sent to Bhaurao Gaikwad from Delhi on 16 March 1948 regarding his choice of me and the decision to get married is extremely important. It gives a realistic explanation for why he chose me as his wife and why he had no choice in the matter of going for a second marriage. The letter is this:[15]

New Delhi
16-03-1948

My dear Bhaurao,

I have received your letter . . .

There are two other matters I wish to write to you . . .

The next thing is about myself. Friends and medical advisers have told me in quite definite terms that while there is every chance of my recovering from the malady I am suffering from it would be fatal if there was a relapse. Diabetes they say is a nutritional disease—and unless there is someone to look after my food insulin etc. the chances of a relapse cannot be altogether discounted. They have been urging me to keep a nurse or housekeeper if I did not wish to marry. I have considered the matter for a long time. I have no doubt that keeping a nurse or a housekeeper would give rise to a scandle [sic]. The better course is to marry. After Yeshwant's mother's death I had decided not to marry. But circumstances have now forced my resolution. The doctor says that for me the choice is between marriage and early death.

While it is easy to make the choice it was of course difficult if not impossible to find [a] wife. A woman to be my wife must be educated, must be a medical practitioner and must be good at cooking. It would be impossible in our community to find a woman who would combine the three qualifications and also suit my age. It also appeared impossible to find a woman outside our community to marry me for the simple reason [that] I have no contacts. My life has been so solitary that I have had no contacts with caste Hindu men much less with caste Hindu women. Fortunately, I have been able to find one. She comes from the Saraswat Brahmin community. The marriage as at present will take place in Delhi on the 15th of April. Keep this confidential.

I came to Delhi on the 11th. I am feeling much better though I feel considerably weak.

With kind regards,
B. R. A.

Meanwhile, D.G. Jadhav had given me the message that Doctor Saheb would arrive in Mumbai on 15 April 1948 and the marriage ceremony would take place in Mumbai. It is difficult to understand why, with nothing of this kind having actually been fixed, Jadhav should have given me this message. Well, actually, very early on, Doctor Saheb's plan was that he would arrive in Mumbai in the first week of March, and we would file an application for marriage with the Registrar of Marriages. He would later go to Delhi and return to Mumbai in the first week of April. The intention was to have the marriage ceremony then. His estimation was that by then 15 April would have dawned. But he later arranged that the ceremony would happen in Delhi.

Now, the reason for fixing 15 April as the date of our marriage. Since 14 April was Doctor Saheb's official date of birth, I was very keen on 14 April. But there would be hordes of friends, well-wishers, colleagues and admirers visiting him to offer their good wishes, and that would have made things very inconvenient. The other important factor was that 15 April was a Thursday, which, as a result of personal experiences, Doctor Saheb regarded as auspicious. As a coincidence, he passed away too on a Thursday, on 6 December 1956.

I wrote two letters to Doctor Saheb, one on 16 March and the other on 17 March. He responded to my letters on 19 March, stating that they were the sweetest letters I had written to him yet, and stated that my language was 'superb and very charming'.

Here is the letter:

12 midnight

Dear Sharu,

> Your two letters of the 16th and 17th have reached me, one today and the other yesterday. They have been the sweetest letters you have written to me so far. Your language is superb and very charming. I make no attempt to emulate you. I am sure I will fail. I don't know how many times I read them. They do not seem to lose their charm and I should say their poetry. From the summary you have given of your letter it must have been very beautiful when you are not inclined to [be] 'mischievous'. I am using your own words [–] you are adorable. I feel certain that you have in you the making of a literary person of high calibre. You should try your hand at it.
>
> I share your belief [that] we shall be the happiest people and nothing is going to come in the way of our happiness. You have

said that in me you have found one nearer to your ideal. I wonder how much away I am from your ideal and would like to know what you will do if you subsequently find someone equal to your ideal. On my part, I can say that in you I have found one who is better than and above my ideal. You need[n't] therefore, have any such fear as I have about you. How I have caught you by your own words!! I am a lawyer with the lawyer's skill in argument. This is just banter. I know you will not exchange me for the world. Will you?

I was, of course, struck with surprize [sic] when you did not shed tears. I was so overwhelmed with grief that I did not stop to find out the reasons. I see you had practised yoga for 3 days. I [did] not think of it else I would have also shown how much power of control I can command. However, I do[n't] mind having shed tears. They were the natural outlet of an [sic] heart that was overflowing with love.

Because of [the] stiff tone of some of my letters you are threatening me with short letters or no letters. If there was a stiff tone the offence is not mind [sic]. You are responsible for it. To inflict any such punishment on me would be wrong. I certainly would not forgive you if you did that. I deserve one letter a day [—] long, sweet and loving. I am prepared to have it every alternate day.

As I have said, there will be nothing to make us unhappy. For we are both magnanimous, forgiving and determined to make each other happy. There is just one thing I am anxious about. I want you to cultivate a motherly affection for my son and my nephew. I have spent all my affection on them so far. I would like you and them to be on the friendliest terms. Although you have had no children, this should not be difficult for you. As you yourself say that doctors are the most humane persons and I am sure you [are] more humane than others in your profession. Would you like to meet them? I can tell Chitre and Jadhav to arrange a meeting. I should like to [sic] you to let me know in your reply your sentiments on this. It will relieve me of great anxiety.

I don't know how many people you wish to bring with you for the 15th. The house is a small one. There is only one spare bedroom. There is also consideration of cost of air travel. I shall certainly write to Dr Malvankar extending an invitation to come . . .

My health is much better. My pain has subsided and its intensity is [sic] lessened much. [The] only thing is I feel very weak and without much appetite.

With deepest love
From Raja
19.3.48

In the letter written to Chitre on 19 March 1948, Dr Ambedkar expresses regret about some improper things that Jadhav had fed to Yeshwant about me and talks about the salutary effect that Malvankar's treatment has had on him. I give below the important excerpts from that letter. The K in the letter is me (Dr Kabir):

PERSONAL

My dear Kamalakant,

I have certain matters purely personal to write about. That is why I am writing them on a separate sheet . . .

Yeshwant writes to me that Jadhav told him not to write any letters to me, because K would not like it. I don't know on what basis he made this statement . . . It's sowing seeds of ill-feelings between K and Yeshwant. But I am quite certain K could not have said such a thing. She is the kindest woman I know. In fact, I want Yeshwant and Mukund should [sic] meet her before she comes over to Delhi. In fact, I want you to arrange such a meeting either in Rajgraha or at some other place. I will write to K and let you know about it . . .

It seems you and Jadhav went to Malvankar after my train left and complained to him that my pain had not vanished. It seems he felt hurt; of course both are right from their point.

Dr Ambedkar received my letter of 21 March 1948 on 23 March. He replied to me in English-Marathi. I had written to him in my letter that he was a treasure given to me for safekeeping by God. I had also written about how much he cared for my health and how he loved me beyond measure. Also, having learnt from experience that Thursday was an auspicious day for him, he had decided on a Thursday (15 April 1948) for our wedding. The letter presented below refers to another historically important point, which is that there is no certainty about 14 April being his date of birth. It is just the date that was entered in the documents as his official date of birth. This is how the letter goes:

[Translated from Marathi]

Midnight
23.3.48

Dear Sharu,

Received your letter of 21st this morning. The fact is that I should have written to you even before your letter reached me, but I couldn't do so because of pressure of work. I express my regret.

The confluence of Ganga and Yamuna finally happened after I had left. It happened at night if it hadn't happened in the morning. You had great will power, you had said, implying that I should have that kind of will power too. Is this, then, the will power you were talking about? Where an entire dam has burst, where is the point in saying that you want to block a current of water? My dam burst and I admit it. I didn't even try to conceal it. But did your dam hold on either? There is nothing improper at all that the dam of both of us should have burst.

I cried during the day, you cried at night. Our love for each other is not going to shrink like the water stocked up in a well. It has a spring at its base. The tears were the result of its overflowing. They arrived in the eyes of both of us, don't you think?

I believe that you too are a great treasure given to me by god for safekeeping. When you told me over the telephone that you had not been keeping well, I felt extremely bad. It is necessary for you to take great care of your health; nay, it is your duty. I being unwell is trouble enough for both of us. If you fall ill too, it will double our problems. This is the time when I want to admonish you. If you fall ill, my temper will rise. The remedy for it is that you should take care of your health and not fall ill.

It doesn't look like you are enthusiastic about writing letters. But I absolutely must keep receiving letters from you again and again. You are thousands of miles away. What other means have we got of nullifying this distance except letters? And then, your letters are so sweet! I at least get the sensation that you are close by when I read them! . . . Such being the circumstances, your not writing means handing down to me the harshest of punishments.

[In English from here on:]

I am following all the instructions you have conveyed to me. I shall be writing to Dr Malvankar in a day or two. As I said, I am feeling very lonely. I am counting days and waiting for the 15th of April. I long to see you and hug you.

You asked me why 15th and why not [the] 14th. I fixed 15th because it is a Thursday and Thursday for me is a very *shubh din* [an auspicious day]. The only thing in favour of the 14th is that it is my official date of birth. Different astrologers have given different dates as my birth-dates. Some have given 14th April, others 17th April, others 15th May, etc. In this state of uncertainty, I prefer Thursday, which my experience shows to be my *shubh din.*

—Raja

I wrote two letters to Doctor Saheb after that: the first on 25 March and the second on 31 March 1948. I received his letter of 1 April. The important excerpt is this:

[Translated from Marathi]

1-4-48

Dear Sharu,

I am aware that it's now a week that I haven't written to you. There are reasons for that too. I fell quite ill from Saturday onwards and only yesterday have I recovered a bit. I had given you the news about my illness on the telephone. Hence you cannot blame me on this matter. But you too seem to have sealed your lips, which causes me regretful surprise. I don't see any reason for this behavior of yours . . . An application has been submitted to the Registrar of Marriages on the 29th. If you are not certain in your mind, the entire game can be cancelled. Should I then wait for you on the 15th? Once I know, I shall make arrangements for getting your things brought over. Chitre has written to inform that he and Jadhav are going to be present for the ceremony. They are coming by train and they can bring your things over. There would then be no need of sending a person from here. I am going to tell them to come by the Frontier Mail. Therefore your luggage should be packed and ready before that. I shall not be able to send trunks to you. You can pack your luggage in trunks available in your father's house or maybe your own. Jadhav also may have some trunks which he will give if asked. Once the luggage has been brought over, the trunks can be returned to the owners.

You asked for two and a half thousand. I sent seventeen hundred. Did you get disappointed? It's possible, but I had no remedy. Not counting the 1700 rupees last sent, I had left behind totally 5300 rupees. I, at least, didn't think that the bill for cloth ran up to two thousand. My understanding was that some amount would remain. You said that the ornaments would go beyond two thousand. I had assumed that whatever was left from cloth [sic] would make good the deficiency for the ornaments. However, I left behind 1300 rupees so that there should be some money left in hand. I had been nursing the surety that the money was more than needed, therefore there would not be much difficulty. It is in order for me to say that the expenditure (seven thousand) got to be extremely big in relation to what I can afford. Someone has caused you to misunderstand that I am a very rich man. How can I be rich? My father did not leave behind any wealth for me. On the contrary, he had left behind a debt of 5/6 thousand, which I cleared. Started practising!! There was that opposition from the Hindu people, particularly Brahmins. Opposition from the Hindu people because I was opposed to the Congress, opposition from the Brahmins because a Mahar was infiltrating into their profession. Not to let me get any court work was the resolve of both parties!! I somehow managed to survive under these circumstances. So, how can I then have a lot of money? *'Motthaa vaasaa aani pokal ghar'* [Massive rafters and hollow house] is the state in which I am. Going by the state of my health, it appears unlikely that I shall be able to stay on a job for many days more. Even if I do work, it will be a political job—here today and gone tomorrow. Besides, I have no hope of receiving a pension of any kind. Under these circumstances, I remain very anxious about what will happen during old age. The water has to be stored and water has to be used with care; only then will the time ahead be happy for me and you. I felt very satisfied at reading your words that you will not be extravagant.

[In English from here on:]

. . . I have no doubt you are more generous than you have shown yourself in your letter. You ask me that if I love my children so much, have I any love for you. I have no doubt what [the] answer is. There is no contradiction in loving my children and loving you. If love was such an exclusive thing, then the conclusion will be that to love one must hate all others. Because you love your father, brothers and sisters, can I say that you don't love me. [sic] How stupid that would be. One can love all and indeed must love all. The only thing is that loving all does not mean that one has the same interest or equal interest in all those in whom he is interested.

In India, people have more interest in their children than they have in their wives and wives have more interest in their parents and relatives than in their husbands. I have always held these views to be wrong. The wife must have her proper place in the affection of her husband and that is why I don't believe in joint family, which is always detrimental to [a] woman.

. . . There is no spirit of revenge in me. I have done more good to the people than anyone else can boast of. There are many who turned enemies, but I have never sought to take revenge. I always welcome [them] as guests [sic]. So you need have no fears regarding my attitude to your relations. They are always welcome as guests.

I wrote to you about my children because I know that the relationship between step children and step mothers are [sic] not always happy. These unhappy relations start with prejudice and end in complete antagonism, which destroy [sic] the happiness of all. I do not wish this to happen. That is why I wanted to induce goodwill and understanding from the beginning between the two sides. I regret you did not show enough response. I hope that this is due to shyness and not to any prejudice. My second reason in writing on this point was that my son, who is in business and has a great business head might be of help to your brothers if you were friendly to him. Evidently, you did not realize this.

You are adverse in [sic] writing and I have no desire to force you myself, I am too busy to write often. The telephone is no use. It causes exasperation, we can only depend upon such intermittent correspondence as we can. I had no communication from Dr Malvankar. Perhaps he has not returned from Ahmedabad.

Fondest love from
Raja

It appears that the doctor opened his heart out to Kamalakant Chitre with regard to everything about our marriage. He probably did not have the same trust in Jadhav. On 3 April, the doctor wrote to Kamalakant in which he spells out the details:

My dear Kamalakant,

. . . One of my close colleagues is sowing seeds of ill feeling between Yeshwant and K . . .

I agree that there should be no postponement of the event. It is irrevocably fixed on the 15th. Postponement will open a field for wider publicity and greater opportunity for evil tongues to wag. I feel no moral turpitude in what I am doing, nobody can have any ground for complaint, not even Y. To the latter I have given about Rs. 30,000/- and in addition a house, which is today worth at least Rs. 80,000/-. I am sure no father can do more for his son than I have done for him. Y's disaffection comes to me as a surprise for I remember his writing to me of his own free will that in the interest of my health, I should marry.

I am sending a cheque for Rs. 100/- to cover the cost of your journey and the costing of Dr K's luggage. Please don't forget to get the following things from Rajgrah with you when you come.

1) Photo of Buddha
2) Chest expander, which is in the inner room along with the book.

With kind regards,
Yours sincerely,
B. R. Ambedkar

I had written a letter to Doctor Saheb on 6 April, which I began with: 'May it please your honour'. I had written further:

> . . . I believe, since the day we decided to enter matrimony, my mission in life is to look after you in such a way that not only to not allow [sic] your physical health to suffer but to see that the integrity of your mind is preserved. To achieve that end, I have to be very submissive—in fact it is to be of so much larger effect that I sort of cease to exist. Under such circumstances, how can I do things which will disturb you? In future I will be very careful for you seem to have a very sensitive temperament . . .

The contents of my above letter would have bitten him quite hard because he too responded to me in a little biting and sarcastic language on 9 April:

9-4-48

May it please Your Excellency

[Translated from Marathi]

The salutation has changed! But what else can I do? If you find it not merely necessary but also natural to abandon your usual practice and address me as 'Your honour', I am also compelled to address you as 'Your Excellency'. And looking at your proud and conceited nature, it suits you too. If you don't mind, I intend to use this address for you from here onwards.

I couldn't help feeling regretfully surprised at reading your letter of the 6th. It is natural for me to feel aggrieved. Who would not feel aggrieved when such piercing words were served out without any rhyme or reason? Who would not be surprised at reading accusation after accusation when there was never any offence? There is repeated mention in the letter that there should not be any misunderstanding and so on, but what's the use of all that? There is a saying in English: Why be afraid of kicking when you can excuse yourself by apologizing afterwards? This looks like a case of the same kind: kick first and apologize later. I am compelled to say that I don't see a straightness in your disposition. I expressed my desire in my letter that there should be a motherly affection between you and my son and that there should be a meeting between the two of you . . .

. . . All I had asked was: how so much expenditure? Any person with a straight disposition would have sent a note detailing the expenditure and be done with it. But you decided not to make use of this straight path. On the contrary, you wrote that you consider all the expenditure as a debt upon you and resolved to pay it off and get rid of your indebtedness to me. I cannot disentangle the strangeness of your temperament here. Is it a crime to say that there should be an increase in affection between you and my boys?

What was improper in my suggesting that money should be spent judiciously?

You have announced that your relatives would rather beg on the street than come to me; I have nothing to say about it. I can only congratulate them on their self-respect. I am extremely grateful that you have promised to look after me during my time of distress. But it is my intention to live my life till the very end by eating the salt and bread that I have earned by my own effort. I do not want a life of dependence on anybody. It is my resolve that when I find it difficult to fill my stomach (and yours, obviously, if you are living with me), I shall commit suicide. So you needn't worry on this matter.

It appears that you think of me as miserly and niggardly. I may be a miser, nay, in fact I am one. I was not born a rich man. I have risen up from the extremes of poverty. It is natural, therefore, that I should get into the habit of parsimony for fear that I do not again fall into the cesspool of poverty; you will agree that this is proper too. Hence, even if I am parsimonious, I am not niggardly. I do not want to be boastful but I doubt whether a more altruistic person can be found anywhere. My entire life was spent in the service of the people. I never looked at a person's caste or creed before helping him. I helped everybody. Your relatives on account of whom you considered me niggardly, I shall help them too, if they ever felt the need, obviously.

When you express your fear about what will happen to your independence, you seem to think that you are marrying a savage, immoral person who is given to the evil habits of drinking, gambling and whoring. If that is the impression you have formed, the remedy is in your hands. I don't have the slightest conception of this independence. All my days were spent carrying burdens like the potter's donkey. I never found the time to stretch myself out in the luxury of independence; therefore, when you lament about whether you will lose your independence, I just don't understand it. If you had asked me how much independence you wanted, I would have been able to give you a definite answer. I don't know how much independence your father had given to your revered mother; but you may rest assured that you shall get that much of independence from me.

There is a resonance in your letter of a thought that seems to have upset you: that marriage would lead to the impoundment of your body. This is mere imagination and nothing else. In marriage at a young age, the sexual desire is strong and man takes forcible possession of his wife's body. My marriage is the marriage of old age. The desire for company is much stronger than the desire for sex. Therefore you have no reason for nursing fears in this regard. Looking at it from another perspective, your ghosts are only the ghosts of your imagination. However strong the sinful thoughts that I may have of commandeering your body, these thoughts cannot succeed, because the law is on your side. If the possession becomes intolerable, you have the right to stay separately. Also, if the hope of bearing a child (through me at least) vanishes, your way is always clear. Such being the circumstances, you need have no fear of subjugation.

We have begun to locate in each other the faults that we have; we will see more later, and who knows, this fault-finding may become a habit. If this happens, then, as you say, the visions that we saw earlier of our future may turn out to be mirages. I have used your own words. If this is the thought that arises, then it is better that the relationship between the two of us is seen as an experiment. Letters should be sweet, you have said, and I feel the same too. But you have forgotten that it needs two hands to clap, I regret to say.

Well, then, I wait for you on April 15. So that you do not carry fear about your independence, I finish with a new title for myself.

Your slave
Bhimrao
Sharu's Raja.

On the occasion of his official birthday, 14 April, I wrote a complimentary letter to him on April 13 in Hindi—just for the fun of it. In another two days' time, that is on 15 April, I was due to go to Delhi; therefore, this would be the last letter I would write to him. I titled this letter 'Mubarak Patrika' [which, loosely translated, would mean 'Congratulatory Message'].

[It is written in rather tacky Hindi, which is where its charm lies. Here is its English translation:]

> This congratulatory note is offered with love and respect in the revered hands of my dearest Rajan.
>
> On this auspicious day, when your birthday is celebrated, it had been my keen desire to be with you in Delhi—it would have been great fun. But you didn't like it. Which is why the work that could have been done by my voice, I am now being compelled to have it done by my pen. I had written to you in one of my earlier letters that by the benevolence of God, I have been gifted with such a great treasure. And many a time I have had this doubt in my mind whether I really am worthy of this. On this day I pray to God that He grant my Rajan a long life, lovely health (all those ailments that have infiltrated into your body and do not want to depart from your body, please remove those ailments as early as possible), successful happiness and great progress. I have all the hope that God will accept this my prayer made with the purest of feelings.
>
> You will be a little surprised at seeing this letter of mine written in Hindi. I have never learnt the Hindi language, therefore, whatever mistakes there are, it is my request that I may forgive you [sic]. A few days back when you were in Bombay, you had once expressed your doubt whether I could talk at all in Hindi. I send a reply now through the medium of this letter.
>
> You had said that after the 15th of April you would never give me a holiday (not for a single day). Therefore there would be no

scope for writing a letter to you. Hence on this occasion I write this letter in Hindi and send to you. Accept it with happiness, that's all. This is where my congratulatory note finishes.

Once again I pray to God that he grant you a long life, progress and successful happiness. All Indian citizens have to get a lot of work done out of you. Therefore your health has to become good and your life should also extend a lot.

My loving salutation.
Sharu

[The next line is translated from Marathi to English]

How I have stumped a certain person! Said I didn't know Hindi!

[The following paragraph is in English]

Being a doctor by profession, I must know as many languages as I can pick up. Patients could be well convinced only if the doctor can speak his (patient's) language.

[What follows is translated from Marathi]

Yes, a few mistakes are bound to occur, that's where the real fun is! Do I once again give you my good wishes in my mother tongue? Whether the date is the real one or not, I should walk in step with all the others, shouldn't I? What a big and proud day it is today! At such a time I should present myself before you with a platter containing a lamp and vermillion in one hand and a garland of love in the other. Whatever the disgust you have against such rituals, I shall do it nevertheless. This kind of a thing will be against your wishes, perhaps. After doing the *aarti*, I shall send my prayer to god: 'Oh lord! Grant a great social worker and a leader of the people like him long life, lovely health, great prosperity and all varieties of happiness.' My daily prayer is: 'Oh God, free my husband of all ailments at the earliest. Give him great health and a good 125 years of life.' You shall continue your march down the path of progress . . .

Some of your people did snitch, finally, and news has begun to arrive in some Marathi papers regarding you and me. That Parvate of *Loksatta* writes very frivolous stuff. He doubts whether, considering your poor health, poor I will get any marital joy, but finds happiness in the thought that I shall get full advantage of your Sarasvati [the goddess of knowledge]. This sort of rubbishy stuff. I haven't told this to anyone. I hate people calling me poor this and poor that. He said you were suffering from mental illness too and all that nonsense. We don't pay much attention to such things, anyway. Whichever way we behave, the world never likes it. So why not do things and please yourself? Nobody can know so much about your health as we do. After considering all possibilities we have decided. There are always going to be people who delight in talking ill of others, there is no remedy against them. It's absolutely a personal affair and no dabbling from outside will be tolerated. Nothing in particular otherwise.

So let me once more send you my most warmest wishes on this auspicious day. Of course, this time in your mother (foster) tongue: May God give you a very healthy and very long life, full of happiness, peace and honour.

So long till we meet on the 15th of April.

Fondest love.

Sharu

This was the last letter I wrote from Mumbai to Doctor Saheb. I reached Delhi on 15 April, which obviously meant that there was no question now of my getting any further letters from Doctor Saheb. This is why I have given the above excerpts from my letter.

Everywhere else, I have given excerpts only from Doctor Saheb's letters without making references to mine.

The Letter Pads for Our Correspondence

The letters I wrote to Dr Ambedkar early on were written on ordinary paper, in fact very often on scraps of paper. Once, when he was on a tour of Mumbai, he came to my house. After tea, he said, 'Get ready to go out.' I got ready, and we got into the car. Dr Ambedkar told the driver to take us to Thacker & Company at Kala Ghoda. Once the car rolled off, the Doctor said, 'Sharu, you write to me on scraps of paper. Come now, we shall place an order for letter pads at Thacker's. From here on, no more writing on scraps. Always use a letter pad.' On reaching the shop, he placed the orders. The speciality of these letter pads was that they didn't carry our names or addresses. Some letter pads had 'B' and others had 'S' printed on them in thick, Roman style, artistic patterns on the top middle of the page. Our correspondence happened on these letter pads after that. I believe that since these letterheads were for our exclusive use, Doctor Saheb used them only when writing letters to me. It is impossible that he would have written letters to others on those letterheads. I did find a letter on this letterhead written to Bhaskarrao Kadrekar.

When Dr Ambedkar was first introduced to me, he knew me only as Dr Kabir. As we got to know each other better, he got to know me as Sharada. He gifted to me all the books he had written before our marriage, on which he wrote:

> To,
> Dr S. Kabir
> With love from the author

He then signed underneath. He would always address me and write to me as Sharu and after our marriage he changed it to Savita. Savita, he told me, meant the glory of the sun. Although he did name me Savita, he would always call me Sharu. There is another thing that I must clarify here, lest readers get into any misunderstanding. It is this: In my letter of 13 April, I have used the words 'bhagwan' and 'god', but they have been used only symbolically, merely as a customary token of expressing feelings. Actually, at that time I had not even been initiated into Buddhism.

We got married on 15 April and from then on till the last moment I stayed with him ceaselessly like his shadow. Doctor Saheb himself never kept me away from him. There was no question, therefore, of any exchange of letters between us. The only exception here is of a meeting of the People's Education Society. Dr Ambedkar was the founder chairman of this society. The meeting was being held in Mumbai and the travel would be by air. Since it was difficult for us to bear the financial burden of two air tickets, he travelled to Mumbai alone. That was when he sent me another letter, which I shall give in its proper place in chronological order. Some would be surprised at hearing that we couldn't afford the expense of two air tickets, but there isn't an iota of exaggeration here. Dr Ambedkar lived with utter probity and selflessness. He was never enamoured by wealth, the consequence being that our financial status was always just about adequate. But we never regretted it and lived our lives with great dignity.

My Travel to Delhi and Our Marriage Ceremony

Dr Ambedkar had decided to go through with our marriage ceremony in Delhi on Thursday, 15 April 1948. He had sent invitations to Kamalakant Chitre, Daulat Jadhav, Bhaurao Gaikwad, Dr Malvankar and a select few friends from Delhi. He had intentionally not publicized the event because the atmosphere in the country was quite tense. India had just been partitioned and tensions ran high everywhere. Waves upon waves of displaced people were flowing in. Against the background of such incendiary and explosive circumstances, Nathuram Godse had shot Mahatma Gandhi to death on 30 January 1948, at Birla House, New Delhi. Riots had broken out everywhere, and we were getting married against this background. The ire of the Congress had boiled over against leaders opposed to Gandhi, and that was why we had not spread word around regarding our marriage. I too had not spoken much about it to our relatives and acquaintances.

I began preparing for my departure to Delhi. My third brother Vasant showed his readiness to come along with me. D.G. Jadhav and Kamalakant Chitre had maintained constant contact with me. They had taken care of all that would be needed. Doctor Saheb would deliver instructions to them on the phone, and they did all the running around accordingly. It was Doctor Saheb who had arranged the air tickets for my brother and me. Jadhav sent me the tickets. I took off from the Santacruz airport in Mumbai with my brother on the morning of 15 April in an Indian Airlines aircraft and landed at Delhi. Jadhav and Chitre were there to receive us with a group of people. Chitre said, 'Doctor Saheb had very much wanted to come to receive you, but we explained to him that it would not be proper. If he were to come himself, his opponents would get an excuse to spread frivolous stories, and it would then become a topic of discussion.' I agreed with Chitre because Dr Ambedkar was then the law minister in the Council of Ministers in the Central government and his coming to receive us would not have looked proper.

During those days Doctor Saheb lived in a bungalow known as 1, Hardinge Avenue, Delhi. We set off for the bungalow from the airport. All arrangements had been made at the bungalow for a civil marriage much before our arrival. About fifteen to twenty of his closest friends were already present. As soon as we reached 1, Hardinge Avenue, Chitre's daughter-in-law hurried out to the porch with a platter on which were five earthen lamps for the ritual welcome. As soon as I stepped out of the car, she circled a piece of bhakari [native unleavened bread] and some water round my face, held my hand and led me into the bungalow. Doctor Saheb himself came out immediately to welcome us. The first thing he did was to apologize for not having come to receive us at the airport himself. He then made courteous inquiries about our travel and whether we had suffered any inconveniences. Next, he introduced me to all the invited guests. Quick pleasantries were exchanged with all present.

Chitre's daughter-in-law then took me to a room upstairs; the bungalow was a double-storeyed structure. She had been specifically invited for the ceremony because there was no lady among the handful of Doctor Saheb's surviving relatives. She took me to an upper-storey room and helped me dress up appropriately. She then escorted me to the drawing hall downstairs. The registrar of marriages had already arrived with all the necessary documents. Our marriage was solemnized under the Civil Marriage Act; our signatures were taken along with the signatures of two witnesses from each side. My brother Vasant and Kamalakant Chitre signed as witnesses from my side while from Doctor Saheb's side, one signatory was Raosaheb Meshram. Who the other person was, I do not remember.

There were fifteen or twenty select people present for this occasion. Included among these was the registrar (his name was either Randhawa or Rameshwar, perhaps). Some of the others were Rao Bahadur Puranchand, engineer; Doctor Saheb's personal secretary and his government secretary Massey, Pillay and Khadse; a government official named Nilkanth; Ramkrishna Chandiwala, the correspondent of a foreign newspaper; Rao Bahadur G.T. Meshram; Kamalakant Chitre; Chitre's son and daughter-in-law; Daulat Jadhav; secretary of the home ministry Dr Bannerjee; Doctor Saheb's colleague Sohanlal Shastri; my brother Dr Vasant Kabir; S. C. Joshi and some other dignitaries. Correspondents of the leading newspapers of India were also present. After signing the documents of registered marriage, we had officially become husband and wife. As the sound of clapping burst out, the people present congratulated us and offered us their heartiest good wishes. The newspaper correspondents took quite a number of photographs and sweets were served. The wedding ceremony thus came to an end amidst a lot of enthusiasm and joy.

This was followed by a small lunch for a few select friends and colleagues. Later, in the evening, a small reception was thrown in the compound of the bungalow. Lord Mountbatten, the then governor-general of India, sent a special envoy bearing his congratulations, gifts and good wishes. A number of very senior government officials were present too. Actually, Doctor Saheb had wanted a function on a big scale, but I had expressed my opposition. Chitre, Jadhav and his other colleagues also persuaded him to scale it down, pointing out to him that the assassination of Gandhiji had seriously vitiated the atmosphere. The atmosphere was peaceful but tense. Holding a gala function under these circumstances with pomp and show would have looked like deliberately provoking the Gandhians, giving them an opportunity to cavil. As the assassin, Naturam Godse, was a Maharashtrian Brahmin, the houses of Maharashtrian Brahmins were being attacked all across the country and set on fire. Nobody bothered about the sub-caste—saraswat, *chitpawan, chandraseniya, deshast, konkanast, karhade*. They were being attacked without discrimination. If we had held our reception on a grand scale, there was a distinct probability of some of my relatives being harassed. If this were to happen, some of my other relatives would have got this opportunity to blame me. The fact was that in their eyes Dr Ambedkar was an untouchable and they had been opposed to the marriage. Taking all things into consideration, we had decided to keep the function small and simple inside the compound of the bungalow.

Meeting with Sardar Patel

Sardar Vallabhbhai Patel, the deputy prime minister and the home minister, had sent us a congratulatory note that read:

New Delhi
15-4-1948

My dear Dr Ambedkar,

I learned from the papers about your marriage which is coming off today. Please accept my warmest congratulations and best wishes for a happy married life. I am sure, if Bapu were alive, he would have given you his blessings.

With kindest regards,
Yours sincerely,
Vallabhbhai Patel

To,
Hon'ble Dr B. R. Ambedkar
Minister for Law.
New Delhi.

Doctor Saheb responded to Vallabhbhai's letter as given below:

My dear Sardar Patel,

I and my wife join in acknowledging your good wishes on the occasion of our marriage and in saying how thankful we are for the same. I agree that Bapu, if he had been alive, would have blessed it.

I hope by now you would have completely recovered.

With kind regards,
Yours sincerely,
B. R. Ambedkar

After the function, Doctor Saheb took me to meet Sardar Patel at his residence. He had suffered some heart problem a few days back. He had begun to feel better, but the doctors had advised him complete bed rest. A bed had been laid out for him on the lawn outside his bungalow so that he could meet people. When we went to meet him, he raised himself up in his bed and welcomed us with a smile. He shook hands with Doctor Saheb and heartily congratulated us. He made me sit next to him on the bed, patted me lovingly on the back, made extremely affectionate inquiries and said, 'Daughter, you have shown great courage by marrying Doctor Saheb. If this auspicious event had happened in Bapuji's presence, it would have been a greater reason for joy. I feel sad that Bapu is not with us to witness this revolutionary event.'

Sardar Patel had actually organized a small function to felicitate our marriage, but his health being poor, we didn't stay with him for long.

Reactions in the Newspapers from India and Abroad

The story of our marriage was flashed in several newspapers in India and abroad. The *Daily Mail* of London, the *New York Times* of New York, and all the newspapers and magazines of India covered the news of our marriage prominently along with photographs. In the process, the India correspondent of *The Daily Mail* of London filed quite a misrepresentative story. When Vallabhbhai Patel noticed it, he shot off a surprised and angry letter to Prime Minister Nehru, asking him what he could do to prevent such happenings. The letter is given below:

> My dear Jawaharlal,
>
> You will be interested in the enclosed copy, a dispatch of the Delhi correspondent of the Daily Mail, London. It is a most mischievous message and a deliberate distortion of the actual conditions. I wonder what we can do to stop such nonsense.
>
> Yours sincerely,
> Vallabhbhai Patel

The Hon'ble Prime Minister Jawaharlal Nehru,
Prime Minister of India,
New Delhi

ENCLOSURE

MESSAGE DATED 13TH APRIL, 1948, SENT BY MR. AZAD, DELHI CORRESPONDENT OF THE DAILY MAIL, LONDON, TO DAILY MAIL

Dr Ambedkar, Scheduled Caste (Untouchable) Law Minister in the Government of India, will defy Hindu Law when he marries a Brahmin girl in Delhi on Thursday. Brahmins – priestly order – are the highest caste in the Hindu religion and it is a crime for a woman to marry outside the Brahmin caste. To avoid embarrassment to other members of the government whose caste forbids them eating [in] or entering the house of an untouchable, no announcement of the wedding is being made and all the Cabinet Ministers will be absent from Delhi on Thursday. Ambedkar's bride is a well-known lady doctor here.[16]

The world-renowned *New York Times*, published from New York, America, published the news of our marriage on 16 April 1948. The news as it appeared is as follows:

Hindu Brahmin weds untouchables' leader forfeiting her caste right to enter heaven

Special to New York Times, New Delhi 15 – To millions of orthodox Hindus, one of the most significant [events] in new free India [was] the marriage today of D. B. R. Ambedkar, an untouchable, to Dr Lakshmi [sic] Kabir, a member of the Supreme Brahmin Caste. Only a few years ago, such a union could hardly have happened in caste-bounded-India and it still is rare enough for front-page display in Indian newspapers.

Dr Ambedkar, Minister of Law in the Indian Cabinet and the President of the All India Scheduled Castes (untouchables) is best known as a champion of equal rights for those 60,00,000 Indians who in the social system are the lowest of the low—a people without caste, doomed to be reincarnated as untouchables throughout eternity. Partly through his efforts over many years, the untouchables are [now] admitted to many Hindu temples as a legal right.

By her marriage to [an] untouchable, Miss Kabir, according to orthodox Hindu doctrine, forever forfeited her right to enter heaven. She has violated the strict bars of caste and thereby, according to a belief still held in the thousands of Indian villages, has placed herself and her descendants beyond the pole [sic] till the end of time.

That a Brahmin girl could thus defy one of the strongest religious conventions in the world is taken here as a milestone on the road of a new age in Hindu India. It is far more significant than a wedding of a royalty to a commoner.

Dr Ambedkar, who was 55 yesterday, studied at Columbia and European universities under the patronage of Maharajah Gaekwar of Baroda. He has had a distinguished career in Indian Politics, becoming famous for his bitter differences with Mohandas K. Gandhi on the issue of a separate electorate for the untouchables, which Dr Ambedkar favoured.[17]

The renowned newspaper *The Times of India* said in its news column:

Dr Ambedkar, the Law Minister, Government of India, was married to Dr (Miss) Lakshmi [sic] Kabir on Thursday morning at his residence at 1, Hardinge Avenue. The bride is a medical practitioner in Bombay. The marriage was celebrated [sic] under the Civil Marriage Act by a few personal friends of Dr Ambedkar who entertained them to lunch. – API

Caravan, the well-known magazine of India, gave the news of our marriage and referred to Dr Ambedkar as the saraswats' son-in-law.

Once the news of our marriage was announced by the newspapers, it began raining congratulatory and complimentary telegrams and letters. A large number of Doctor Saheb's friends, colleagues and followers expressed their joy. Members of the Constituent Assembly, parliamentarians, members of the Council of Ministers, Prime Minister Nehru, the president of the Constituent Assembly and later the first President of India Dr Rajendra Prasad, the first governor-general of Independent India Lord Mountbatten, the first Indian governor-general of India C. Rajagopalachari and many other eminent personalities offered us their congratulations and good wishes through letters, on the telephone, through telegrams or through meeting us personally. Doctor Saheb's friends in England and America also sent us letters and telegrams to congratulate us and to wish us success.

Dr Ambedkar and Naval Bhathena—an Indestructible Friendship

A letter of congratulations arrived from Doctor Saheb's Parsee friend Naval Bhathena. I consider the friendship between Dr Ambedkar and Bhathena to be an example of an ideal friendship. I doubt whether Dr Ambedkar would ever have had another friend as self-effacing and as eager to rush forward to offer selfless help in every single difficult circumstance. Bhathena and Doctor Saheb used to live together when they were in America. Since Dr Ambedkar needed financial help so as to be able to complete his barrister's course, Bhathena had arranged two tuitions for him. It was through Bhathena's efforts that he got a job with the Batliboi firm where he worked for a few days. After he finished his Bar-at-Law, he didn't have the money to procure a licence, for which again Bhathena gave financial help. When he went abroad for the second time for further education, he did so with financial help from Bhathena. The Doctor's son Yeshwant and nephew Mukund had to be settled into decent jobs, and here too Bhathena exerted himself, and all this without any fuss and bother or any expectation. Doctor Saheb later became the drafter of the Constitution and still later the law minister of India, but never did Bhathena hold any expectations, nor did he try to make capital out of his friendship.

A special thing to note here is that Bhathena was a devotee of Gandhiji and Dr Ambedkar was his bitter opponent, but these differences of principles never came in the way of their friendship. It was a keen desire with Dr Ambedkar that Bhathena should participate actively in the People's Education Society and share the responsibility of the society, but this wish could not be fulfilled. He had called Bhathena over and made this request to him, but within a month of this meeting, Doctor Saheb passed away.

Naval Bhathena sent a congratulatory letter on the occasion of our marriage and laid emphasis upon the need that existed for him to get married. Doctor Saheb responded to his letter on 19 April:

> 'My dear Naval,
>
> Thank you very much for your letter of good wishes on my marriage. I am glad you appreciate the necessity for it . . .'

The Beginning of Our Life Together

Within a few days Doctor Saheb took me to Simla (7 to 16 June 1948). It was the first time after our marriage that we were going for a holiday. In fact, it was the first occasion for me to travel anywhere with Doctor Saheb. We stayed at the government dak bungalow in

Simla. By sheer coincidence, N.V. alias Kakasaheb Gadgil had also remarried, and he too had come holidaying with his newly wedded wife to Simla. Kakasaheb Gadgil was also a minister in Nehru's Council of Ministers, holding the post of minister for public works. The two enjoyed a warm relationship. Doctor Saheb expressed his delight at meeting him there. Whenever the two met, they would talk for hours on Maharashtra politics. We also met Tekchand[18] Mahajan who was a judge in the Supreme Court of India. He was later appointed the chairman of the Mahajan Commission, which was set up to resolve the boundary dispute between Maharashtra and Karnataka. He is the Mahajan of the Mahajan Report that is mentioned so often.

Justice Tekchand makes reference to his meeting with us at Simla in his autobiography *Looking Back*. He says:

> 'It was during my stay at Simla that I met Dr Ambedkar, who was then the Law Minister in the Government of India and Kaka Gadgil, who was then the Minister of Housing at the Centre. Both of them had recently remarried and were enjoying their honeymoons at Simla. Since my first meeting them, I had the privilege of cultivating their friendship.'

We stayed in Simla for a few days. Doctor Saheb looked very joyous and enthusiastic. Very few people know that Doctor Saheb had a very sharp sense of humour. It was in Simla that I experienced listening to humorous tales from him—complete with histrionics thrown in. He would so embellish his stories in the telling that my stomach would begin to ache with laughing. Once he got into the rhythm, every one of his anecdotes would bring a crick in the stomach with all the laughing. Raising or lowering his voice according to the demand of the narrative, throwing in gesticulations along with theatrics, he would give us a sampling of his sharp sense of humour.

After holidaying for a few days after our marriage, we came back to Delhi and our joint venture began. Looking at the history and the background of the two of us, it was an act of courage. For me, particularly, it was a big act of courage, and I feel not only surprised but most certainly proud that I did perform it.

Doctor Saheb was then the law minister in Nehru's Council of Ministers. As the chairman of the Drafting Committee, he had the primary responsibility of drafting the Constitution. He endured enormous trouble for completing the great, historical work that the nation had placed upon him.

Dr Ambedkar had already been suffering from diabetes, rheumatism, neurological pains and a host of other ailments. The pain in his legs would flare up every now and again, as a result of which he would not be able to sleep for fifteen days at a stretch, writhing in bed all through the night. Pressing his limbs, giving his legs an oil massage, fomenting his legs with a warmed-up brick wrapped in a towel whenever his neural and leg pains flared up, I would always be anxious to find ways to bring relief to him in some way or the other.

Carrying the responsibility of running the law ministry and doing the work of drafting as the chairman of the Drafting Committee of the Constituent Assembly meant that he carried dual responsibilities on his shoulders. That required him to be busy night and day, despite his seriously compromised state of health.

Our Daily Routine

After entering his life, I ploughed in all my efforts to prepare a meticulous schedule for him. I prepared a finely calibrated timetable for his meals, his rest hours, his medicines and for his great work of preparing the Constitution. Since Doctor Saheb was already diabetic, extreme care in the matter of food, dietary discipline and medicines were critically important; therefore, I was always alert to establishing a nice balance among all these things.

Doctor Saheb was not an early riser. His reading and writing would go on till late into the night; occasionally he would spend the entire night reading and writing. When he was busy thus, he would forget not merely the world, but his own self. He would lose consciousness of time, sleep, rest, food, the rest of the world and of himself. If he so often went to sleep just before dawn, it was natural that he would not be able to get up early. It was my duty to wake him up every day sometime between half past seven and eight o'clock.

I, however, would be up and about at half past five or six. This routine has been with me since my student days and remains with me till today. As soon as I got up, I would take a round of the two expansive gardens around our bungalow. I would then go to our gardener's room, which was alongside the gate of our bungalow. I would have a cup of black tea with the gardener and his family. After spending some time with the family, I would go brush my teeth, wash my face and finish off with my toilet activities. I would then take a bath and prepare the English-style tea for Doctor Saheb: the brew in one pot, milk in another and sugar in a separate container, so that the three could be mixed in the desired proportion. The tray thus readied, I would carry it into his bedroom and wake him up. Once he was awake, I would make his tea and the two of us would then have our tea together. As Doctor Saheb had lived in England and America, he had got into the habit of having bed tea. He would skim through the newspapers as he had his tea. After the tea was over, he would continue looking through the papers.

Yoga asanas are quite efficacious for controlling neuritis and blood pressure; since Doctor Saheb had both, I had taught him a few asanas. I would insist that he performed these yogic exercises regularly. After finishing his tea and skimming through the papers, he would do his exercises. He would then go to the veranda of the bungalow and stretch himself out in an easy chair.

Our driver would then arrive, apply massage oil on him and give him a nice rubbing down, so his blood circulation would improve and his nerves would get energized. This massage would carry on for about half an hour, during which time our driver would be bathed in sweat. Both yogic exercises and the massage were a part of his treatment, which was why I had forced this routine upon him.

Doctor Saheb would then go to brush his teeth, wash his face, finish his toilet activities and go for his bath. He needed hot water for his bath. Very often I would give him his bath too. He would love it when I soaped him, scrubbed him and rinsed him. He would sit like an innocent and obedient child when I gave him his bath. I too thoroughly enjoyed this innocence of his. After the bath was over, I would help him dry himself. I would then dust talcum powder all over his body. He loved it all.

He would then come to the dining table for his breakfast by about half past eight or nine. You could call it an obsession, but it was his intense desire that I should prepare the breakfast items myself and serve them to him hot and fresh. We had a cook at home, but no! When Saheb sat for his breakfast, whatever he wanted had to be prepared right there and served piping hot. I had arranged for a hotplate and placed it right next to the dining table. As with his other meals, for his breakfast too he liked variety in what he ate. Whatever item he asked for, I would prepare it for him according to his liking and desire and serve it hot.

The first course in his breakfast was porridge. Porridge is boiled oats. Just mix milk in these boiled oats and the porridge course is ready. I would add some almond paste to it. It is called *pej* or *kanji* in our language, but in English it is known as porridge. He would occasionally take cornflakes for a change. While he was having his porridge or cornflakes, I would ready for him some egg dish on the hotplate. He liked his eggs done in a variety of ways. Actually, I learnt how to cook a number of dishes from him. I had also bought quite a few recipe books during those times. I would make a new dish for him almost every day and he would consume it with great joy and relish. Even with eggs I would do them for him in various forms turn by turn: boiled, half-fried, full-fried, omelette, mashed, scrambled, etc. There would be hot toasted bread with butter to go with the eggs. He loved different kinds of jams too. He would then wash his eggs and bread down with coffee. He absolutely loved coffee.

He was very regular with his breakfast—this was his main meal. He didn't eat much for lunch. He loved China crockery and we had a whole range of sets for different meals: for breakfast, for tea, for coffee, for lunch and dinner. His instructions were clear—the sets should be used only for the purpose for which they were designed: tea set for tea, coffee set for coffee, breakfast set for breakfast, meal set for lunch and dinner. Different sets for different occasions. We had a lot of crockery and cutlery sets too. He always insisted that there should be plates, forks, spoons and other dishes according to the kinds of styles and services. Since he had spent a good part of his youth in the Western world, all these things had been imprinted in his mind.

Once breakfast was over, he would get ready for office. He wanted me to help him get dressed. The trousers he would slip on himself, but I was required to help him put his shirt on. He would lift his arms up and I would slip the shirt on him and button it up for him. I had to help him put on the jacket too. He would again stand with his arms raised so that I could put the jacket on him. Once the jacket was buttoned up, I would then be required to place a handkerchief in the breast-pocket. The handkerchief had to be folded in a specific way so that one triangular edge showed neatly over the breast-pocket. He would stand before the dressing table like an innocent child. Once he had his clothes on, our cook Sudama would be ready to help him put on his socks and shoes.

Once he was properly dressed, he would set off at around nine or half past nine. His car would be waiting for him in the porch. Once Saheb began to move towards his car, I was expected to accompany him, open the door for him and shut it once he was seated inside. He would then wave goodbye and I was required to stand on the stairs and keep waving to him till the car had driven out of the gate. He too would keep his eyes on me right till the time the car turned out of sight. This activity had settled into a routine and would happen automatically. He loved it all and therefore I would do it all with joy and excitement.

Favourite Dishes

Saheb would ordinarily return home around half past one or two and we would have our lunch together. His lunch was very frugal. He would have two wheat chapatis and a little bit of rice. He loved non-vegetarian food. Although he didn't eat much, he wanted variety—a variety of items cooked in a variety of ways. Roast mutton, cold mutton, special kinds of soups, pudding and baked items were his particular favourites. He loved the hilsa fish of Calcutta. He would get D.G. Jadhav, who was working as labour commissioner in Calcutta, to pack it in an icebox and send it over by flight. He loved chicken fry and fried pomfret too. Chicken too he liked cooked in different ways. I would do chicken fry, chicken curry, tandoori and other dishes for him. He wanted soups and pudding with his meals. It had become a principle with me to do for him everything he liked with joy and enthusiasm.

Although he liked meat on his table, he wouldn't each much of it—a piece or two at the most. If the subject of the Constitution came up for conversation during meals, we would talk about its articles. Since I did enough reading and because I loved it, I would be able to talk with him point-wise and logically. He would feel very pleased about it. We would finish our meals chatting thus.

After his meal, Doctor Saheb would want to return to his reading and writing. He had then to be compelled to go into the bedroom for some rest. The intention was that he should be made to rest under any circumstances. Neither Doctor Saheb nor I could sleep if there was light in the room and therefore after he had gone to sleep,

I would shut the doors and windows and draw the curtains so that he could sleep well in the darkness.

We had a telephone in our bedroom. I used to cover the telephone with a pillow so that his sleep wouldn't get disturbed if it rang. If it ever rang, he would raise himself up and ask who was calling. This was why I had to take additional care.

Ordinarily, I didn't sleep in the afternoon. I would generally busy myself with finishing off other domestic work or take the car to the market to fetch things or read the newspaper and books (which were most often on Buddhism).

Saheb would get up from his afternoon siesta at around half past three. He would brush his teeth and wash his face, and we would then have our tea together. He would then return either to the Parliament or the Constituent Assembly office. He would return home sometime between nine and ten in a state of great exhaustion. The tensions of the day would drain him out. I suspect nobody else carried the kind of responsibility that he did during those times. When he returned home, it was I again who was required to undo the buttons of his jacket and remove his jacket and shirt. Once he had changed into either a lungi or pyjamas, he would go out to the lawn. I had placed tables and chairs on the lawn so that he could sit there in the fresh air. We had a beautifully maintained lawn at 1, Hardinge Avenue. We had a small pond there in which we had put some lotus plants. The lawn had a small but attractive fountain in it. It was near this pond that we would sit in the evening.

After all the work at the Constituent Assembly offices, at the law ministry, providing information to the members about the articles to be presented to the Constituent Assembly the next day and clearing their doubts, and a whole lot of other work, he would return home dead tired. As a result, he would often turn obstinate and keep saying, 'I don't want any food', or 'I don't want this' or 'I don't want that'. This would often place me in a fix. I would then try to cajole him as one cajoles a child. Sometimes he would insist on a certain dish, leaving me with no choice but to bring out a stove and all the items needed for the dish to the lawn and prepare the dish that he desired. That was how he would finally be persuaded to eat something. After resting on the lawn for a little while, he would go to the first-floor bedroom of the bungalow. It would then be back to reading, writing and preparing notes for the Constituent Assembly till an hour or two past midnight. I would look in every little while and ask if he wanted anything. At around one or two he would finally go to sleep.

My First Public Felicitation

I had not met my family members even once since I had got married. It was by a stroke of luck that a big welcome programme was organized by the Mumbai Dalit Women's Association at the St Xavier's ground on 12 October 1948. Doctor Saheb was also requested to be present for the programme, and he had sent his acceptance and assured them of his presence. We went to Mumbai for this programme. The unrest related to the question of a *samyukt* (composite) Maharashtra state was on the boil during those days. The movement had gathered roots. There was suspicion everywhere that the Central government was plotting to separate Mumbai from the rest of Maharashtra. A number of intellectuals from the erstwhile Bombay State and from other parts of Maharashtra had joined forces. Because of getting caught up in this work, Saheb could not go for the meeting. Since the programme was organized to felicitate me, there was no way that I could opt out. The chairperson of the meeting that day was Mrs Sarojini Jadhav, the wife of D.G. Jadhav. Although entry was allowed for people who had bought a ticket of either one rupee or eight annas [half a rupee], thousands of men, women and even children had come crowding into the ground. I explained to the organizers that Doctor Saheb could not come for the function because he was busy with work related to the reorganization of states on a linguistic basis and because he was not keeping very well.

The function began at around six or half past six in the evening. I was felicitated by the chairperson by being given a bouquet of flowers and a sari. This was followed by speeches from Shantabai Wadlavkar, Champubai Kamble, Mrs Subhadrabai Kasare, Mrs Muktabai Kamble, Mrs Sushilatai Pawar, Mrs Borikar, Mrs Rukhmabai Shirkey, Mrs Sakhubai Mohite and a few other women workers in praise of Saheb and me.

Finally, amidst thunderous applause, I rose to reply to the felicitation and addressing the vast audience, I said [translated from Marathi]:

> Brothers and sisters,
>
> I am delighted at receiving such a warm welcome from all of you. Please don't be disappointed at the absence of the revered Babasaheb from this function. You are aware that his health has been in a delicate state lately. Besides, he is also busy in extremely important work today. I am convinced that soon his health will improve, and he shall come and meet you.
>
> You ladies are uneducated. There has to be spread of education among you. I feel that you must at least turn literate. Doctor Saheb, I and many others feel sad that there is no one to be seen who can carry Doctor Saheb's mission forward. You must bring his philosophy of life into your conduct.
>
> Like me, you also feel that Mumbai should stay in our Maharashtra. Babasaheb's opinion in this matter carries a lot of importance. It was because he was involved in this Mumbai-Maharashtra work that he could not come.

Every one of my statements was greeted with thunderous clapping. It doesn't need mentioning that Dr Ambedkar was the original promoter of the Samyukt Maharashtra Committee. But there are people who were not even remotely connected with the resolution of the Mumbai-Maharashtra matter who go about shouting slogans of 'Our Mumbai, Marathi Mumbai' or 'Jai Maharashtra'; they seem to carry the delusion that Maharashtra has come to them as a marriage gift.

The very first function held for felicitating me was thus held in an extremely grand manner. Doctor Saheb expressed his happiness on reading the news report of my speech in the next day's *Janata* and patted me on the back.

The Golden Moment of My Life

The Bhim Memorial [the Constitution] of this country was given its shape and came into existence in my presence. Once it was adopted, it became known universally as the world's most voluminous written constitution of a democratic country. I was witness to every one of the developments that took place during the creation of the Constitution. The Constituent Assembly was handed over the [draft] Constitution of India in November 1948. This was the golden moment of both of our lives.

I remember vividly that when Dr Ambedkar handed over a copy of the [draft] Constitution to Dr Rajendra Prasad, the president of the Constituent Assembly, a special foam chair was brought into the Central Hall for Saheb with the permission of the President. The large hall in which the work of the Constitution was being conducted was furnished with wooden benches on which the members sat. The reason for calling for a special chair for Doctor Saheb was that a boil had developed just below Saheb's navel. Readers would be aware that the wounds of people suffering from diabetes do not fill up easily, nor are they amenable to a quick cure. Since Doctor Saheb was suffering from diabetes, the boil was refusing to heal despite all efforts. It had begun to cause him such pain and discomfort that even sitting down in comfort had become impossible for him. I would dress that boil every day. The lesion had become so large that an entire swab of cotton would comfortably sit inside the cavity. But the work of presenting the Constitution was so important that a special chair had been prepared for him. I have preserved that chair as an important memento of that historic occasion. People will be able to see it in the national memorial called 'Dr Babasaheb Ambedkar Museum and Memorial', which is being constructed by the Symbiosis Institute of Pune. The Gita, the Bible, the Koran and the Tripitaka of the people of India, it is the Supreme Constitution of the country. I experienced that moment personally, saw it with my own eyes. My eyes were thus consecrated.

The unforgettable occasion celebrating the writing of the Constitution by Doctor Saheb keeps playing in my mind's eye like a movie. The heartfelt invocation for national integration that Doctor Saheb made in his historic speech[19] still resonates in my ears:

> 'I came into the Constituent Assembly with no greater aspiration than to safeguard the interests of the Scheduled Castes. [. . .] I was therefore greatly surprised when the Assembly elected me to the Drafting Committee. [. . .] I am grateful to the Constituent Assembly and the Drafting Committee for reposing in me so much trust and confidence and to have chosen me as their instrument and given me this opportunity of serving the country.'

After analysing the attributes of the Constitution, he finally made a fervent appeal to his countrymen:[20]

> 'In India there are castes. The castes are anti-national. In the first place because they bring about separation in social life. They are anti-national also because they generate jealousy and antipathy between caste and caste. But we must overcome all these difficulties if we wish to become a nation in reality.'

The speech of Dr Rajendra Prasad, the president of the Constituent Assembly, gives a fair picture of the work that Doctor Saheb performed and the responsibilities he fulfilled. He said:[21]

> 'I have realized as nobody else could have, with what zeal the members of the Drafting Committee and especially its Chairman, Dr Ambedkar, in spite of his indifferent health, have worked. We could never make a decision which was, or could ever be, so right as when we put him on the Drafting Committee and made him its Chairman. He has not only justified his selection but has added lustre to the work which he has done.'

The historic work of drafting the Constitution brought worldwide praise to Dr Ambedkar. The country extolled him as a 'modern Manu'. We began getting felicitous invitations from a number of places. The Scheduled Castes Federation too organized a function on 22 December 1948 at the R.M. Bhatt High School in Parel, Mumbai. We reached Bombay Central from Delhi. It would be appropriate to present here the enlightening thoughts that Doctor Saheb placed before his followers in the huge audience [translated from Marathi]:

> 'I don't exactly remember, but we had held a meeting here during the elections that took place in 1943. I was present then. As I stand before you today, I vividly remember that meeting. In 1946, it must be said here, we and our party had suffered a big defeat. There is no reason for us to feel regretful for having lost the election. I never feel particularly unhappy about defeats. In cricket matches, sometimes one team loses, sometimes the other team loses. The defeated team can win later, while there is always the probability of the winning team losing. Wins and losses in elections are the same. Therefore, if the Congress had merely defeated us in the elections, there would have been nothing much to ponder about.

'There is no provision here for wondering what we should have done in the previous election. We should see which are the parties that stand for the election. We are in a minority. We will not be able to manage without cooperating with some party or the other. We will have to look at the manifesto of each party for deciding which party to cooperate with. Even if we have to form an alliance, we shouldn't be joining them by breaking up our own party. Our policy should always be of forming alliances with other parties while keeping our own party intact. We shouldn't be reduced to the same pitiable state as the 'Brahmanetar' [non-Brahmin] parties have been reduced to, and that's why it is important to sound this alert. The Brahmanetar party dismantled its own organization and went and joined the Congress. Now it has come out of the Congress and has started forming its independent organization. There is no sense in following this circuitous policy of first getting into somebody else's house, then moving out of the house and rebuilding the demolished house.'

Both Saheb and I were grandly felicitated at the meeting. After staying in Mumbai for a few days, we returned to Delhi. But before leaving for Delhi, I insisted that the state of his health be investigated. We went to the St George Hospital and got his teeth examined. We also visited the renowned heart specialists Dr Tulpule and Dr Malvankar and began treatment accordingly.

While out on an official tour, we were given a grand felicitation on 15 January 1949 at Manmad, which lies on the Hyderabad Road. Saheb said there [translated from Marathi]:

'I have not been talking on politics recently for quite some time because right now I am working under political constraints. I have no doubt at all that the untouchable community is far more politically knowledgeable than any other community. The progress of any community depends upon the progress it makes in education.

'For making our politics successful, our community should get positions of authority—meaning, as I've been telling you—sensitive positions under our control.

'We are seventy million people. If we can stay together, what we have gained is enough. If we can combine that with organizational strength, we need to fear nobody. We should always stay attached to our political party, the Scheduled Castes Federation. Even if we are a minority, because of the strength in our wrists, we have no reason for fear.

'Demolishing our own house and getting into the mansion of another person is foolishness of a high order. Let us keep our huts intact, otherwise nothing will stop our situation from getting as bad as that of the Brahmanetar party. Look what a terrible state the Brahmanetar party is in! We were working together till 1932. Some of the Brahmanetar leaders then felt that there was no advantage in staying out of the Congress. They got into the Congress with the understanding that the Congress fort could be hollowed out from the inside and demolished; it could not be demolished from the outside. So often did I try to explain things to them, but they refused to listen to me. Now the non-Brahmin party has been wiped out.

'From very early times I have been accused of subverting my country, but now the hollowness of that accusation has become visible to everyone. Our party was never against the interests of the country.

'We are the ones who will establish real socialism. We shall establish the state of the peasant and the worker, because we have no affluent class and no middle class. We are all workers, we are all poor. We are the ones who will create a democracy. If a real democracy has to be brought about, it will not happen without the real revolution of bringing down the upper classes that have been dancing on our heads for thousands of years and lifting up the downtrodden class. The wheel of revolution has turned only half. There can be no revolution without turning the wheel fully. We shall turn this wheel fully round.

'I have made arrangements for the reservation of seats in government jobs for the untouchables, but suitable candidates for these reserved jobs are not available. We have now acquired the official rights, but the proper implementation is not happening because the officials belong to the upper class. That is why these critically [sic] critical positions should come under our control.

'Educational institutions occupy as important a place as politics. The progress of a community lies in the hands of the intelligent, enterprising and enthusiastic young persons of that community. Moving in this direction, for the past few years I have been concentrating my attention more on educational institutions than on politics. I started the Siddharth College in Mumbai in which, out of a total of 2,400 students, 160 are ours. I spend Rs. 21,000/- for them. My entire attention is focused on this matter. I've been thinking of opening up a college in Aurangabad. It's like the god Pandurang helping his devotee Namdev out with his wedding.

'I have made provisions for the untouchables in the proposed Constitution. Article 19 of the Constitution has completely demolished the concept of untouchability. All kinds of caste discrimination and feelings of superiority-inferiority have been exterminated. The barber now necessarily has to cut your hair, the washerman has to wash your clothes, we have to be treated in the same manner as the upper castes in temples, in eateries and restaurants. Everybody has to interact with us as equals.'

It was the first time after finishing the great work on the Constitution that we visited Mumbai, because of which every meeting of ours was attended by mammoth crowds. The air would resonate with shouts acclaiming Doctor Saheb. Everywhere we were welcomed with the deafening sound of claps. The meeting ended with some refreshments served.

Dr Ambedkar in Hospital

This incident is from 1949. Dr Ambedkar returned home after finishing his work at the Parliament and in his ministry. I had been to the market in the afternoon for some purchases and spotting some fresh ears of corn with nicely filled out kernels, I had bought some. After Saheb returned, we sat on the veranda chatting in the company of my father, who had come to Delhi to spend a few days with us. As we sat chatting, I remembered that I had asked our cook Sudama to boil the corn with salt. I told him to fetch the corn. The three of us then picked up a ear apiece and sat chatting and eating. As he ate the corn, he told us, 'There are lots of vitamins in the ears.' The salted and boiled ears were delicious and Saheb ate two or three of them. Even so, I alerted him not to eat too many, for all the vitamins it contained. But he responded, 'What can happen with a bit of corn?'

As we were chatting, his colleague Sohanlal Shastri also arrived. Doctor Saheb offered him the corn too, informing him that it was full of vitamins. After Sohanlal departed, we had our dinner and Doctor Saheb retired to his study and got submerged in his reading and writing.

Suddenly, during the night, Doctor Saheb began writhing in stomach pain. We all woke up. Along with the pain, he had also started passing stool. These loose motions continued right through the night. I gave him some medicines, but the bout being rather severe, the medicines didn't help much. I had to be very careful while administering medicines to him on account of his diabetes, neuritis and high blood pressure. The dysentery got to be so severe that he couldn't hold himself long enough to reach the toilet, with the result that his bed sheet and his pillows too got soiled. We wanted to admit him to hospital, but he turned obstinate. 'I have never been admitted into a nursing home before,' he insisted, 'and I don't want to get confined in one now.' My father, Sudama and I took care of him as well as we could and kept pleading with him to get admitted into a nursing home. But he continued with his obstinate refusal. Because of his excessive bowel movements, he had become extremely weak. We spent the whole night without sleeping a wink.

The next day we decided that we would have to shift him to a nursing home, come what may. Sohanlal Shastri also arrived, and we all began to make him see sense. Finally, after much effort, he was persuaded to accept our plea. I called an ambulance and we got him admitted to Willingdon Hospital (now called Ram Manohar Lohia hospital). Treatment began as soon as he was admitted, and he was put on a saline drip. He had turned so limp with weakness that he did not even have the strength to talk to anyone. After about three or four days of treatment and rest, he found relief.

The reader would be aware that Doctor Saheb had off and on been suffering from loose motions from very early days. I have given excerpts of his letters to his friends in the early part of this book in which he makes mention of this condition.

Another such memory is from Aurangabad. Doctor Saheb and I had gone to the city for some work related to Milind College and we stayed at the Railway Hotel. We set out in the morning, but just as we were stepping out of the lift, the putrid smell of faeces struck me hard. When I looked down, I saw his trousers and even his shoes stained with stool. This obviously meant that he had not even realized that he had passed stool. We turned around and I took him back to the room and helped him change his clothes. I quickly washed off the muck from his underclothes and trousers. He wore another set of clothes, and we finally left for the arranged programme.

The first time that we had gone to Aurangabad was to see the caves of Ajanta and Ellora. It was in execution of a deliberate plan that he had taken me on 22 January 1949 to see the caves. He had given me a detailed commentary of the pictures and statues in each one of the caves and the Jataka tales related to them. I was left speechless. His fascination for the Buddha was limitless. He was quite attracted to Aurangabad. He would talk with great enthusiasm about the relics associated with Buddhism scattered all over the Ajanta-Ellora precincts. He felt very proud of these world-renowned caves that revealed information on the golden period of Buddhism. How vibrant this place would have been with the presence of the Buddhist monks! With what passion would knowledge have been pursued here! Doctor Saheb would get lost in contemplating how these caves were the centres of learning, of culture and of the propagation of religion during those times.

A region that was at one time the centre of learning had now become very backward, and this knowledge would distress him. If all of Marathwada was so benighted in the matter of education, the state of its untouchable denizens was not even worth imagining.

In Education: Siddharth and Milind

Doctor Saheb was very sharply aware that the upliftment of the untouchables was possible only through popularizing and spreading education among them. It was in furtherance of this mission that he established the Depressed Classes Education Society in 1928 and started two hostels. Later, in 1946 he founded the People's Education Society and started the Siddharth College in Mumbai on 20 June of the same year. It became the first college in the history of Mumbai University to begin morning classes. This made it possible for the untouchables as well as for the touchables to go for higher education while retaining a day job.

Following that, since Marathwada was regarded as a backward region, he wanted to establish a good educational institute there. Thus began his effort to raise a college in Aurangabad. His endeavours bore fruit and Milind College came into existence. Dr Ambedkar thus became the first person to establish a college in such a remote region as Marathwada.

Doctor Saheb had got the maps of the land on which he wished to set up a college in Aurangabad readied by an engineer in February 1949. He marked the maps and wrote to Bhaurao Gaikwad asking him to get all the information on the plot of land including the survey number from the collector's office in Aurangabad and provide him with information on matters related to its cost.

Also, if the land required for the college could not be made available through private negotiation, Gaikwad was instructed to meet the collector and ask whether it was possible for him to recommend to the Hyderabad government the grant of those lands for public purposes.

Readers are aware of the hard work with which he raised the magnificent college in the barren wilderness of Aurangabad. Its earlier name was People's Education Society's College. I record here with pride that it was I who was responsible for naming the college Milind College and for naming the splendid and extensive precincts around it the Nagasena Vana or the Nagasena Woods. It happened thus that a discussion was going on between us on a proper name for the institution and I suggested Milind, after the name of a Buddhist scholar; for the land that spread all around the building I suggested Nagasena, the name of another learned devotee of the Buddha. Doctor Saheb liked the names and thus the college was named Milind College and the area around it was christened Nagasena Vana.

Readers would be surprised to hear that the Doctor had himself prepared the plans for the buildings of the Milind Science College Hostel, the Arts College Hostel and the Milind High School at

Aurangabad. A look at the buildings today shows how competent Saheb was in architecture. When he was the labour minister in the Viceroy's Executive Council, the Public Works Department was under him, and that was when he had gained proficiency in architecture through his own efforts. While he was the labour minister, he had astounded the engineers assembled for a conference from all over the country by his excellent lecture on architecture.

He would always be occupied in beautifying the Nagasena Vana premises in Milind College. He had mandated that whoever came visiting would plant a tree. He had got hundreds of saplings of various kinds planted under his own supervision. He had visualized a Buddha Vihara, staff quarters, a guest house, a rich library, a playground and a big clock tower in front of the Milind College building. Some of his dreams took physical shape, while some just dissolved after his passing away.

Our plan was to build a bungalow on a plot that B.H. Varale had taken near the Science College. (Varale, an associate of Dr Ambedkar, looked after Dr Ambedkar's educational institutions.) Our intention was to spend the remaining part of our lives in Aurangabad. Saheb had also been thinking of establishing an orphanage near our bungalow. He would derive great contentment by serving the orphans. He would always say, 'It is a very deep desire with me to take orphans—the poor and the infants abandoned by unwed mothers—into the orphanage and be of service to them.'

Doctor Saheb's Health

Doctor Saheb fell very ill in the first week of April. I remember it to be a Sunday. Joint ache, toothache and high blood pressure had reduced him to a state of distraction. The sugar level had shot up too. I stayed up for the entire night that Sunday, pressing his limbs to provide him with some relief. He stayed in bed for about ten or twelve days. He writes to Bhaurao in this context:[22]

New Delhi
11th April 1949

My dear Bhaurao,

While you & Chitre had been to Aurangabad I had been seriously ill in New Delhi. Sunday 3rd was a very critical day. I am better now. I am not able to move out or do any work . . .

Yours sincerely,
BRA

The Hindu Code Bill

After finishing with the historical work of the Constitution, Doctor Saheb took another extremely important work in hand and that was the Hindu Code Bill. The vicious propaganda that is spread about Dr Ambedkar being anti-Hindu is altogether wrong. The service Doctor Saheb has done for the Hindus is more than he even did for the untouchables. He shook awake society by launching a vigorous attack on the doltish imaginings of the Hindu religion and the religious customs that stood in the way of human progress. He provided for equal rights for Hindu men and women. Several laws emerged later from this Hindu Code Bill that brought equal rights and independence for Hindu women. He opened the eyes of society by his sharp criticism of the evil practices prevalent in the Hindu religion, which is why one sees progress among the Hindus.

Being a woman myself, it is natural for me to understand a woman's mind. Doctor Saheb and I, therefore, would have long discussions on the Hindu Code Bill. He was always deeply concerned about women's education, women's independence and women's liberation. He was a staunch votary of the emancipation of women.

I have always been a vigorous supporter of women's independence. While the work of the Hindu Code Bill was in progress, I would put forth my opinions with great ardour. Doctor Saheb too appreciated my thoughts and opinions greatly.

Even now I dislike the idea that women should wear the mangalsutra round their necks to display their marital status. Doctor Saheb was of the same opinion too. If the readers were to examine all my photographs, they would see that I never wore a mangalsutra. I would always wear the chain with an anchor for a pendant that he had sent to me before we got married. He would always tell me, 'An anchor is used for stabilizing unstable, drifting ships. It's because of you that my unstable life has acquired stability.'

As a woman, I well understood the torment that women were subjected to. Particularly, I would update Doctor Saheb about the distress that helpless women, abandoned by their husbands, suffered in their in-laws' house, often in their own mother's house too. I would lay a lot of emphasis on the two issues of alimony for divorced women and equal property rights for them. I would insist that the Hindu Code Bill should make provisions for matters such as equal rights, equal distribution of property and prohibition of bigamy. I feel proud that I too contributed to the Hindu Code Bill, even if it's just worth a grain.

Saheb had appointed a few Sanskrit scholars for translating the commentaries and shlokas in the religious books. The room was literally full to the brim with translations and commentaries on religious books. The Hindu Code Bill was being sculpted with Saheb sitting in conference with Hindu religious pundits, resolving doubts, holding discussions and arguments and finding ways out. I have taken detailed cognizance of it at an appropriate place in this book; that should give an idea of how the bill was cast aside during his time. Its articles and sections were, however, later adopted in bits and pieces and the Congress, which was in power, took the credit for them.

The Hindu Code Bill in Milind College

While the Hindu Code Bill was in the making and while the work for securing appropriate land for the college in Aurangabad was in progress, we would also have to visit Mumbai frequently. There were two main reasons for these trips to Mumbai: one was for work related to the progress of Siddharth College, including holding meetings of the governing board of the People's Education Society, and the other was to get Doctor Saheb's health examined.

He would make it a point to attend every special programme that the college organized. The college arranged a function on 11 January 1950, in which the main speaker was Saheb himself. Saheb had decided to speak on the subject of the Hindu Code Bill. I would always insist that in every meeting and sitting he should resolve doubts that people carried on the Hindu Code Bill and publicize it; that would help form public opinion. It was from this perspective that Saheb had selected this topic. This lecture was delivered at 8.30 in the morning in front of the people assembled in Siddharth College. It would be appropriate to give here excerpts from Saheb's speech related to the Hindu Code Bill [translated from Marathi]:

> 'The opponents say that this Code is of an extremely revolutionary nature, but this is wrong. This Code has been prepared after a detailed study of the good and bad customs among the Hindu society from the perspective of the welfare of the society. This propaganda of the opponents is wrong. The opponents' wilful persistence that the government has no right to make laws relating to customs of different castes is wrong. The government has the fundamental right of making laws related to the welfare of all the castes. The Constitution of India has made clear provisions for the government to prepare a Code of such native laws as are beneficial for the country.'

The two matters in the Hindu Code Bill that had become controversial were the joint family system and equal property rights for women. The conservative elements in the Congress were bitterly opposed to this bill.

Felicitation of the Constitution-Maker by the SCF

After seeing through the responsibility of the monumental work on the Constitution, Dr Saheb began looking after his work as law minister regularly. He was being hailed across India as the 'sculptor of the Constitution'. A community that had been denied education, humiliated at every step of the way, for one among them to write the Constitution of a subcontinent-sized country and become its sculptor—this was nothing short of a miracle that Saheb had wrought by dint of his efforts. The Scheduled Castes Federation (SCF) was a creation of the doctor himself. How could it stay silent when the entire country was felicitating its benefactor? They organized a magnificent function in Mumbai and invited us for it.

The Siddharth College function was in the morning, while our followers had organized this grand felicitation for seven in the evening at Nare Park, Dadar. People had begun lining up outside Nare Park from the afternoon.

The entire park had been done up in blue bunting and thousands of followers had poured in, filling up the park and overflowing on to the main road outside. Both of us were welcomed with garlands of flowers, so many of them that we were virtually buried under them. Jagannath Bhatankar, the secretary of the SCF, presented a copy of the Constitution to Saheb in a golden casket. This copy was presented as a symbol of love for the deed that Doctor Saheb had performed in the service of the country and for his boundless service to the untouchables. Doctor Saheb expressed his gratitude to all the workers of the SCF and the organizers of the function and said [translated from Marathi]:

'It's been many days since a meeting was held under my chairmanship and guidance and I too didn't have the occasion to say a few words to you. That led many people to say that since I was living in Delhi, the sand had begun to run out from under my feet in the political arena. If the people who have said this are present here, they will see with their own eyes that the sand, instead of running out, has only solidified under my feet. I do not think it possible that such a huge meeting called by a political party can be assembled under the chairmanship of any other leader.

'The responsibility of the work of preparing the Constitution of our nation falling upon my shoulders was a mutually beneficial event.

'I had nursed no ambition of creating the nation's Constitution. Where even becoming a member of the Constituent Assembly was a far cry, it was impossible to imagine that I would be able to exercise some authority and do some high quality work. It had been decided that any other person would be allowed in except Dr Ambedkar. The doors of the Constituent Assembly were of course closed to me, but the windows had also been closed. The holes had been filled up too. It was on account of our good fortune that I was able to get inside.

'Destiny had ordained that the person who was not even to be allowed inside was trusted with this stupendous responsibility. Whatever happened happened for the best, because the opportunity for doing a phenomenal work of this order falls to the rarest of the rare person. This matter is of outstanding esteem to me and so it is to you.

'All kinds of accusations were being laid at my door for the last twenty years: I and my party are anti-national, I am in league with the Englishmen, I am a lapdog of the Musalmans, such outrageous accusations were made against me. The Hindu people are now quite convinced that we are not that kind, and the Scheduled Castes Federation is a well-organized, strong party that has a strong political stance, it's also a party that will never join any seditious activity; of this, everybody is now fully convinced.

'There is one thing now that we must keep firmly in mind: we had been looking after the welfare of our community, that, of course, we must continue to do, but along with that we should also consider how we can preserve the independence that our country has got. In spite of having gained independence earlier, it has had to suffer servitude. Earlier, the Musalmans and then the English had taken away our independence from us. Independence is as important to the lower classes as it is to the upper classes. We have become free from slavery to the English, but it will be a terrible tragedy if we were to get enslaved again to a foreign power. Therefore, we should consider it our most important duty to defend the independence of this country.'

Dr Ambedkar spoke in detail about the Constituent Assembly, the work on the Constitution and about the Scheduled Castes Federation and then gave them the message of keeping the independence of the country intact.

Doctor Saheb's health again took a hit sometime during the middle of 1949. His neuritis flared up and he suffered extreme pain in the legs. We nursed him night and day. We would foment his legs and back, and massage them.

During this period, Jayaprakash Narayan, Sarat Chandra Bose, Comrade More and some other leaders would meet Saheb to discuss the issue of cooperating with the Scheduled Castes Federation. Even when Doctor Saheb was in Delhi, he would pay close attention to his institutions, the political happenings around the country, party work, his workers and such other affairs. We would always discuss all these matters. Since I had always been an alert reader, I would update him on all the political happenings. I would also assist him in the construction of our own party and in all other matters. Saheb too never felt it below his dignity to take my suggestions. If my stance was not proper, he would convince me with supporting evidence why it was not proper.

The Thought of Getting Yeshwant Married

Doctor Saheb had begun to stay in Delhi after he was nominated to the Viceroy's Executive Council. Yeshwant and Mukund lived [at Rajgraha] in Mumbai. Saheb had also got two independent houses constructed for them at the Konkanast Mahar colony in Khar. We had begun to think about getting Yeshwant married because his settling down into his household would free us of a major responsibility.

Yeshwant too had told a few colleagues about his readiness to get married. We had been making efforts to find a suitable bride for him. Doctor Saheb held the desire that a girl from among my relatives should be selected for Yeshwant. In my opinion, though, there was no girl among my relatives who would match Yeshwant. Basically, Yeshwant* wasn't as well educated as I would have liked. Besides, since there was no suitable girl in our family to match Yeshwant, I gave Saheb a clear 'no'. Now, when I think of that refusal, I feel that that was a good thing to happen; otherwise, she too could have suffered at the hands of the self-servers among Doctor Saheb's followers as I have suffered for the past thirty years. Even beyond that, the people of those times who proclaimed themselves to be the heirs of Ambedkar would also have found an opportunity to malign me. Well, whatever it was, it is said that everything happens for the best, and I experienced the truth of this saying in the matter of Yeshwant's marriage.

My refusal had already been given and Saheb himself had not been able to locate a suitable girl for Yeshwant among my relatives. Therefore, the responsibility of finding a girl was placed upon Bhaurao Gaikwad, Rajbhoj and Kawade from Nagpur. Bhaurao and Kawade had identified a few girls along Doctor Saheb's expectations. We had a few expectations regarding how our daughter-in-law should be. Saheb had noted these in a letter he had written on 3 June 1949. The relevant part of the letter is given below:[23]

New Delhi
3/6/49

My dear Bhaurao,

. . . There is one other matter about which I have been wanting to write to you but have not found [the time/occasion] to do so. Yeshwant wants to get married. I am in search of a girl. Do you know of anyone [?] The girl must be (1) fair looking (2) must have a personality and [a] dignified appearance (3) must be coming from a good family having moral traditions (4) must not be too young and (5) must be educated though it is not necessary for her to be a graduate. I shall be glad if you will treat this matter to be urgent. I would like you to write also to Kawade if he knows any such girl in CP.

With kind regards,
Yours sincerely,
B R A

Saheb wrote yet another letter to Dadasaheb Gaikwad on 5 June regarding Yeshwant's marriage and his health:[24]

Bhimrao R. Ambedkar
M. A., Ph. D., D. Sc.,
BAR-AT-LAW

New Delhi
5th June, 1949

My dear Bhaurao,

You must have got my last letter. In it I have written to you about Yeshwant's marriage. It would be better if you came here.

We could discuss it personally. It is possible the Assembly may close for a short holiday. I am so tired I want to go to Simla & Massourie [sic]. To avoid your missing me I suggest you come here at once.

With kind regards,
Yours sincerely
B R A

Revaram Kawade of Nagpur came to us in Delhi with regard to Yeshwant's marriage. He had identified three girls of the kind we had been looking for in Nagpur and we had even had discussions on it. Saheb said that Yeshwant could select any one of the three girls he liked. Accordingly, we informed Bhaurao that he should arrange for a meeting between Kawade and Yeshwant. In due course Yeshwant saw the girls but he rejected all three of them. We didn't know then why he had rejected the girls, but Bhaurao informed us that Yeshwant wanted to marry a girl of his choice.

After Yeshwant had rejected the Nagpur girls, Rajbhoj of Pune suggested his own girl for Yeshwant to Bhaurao, but Yeshwant rejected her too.

Disillusioned with the matter of Yeshwant's marriage, Saheb decided not to give any further attention to it. He never wrote to anyone regarding his marriage after that. It appeared that a self-seeking clique had gathered around Yeshwant, and he conducted himself according to their advice. He rarely came to us (to Delhi). I would tell him quite often that Saheb and I lived alone and that he should live with us there. But he would be ill at ease in Delhi. Whenever I insisted on his staying, his response would be fixed: 'I feel afraid of Babasaheb. He is always getting irritated. I am better off in Mumbai.'

Later, Yeshwant married a girl of his choice. By chance, we were in Mumbai that day (19 April 1953). I pressed Saheb quite hard to go for Yeshwant's wedding ceremony. He was reclining on a sofa in a room in the basement of Anand Bhavan [Siddharth College]. I got dressed to go for Yeshwant's marriage ceremony and pleaded with him too to get ready. When I went up to him, he sat up and said, 'I'm not feeling well. I don't want to go. You go by all means, if you want to. I'm not holding you back.' He was just not ready to go. He picked up a pencil and paper and got absorbed in making sketches of the Buddha.

Finally, I went with my sisters and a couple of relatives to Yeshwant's wedding [R.M. Bhatt High School Hall, Parel] and returned to Anand Bhavan at Parel. I saw that Saheb was still busy with his sketching. He saw me and said, 'Ah, you are back,' and again immersed himself in his sketching.

Yeshwant later came with his bride to the college. They touched Saheb's feet, but Saheb just about muttered, 'Stay happy,' and without paying much attention to them, he remained busy in his work. The couple left.

Sovereign Democratic India

Dr Ambedkar placed the Draft Constitution before the Constituent Assembly on 4 November 1948 for its deliberations. While presenting the draft to the Assembly, Doctor Saheb delivered an extremely scholarly address. After analysing the American political system and the position of the American President, he talked about the special features of the Indian Constitution.

After the articles were discussed, they were approved one after the other. Article 11 [sic] of the Constitution relates to untouchability.[25] With the approval and adoption of this article on 20 November 1948, untouchability was given a statutory burial. This was Saheb's biggest victory in the crusade of his life. During the Mahad satyagraha, he had publicly torched the Manu Smriti, which propagated inequality, but on 20 November 1948, he truly burnt down the Manu Smriti for good in its truest sense and brought into the country Bhim Smriti, which propagated equality.

The Constitution came into effect on 26 January 1950 and was officially recognized as the most voluminous written constitution of a democratic country, and India arrived as a sovereign, democratic country in the map of the world.

I believe that Doctor Saheb has been a really fortunate person. Very few great men worldwide would be blessed with the destiny that fell to his share. Saheb fought many battles for the establishment of independence, equality and fraternity; in fact, he expended his entire life for this mission. That he could pour the essence of this holiest of holy missions into the Constitution with his own hands, can there be a bigger fortune than this?

On 25 November 1949, Doctor Saheb sounded a warning bell for the country in the Constituent Assembly. I believe that even today every Indian should contemplate it. That trenchant speech reverberates in my ears till today. Saheb sent an alert to the listeners by saying:[26]

> 'On the 26th of January 1950, we are going to enter into a life of contradictions. In politics we will have equality and in social and economic life we will have inequality . . . We must remove this contradiction at the earliest possible moment or else those who suffer from inequality will blow up the structure of political democracy which this Assembly has so laboriously built up.'

Ill Health Again

A programme for felicitating us was organized jointly by the various Maharashtra 'mandals' of Delhi on 29 January 1950. We went for the function with the greatest affection. Saheb always felt proud of being a Maharashtrian. I too have always carried a sense of pride at being a Maharashtrian. Saheb expressed his adulation for the people of Maharashtra in this meeting of the Maharashtra mandals.

After we returned from Mumbai, his health again took a dip. For the entire month of February, he was mostly bedridden. For an entire month an embargo had been placed upon his reading and writing. If I ever saw him reading, I would literally snatch the book out of his hands. He was suffering from sharp pains in his legs. His extreme weakness would make him feel dizzy and out of this dizziness he would have convulsions. This ill health remained for a month. He was administered treatment by Dr Malvankar in consultation with doctors from Delhi. After a month, he started feeling better.

The Buddha's Birth Anniversary in Delhi

We decided that we would embrace Buddhism. It was our resolve to spend the rest of our lives as Buddhists. But there was the matter of the upliftment of the millions of untouchables, and that would not have been possible without the acquisition of political power. With no other remedy in sight, it had become not only necessary but imperative for Saheb to stay on in politics. But it was equally important that we declared our strong and open support to the religious movement and began taking active steps in the direction of religious conversion later.

We had been invited for a function organized to celebrate the birth anniversary of Mahatma Gautam Buddha in Delhi on 2 May 1951. This programme was to be held under the chairmanship of Sir Maung Gyi, the Burmese Ambassador to India. In this very first public address on Buddhism, Doctor Saheb sent the message that there was no emancipation for the untouchables except through the espousal of Buddhism. In his address, he listed out the merits of Buddhism, compared it with other religions and presented convincing arguments for its superiority. I give below to the readers an important excerpt from this address. It is of particular interest that Doctor Saheb delivered this address in Hindi in the presence of renowned Buddhist bhikshus from India and abroad. Addressing this sea of humanity, Doctor Saheb said in his half-hour address [translated from Marathi]:

'The resurrection of Buddhist philosophy has begun again in India. The President of democratic India had to ultimately go to Buddhism for the Ashoka Chakra [the Ashoka Wheel] on the national flag of independent India. The three lions that constitute the national seal of independent India are also symbolic of Buddhism. Also, during the historic occasion of the swearing in of the President of independent India, it wasn't the statues of the countless Hindu gods and goddesses, but the magnificent statue of the Buddha that was installed in the spacious hall. It was with the statue of the Buddha as witness that the President had taken his oath of office.

'No god can stand comparison with the Buddha – not Rama, not Krishna, not anyone else. The fact is that no prophet and guide can ever be born who is greater than the Buddha.'

Going over many events in the Ramayana and the Mahabharata, Saheb remarked on the conduct of Rama and Krishna, and raised questions and doubts about the greatness of the two.

He further said:

'The foundation of Buddhism rests on ethics. The Buddha is a great guide. In contrast, Shri Krishna says that he is the god of gods; Jesus Christ says that he is the son of god and Hazrat Paigambar says he is the last prophet of god. The founder of every religion has adopted the role of the deliverer; in sharp contrast, the Buddha has taken the role of a guide. In Buddhism, it is ethics that has taken the place of god. It was the Buddha who introduced for consideration this revolutionary meaning of the word dharma. In the opinion of the Brahmins, religion is yajna and the oblations made to god. The Buddha, however, made ethics the main basis of dharma instead of karma. The social principles of Hinduism are based upon inequality, while Buddhism is founded on equality. The Gita too has endorsed the four-caste system.

'Further, dharma should not be passed on from father to son as property. The time has arrived when everyone should personally examine every religion wisely and judiciously before embracing it.'

An article published in *The Bharat* of 3 May 1950, gives a fair estimation of the importance of this address. It says:

'A dramatic development of great national importance and interest throughout South-East Asia took place in the capital tonight when Dr Ambedkar, India's Law Minister, called upon 70 million Harijans to embrace Buddhism, speaking at the triple [sic] anniversary of Lord Buddha at a crowded meeting.'

Talegaon

We had a small piece of land in Talegaon on which there was a three-room construction. When we were in Mumbai, whenever we could find the time, we would go and stay there for a day or two. The air in Talegaon was clean and Saheb loved its atmosphere. We would go to Talegaon particularly for rest, and we were always eager to go there.

Whenever we visited Talegaon, the news of our arrival would immediately spread in the neighbouring localities and people would line up to have a glimpse of us. We had made arrangements for cooking and had stocked the house with vessels, mattresses, bed sheets and such things adequate for our needs. But ordinarily, the need for me to cook would not arise because the people of the neighbourhood would bring over bhakari, Bombay-duck chutney, pooran-poli as sweet dish, sometimes mutton and many such dishes with a lot of love, affection and reverence, and serve us with great entreaty. We too would consume the food with great joy and relish. Both of us loved bhakari and Bombay-duck chutney. This innocent and limitless love coming from the people of our community touched us greatly. Doctor Saheb would make sincere and courteous inquiries about them and offer them guidance and fortitude.

The Ahmednagar College

Once, while answering questions from journalists, Saheb announced his intention of opening an arts and science college in Ahmednagar along the lines of Siddharth College. The topic of starting a college in Ahmednagar had featured in our conversations quite often. Relatively speaking, the Nagar area was backward in education and was famine-prone. An enthusiastic worker by the name of P.J. Roham had done a lot of hard work towards establishing a college in Nagar. Saheb had asked him to reconnoitre for a suitable place in this regard. However, nothing further materialized, and the Nagar college never came into existence.

Trip to Hyderabad

A sitting of the Working Committee of the Hyderabad State Scheduled Castes Federation had been organized on 19 May 1950. The chairman of the meeting was J.H. Subbiah. Dr Ambedkar, as the president of the SCF, and I were special invitees to the meeting. Also present was P.N. Rajbhoj, the secretary of the Federation. While we were in Hyderabad, we had discussions with government officials regarding the Aurangabad College.

Saheb delivered a speech at the Boat Club in Hyderabad in which he spoke in detail on the position and importance of religion in human life and on other related issues.

Our Trip to Okhla

In the June of 1950, a colleague of Saheb's by the name of Balwant Varale came visiting Delhi. Saheb held Varale in particular affection.

As soon as Saheb returned from the Secretariat in the evenings, we would take him out to show him the historically important sites in Delhi: sometimes to the Jama Masjid, some other times to the Red Fort, the Qutub Minar, to Humayun's Tomb, to Okhla and other such places.

The shops that we patronized were fixed: for household things, for sweets, for stationery, bookstores and so on, and we would take Varale with us. Even during the day, if there were household things to be brought, I would send Varale for them and he would be delighted to buy those things for us.

One day I planned an outing to Okhla with the help of Varale and persuaded Doctor Saheb to join us. Varale insisted on picking up the expense for this trip. Neither Saheb nor I were agreeable to it, but because of Varale's insistence, we relented. By a coincidence, both my brothers and Dr Malvankar too had come to see us. The doctor had, of course, come to check up on Saheb's health.

Doctor Saheb's personal secretary Massey and assistant secretary Pillay came forward to help arrange the trip. Saheb, I, my two brothers, Dr Malvankar, Varale, Massey, Pillay, a journalist friend of Saheb named Shrikrishna, our cook Sudama and a few others set off. Okhla was about seven miles from Delhi. We reached the guest house at Okhla with our mutton, rice, spices, ghee and other such ingredients.

On reaching the spot, all of us had some tea. Saheb insisted that he would himself do the cooking and got busy immediately. The first thing he did was to instruct the cook to lay out the spices for each of the dishes: for marinating the chicken, for dry mutton and for biryani. The proportions of each item that went into the masala were instructed for each dish: how much of chillies, how much dry coriander powder, how much garam masala, how much of opium seeds, how much of fresh coriander leaves, how much cinnamon. I was amazed that Saheb was a bigger expert in this matter than any woman could be. There were constant instructions given to the servants on what to put when.

He would say, 'The masala should be ground soft like butter and should be so fine that a person should not notice it even if it is put into one's eyes.' While the cooking was in progress, he would lift the lid of a vessel, scoop out a little bit of the dish being cooked with a spoon on to his left palm and lick it to see how it was coming out. He would then issue instructions for the adding of this thing or that.

That day he didn't allow me to get into the cooking at all. 'Sharu,' he said, 'you just keep watching and see what delicious stuff I cook. I doubt whether any of you women can cook such delicious stuff as this.' He also prepared wet chutney of tender coconut to go with the food. Chicken curry, dry mutton, potato curry, biryani, Saheb made everything himself.

We then spread sheets out on the ground and sat for our meal. There was a lot of chat and fun and laughter right through the meal. Saheb would force extra helpings on each one of those assembled. As the meal progressed, he would look victoriously at us and ask, 'So, how was the cooking?' The meal ended in a very convivial atmosphere. Everyone came forth with genuine praise for Saheb's culinary skills. He would feel a great sense of contentment in cooking and serving his dishes to others.

The Colombo Conference on Buddhism

The Young Men's Buddhist Association of Ceylon had invited us for a conference on Buddhism to be held in Colombo (Kandy).

We left for Colombo on 25 May 1950. Rajbhoj, the secretary of the Scheduled Castes Federation, had come along with us. Representatives from twenty-seven countries had assembled at the Temple of the Sacred Tooth Relic (where Lord Buddha's tooth is preserved) to inaugurate the World Fellowship of Buddhists. Our main objective in attending this conference was to observe the ceremonies and rituals associated with Buddhism and study what could be done to propagate Buddhism in India.

Arrangements for our stay were made in Kandy, the ancient capital of Sri Lanka. Doctor Saheb was requested to deliver an address at one of the official sessions of the conference, which he turned down, but once the resolution of the inauguration of the conference was passed, he addressed the representatives of the Buddhist countries of the world [on 26 May 1950] and said:[27]

> 'You probably know that there are people in India who thought the time had come when an effort might be made to revive Buddhism in India. I am one of them . . . Buddhist countries should have not merely fellowship, but promote religion and make sacrifices . . . [C]ountries where Buddhism exists should make sacrifices, establish missions and find funds, so that they can carry on the work of . . . spreading the gospel . . .'

Addressing the Young Men's Buddhist Association on 5 June[28] on the topic 'The Progress and the Annihilation of Buddhism in India', he said:

> 'Buddhism in its material form had disappeared, I agree, but as a spiritual force, it still exists.[29]
>
> 'The religion of India has undergone three changes. Vedic religion which was practised first gave way, in course of time, to Brahminism and this, in turn, to Hinduism. It was during [the] Brahminic period that Buddhism was born. This was because Buddhism opposed inequality, authority and division of society into various classes which Brahminism had introduced in India.[30]
>
> 'I do not agree with the suggestion made by many people in India that Buddhism was destroyed by the dialectics of Shankaracharya. This is contrary to the facts as Buddhism existed for many centuries after his death.'[31]

While analysing the decline of Buddhism in India, he said:

'Buddhism declined in India because of the rise of Vaishnavism and Saivism, the two cults which adopted and absorbed many good points of Buddhism.[32]

'The second reason is the invasion of India by the Musalmans. When Allauddin marched against Bihar, he killed well over 5000 Buddhist monks, which resulted in the surviving Buddhists fleeing to neighbouring countries like China, Nepal and Tibet for saving their lives. During the later period, the Buddhists of India tried to resurrect Buddhism, but they were not successful because almost 90% of the Buddhists had embraced Hinduism.'[33]

During our trip to Colombo, we visited a number of Buddhist viharas and observed the customs and ceremonies of Buddhism.

We were given a grand reception in the Town Hall of Colombo on 6 June 1950. Saheb appealed to the untouchables in Colombo to embrace Buddhism. He also appealed to the citizens of Ceylon to strive with the affection of parents for the welfare of the Dalits and give them a place in their religion.

After the conference was over, we set off on our return journey to India. On way to Mumbai, Saheb delivered lectures in Trivandrum and Madras. He had long discussions on the Hindu Code Bill with the chief minister of Travancore, the advocate general, rationalist scholars and judges in the state dak bungalow. We stayed in Trivandrum for two or three days during which time we were shown a few temples. Doctor Saheb expressed his deep vexation at seeing the dominance of the Hindu priests and the wastage of food.

Doctor Saheb's Statue

On 19 July 1950, Varale brought a gentleman along with him to Delhi. The next day he told me the reason for that gentleman's arrival. He was a sculptor named Madilgekar who wanted to make a statue of Saheb. He had brought along with him the tools that would be required for the sculpting.

I didn't think Saheb would want to get his statue sculpted; also, since I had no experience of the man's talent, if the statue came out badly, Saheb would be upset; hence I resisted the proposition and showed no excitement.

One day Varale himself broached the subject at the dining table. Saheb said, 'What? No! I am no king or any ruler of a state. There's no need for any statue of me. Importantly, I have no time for sittings.'

Saheb was to depart later for a pre-arranged trip to Manmad, Aurangabad and Mumbai. He was going to be presented a purse in Aurangabad. There was also work related to land for the college.

He was presented with a purse of Rs 2001 at Aurangabad at the hands of Subbiah of SCF and news of the programme appeared in the newspaper *Janata*. I consider it important to give excerpts of the speech he delivered there, because it is worth pondering over even today by Dalit leaders. He said [translated from Marathi]:

> 'There was no need for the presentation of this purse. I have never served out of inducements and greed. It is my prime duty to keep serving you. Whatever little money I have received as purse I have never used for my own self. Gandhi was presented with a purse of a few million rupees; Tilak was given a purse of nine lakhs of rupees, but ours is not like that.
>
> 'My only ambition is to keep serving you selflessly. What my friends said in their introductory addresses gives me goosebumps. There's a great difference between the situation earlier and the situation as it exists now. Once we had come to see the Daulatabad fort; my colleagues had drunk water from the pond there to slake their thirst, a 15-20-year-old Musalman boy had rained abuses at us.
>
> 'When it rains on a flat field, the water dissipates; when it falls in a pit, it gets collected. Therefore, I invite you to come together

with a single purpose under the banner of the Scheduled Castes Federation. You have human rights; if somebody snatches them away, you can now go to court against the government. Therefore, there is no reason to be afraid. All I have to tell you is that you must stay united.'[34]

On returning from Aurangabad, he expressed his attraction for Buddhism at a function organized by the Mumbai branch of the Royal Asiatic Society. Professor N.K. Bhagwat presided over this function.

After our Aurangabad and Mumbai programmes were over, we returned to Delhi on 26 July. During Saheb's absence, Varale had gotten me to send him a picture of the Buddha. He decided to ready a model on the basis of that picture. After the statue was ready, he showed it to me. I loved the sculpture made by Madilgekar and told Varale, 'He has prepared an excellent statue. We'll show it to Saheb. He will surely like it.'

During dinner I told Saheb that Madilgekar had sculpted a beautiful model of the Buddha's photograph we had at our bungalow and that he would surely like it. After dinner, at around ten, all of us, including Varale, went to the room we had given to Madilgekar. Saheb applauded Madilgekar and later posed before the statue along with Varale and Madilgekar.

Since I had liked the Buddha's statue, I requested that Madilgekar should also sculpt a statue of Saheb. Varale also joined in the plea. Saheb didn't voice any objection. That, in a way, was a mute acceptance. As luck would have it, the People's Education Society had wanted a statue done too. Patankar, the principal of Siddharth College, had also made inquiries in this regard. I too was very keen that a statue of Saheb be sculpted, and therefore I procured his agreement to sit for the work. Since Madilgekar was also resident at the bungalow then, we got the work started immediately. The modelling would happen every day as soon as Saheb entered the dining room for his meals. One day a number of photographs of Saheb were taken from different angles. In a few days, a clay model of the statue was ready. As per the demand of the Society, this was converted into a bronze statue, and at the initiative of Kamalakant Chitre, the secretary of the Society, the statue was installed in the library.

Lifelong Student Dr Ambedkar

Till as long as Varale and Madilgekar were staying with us, Saheb would take lessons from Madilgekar on drawing and sculpture. Under the guidance of Madilgekar, Saheb also sculpted a statue of the Buddha. The joy he derived from sculpting that statue is beyond description because it had been a long-time desire of his to make a statue of the Buddha himself. He had keenly wanted to make statues of the Buddha with Indian features in the pose of delivering his sermon, as also a number of other statues with his eyes shown open. He wanted to send these statues to different parts of India and abroad. Likewise, it was his hope to install some on the campus of the college at Aurangabad. Saheb remained a student all his life. He was always ready to acquire knowledge of all kinds. He was forever curious to learn sketching, sculpting, tabla-playing, playing the violin, music, cooking, driving, Pali, Sanskrit and to learn different forms of art.

Saheb didn't know how to drive, so that did it! He just got this into his head. 'You know how to drive a car, right?' he said with the obstinacy of a child. 'Well, I have to learn too!' After he returned from the Parliament, we would set off, Saheb, the driver and I, and go somewhere far from Delhi, find a less crowded road and our driving school would commence. He would occupy the driver's seat with great excitement, and I would sit next to him and give him instructions. Our driver would pipe in from his seat behind us. He would get the car started all right, but when I asked him to press the brake, he would press the accelerator, and when the instruction was for the accelerator, he would press the brakes. He would thus get thoroughly confused between clutch, brake and accelerator and create a mess. This driving school enterprise went on for almost a week off and on, and he finally got bored. He said, 'I won't be able to handle this, for sure. How you can drive the car so expertly, you know best, but I know I won't be able to do this.' I responded, 'Whoever asked you to learn?'

Our Dehradun Trip

Towards the end of 1950, Varale came to Delhi once again with two or three of his friends, the sculptor Madilgekar being one of them. My brother Balu Kabir was also with us then. I told Saheb, 'Varale has come with his friends, my brother is here too, so let's go for a trip somewhere.' Saheb liked the idea, and he instructed his secretary Massey to make arrangements for going to Mussoorie. Accordingly, Massey looked through his other engagements and planned the trip. We set off in two cars early in the morning and reached Dehradun at six in the evening.

The district collector of Dehradun was personally present to welcome us. He had requisitioned the huge bungalow that was earlier used by the viceroy. Tea and snacks were laid out as soon as we reached there. The district collector had himself made special arrangements for our dinner. We took our meal in an atmosphere of fun and laughter. The staying arrangement was of the best kind and the weather was wonderful too.

The vegetation and the lawns around the extensive bungalow were extremely attractive. We would sit peacefully on the lawns and chatter to our heart's content.

One day Saheb gave the car to Varale and asked him to pay a visit to a nearby place called Kalasia. There was a monastery on the banks of the Yamuna in which Tathagat Lord Buddha had stayed;

that was why Saheb had sent Varale and company to visit that place. Saheb had taken me there in 1949. Sanctified by the presence of the Tathagat, the place exuded peace, sacredness and serenity. The tea gardens all around it were very attractive.

Eye Problem

Doctor Saheb would be reading and writing ceaselessly. He worked on the Hindu Code Bill with the same intensity with which he had earlier worked on the Constitution. For this purpose, he was required to study the Smritis, the Shastras, the Vedas and the Puranas. There was the relentless reading of hundreds of books, other writings, and the making of notes. Alongside that went his own reading and writing of books. There was never a break in this routine. The doctors had advised him to take a few days' break from all this reading and writing; I too would try to persuade him to take a break. But there would be Hindu experts and scholars coming over to discuss matters related to the bill and that would obviously lead him to return to all his reading and writing. As a result of all this, Saheb further damaged his eyes that had in any case not been in good health.

The eye problem had been bothering him persistently for a good two or three months. When the discomfort got to be too much, he would stop his reading and writing for a few days, but it was simply not possible for him to stay inactive for too many days. He would go back to his work and his eyes would begin to pain. We even visited Mumbai to get his eyes treated. There was a celebrated ophthalmologist in Bombay Hospital, a Parsee gentleman named Master or Mistry, I can't remember exactly, who treated his eyes.

His eyes had become so bad after all the reading and writing that the power of his lenses would change every few months. He would often say in agitation, 'What will happen to me? What would be the purpose of living if I can't read and write?'

The Concern about the Aurangabad College

We had started a college in Aurangabad in 1950 called PES College, which was later rechristened Milind College in October 1955. The cornerstone of the building was laid by the first President of democratic India, Dr Rajendra Prasad, during a function organized on 1 September. A special envoy of the Nizam was present for this event too.

In the speech that he delivered on this occasion, Dr Rajendra Prasad lavished fulsome praise on Saheb for his boundless scholarship, his vital role in the writing of the Constitution and for passionately pursuing the mission of spreading education among the poor and downtrodden. The next day, Dr Rajendra Prasad, Saheb, the principal of Milind College Manohar Chitnis, Varale, a few government officials and I went to see the caves at Ellora. Doctor Saheb explained to the President the details and the entire history of each one of those caves. The President was awestruck by all the information that Doctor Saheb gave on the art and the Buddhism-related background of the caves.

Although the college had started in June, there was little money for its expansion and its balance sheet of revenue and expenditure was in a poor state. The Aurangabad division was under the control of the Osmania University, and the vice chancellor of the university had met Saheb in Delhi, but looking at its financial state, he hadn't been very keen on extending help. We had been informed that the college would incur a loss of a hundred thousand rupees that year. The college, therefore, had become a matter of great concern for Saheb. The vice chancellor had gone to the extent of advising that the college be shifted to some other place.

But later on, Saheb helped the institution to develop phenomenally; in due course the college gained tremendous recognition as a great institution of learning.

At the Worli Buddha Monastery

When the Lok Sabha was prorogued on 22 December till 5 February 1951, we decided to use this break in the service of religion and therefore went to Mumbai. Saheb's eyes also had to be tested.

Workers had organized a meeting on 14 January 1951 at the Buddha monastery in Worli. A conference had been going on there for a few days. Professor Bhagwat came to visit us at Siddharth College and invited us to visit the Buddha monastery, which Saheb accepted. At the insistence of the gathering present there, he delivered a speech in which he expressed his opinion on Buddhism. Saheb said [translated from Marathi]:

> 'The Buddha lived in this land for eighty years and spent 45 years of his life in proselytization. He did not have a car with him as the Shankaracharya has today. He didn't even have a simple horse-carriage. He didn't have any mode of conveyance, but for the welfare of the country, he travelled literally on foot right from Jammu to Kanyakumari. Buddhism was prevalent in the country for 1200 years. A person who lived his life by begging, a person who suffered all kinds of travails, his name is no longer brought up in this country.
>
> 'It happens sometimes that untruth wins and truth is not hailed. This matter falls into that category. But everybody needs to keep in mind that truth is bound to prevail one day and that day has now arrived. I am convinced that after 1200 years, it shall again become the religion of the country.
>
> 'Some of my bhikshu friends here have said they want to give deeksha to a number of people, but I have told them that it is not easy to become a Buddhist. That is the reason why my people and I are going to prepare some rules. Only those who observe these rules should be given the deeksha. Once you have embraced Buddhism, you will not be allowed to bring Hindu ideas and

Hindu gods and goddesses into Buddhism. Khandoba inside and the Buddha outside will not be allowed.

'Religion seems to have exhausted itself, but I believe that religion is necessary for everyone. One thing, in my opinion, is certain: a society cannot survive without religion and that religion has to be Buddhism alone. The three attributes – equality, love and fraternity – necessary for the upliftment of the world are present in this Buddhism. For the last twenty years I have studied every religion and after this study I have arrived at the conclusion that the entire world should embrace Buddhism.'

The Hindu Code Bill Debate

The probability existed that the Hindu Code Bill would be tabled on 5 February [1951]. The *sanatanis* among the Congress had been opposing the bill and the other Congressmen were opposing it with an eye on the elections to be held soon. Stormy debates were being held across the country on the matter.

The main accusations of the opponents were as given below:

1. People's opinion on this subject had not been gathered, hence the bill should not be submitted before the Parliament in a hurry.
2. The circumstances were not favourable for bringing about revolutionary social changes. The controversial bill, therefore, should not be taken up for discussion now but should be discussed later at a suitable opportunity.
3. If this bill were to be adopted, the Hindu community would be split.
4. The present Parliament has been constituted through indirect elections; therefore, it does not possess the people's mandate for making laws on such a fundamental issue.

5. The present government calls itself a 'caretaker government', therefore, such a caretaker government does not have the authority to make laws that can affect the social life of a country.

Dr Ambedkar nursed the great dream of restructuring within the framework of equality a Hindu society that was based upon inequality. To clarify the aspects of the Hindu Code Bill, Saheb had got a thirty-nine-page booklet printed and distributed among the members of the Lok Sabha. In this booklet, he explained how he had held discussions with representatives of different strata of the country and gave a detailed analysis of what changes he had made in the basic Hindu Code and how.

Prime Minister Nehru had just returned from a tour of America when Saheb met him and got from him the approval to table the bill. Nehru assured Saheb that he would get the bill approved. He went so far as to say that if the bill were not passed, his government would resign. 'I will die or swim with the Hindu Code Bill,' he thundered. Prime Minister Nehru was not against the bill, but Speaker Mavalankar, President Dr Rajendra Prasad and Home Minister Vallabhbhai Patel were openly against it.

It was under these difficult circumstances that Doctor Saheb tabled the Hindu Code Bill in the Lok Sabha on 5 February 1951. As was expected, a storm broke loose. Sardar Hukum Singh, the Sikh representative, was a hardcore Hindu supporter. Pandit Thakurdas Bhargava also bitterly opposed the bill. Saheb responded to the critics with suitable and well-argued analyses. The debate went on for three days, but the opponents of the bill refused to be satisfied. The sanatanis had come with the determination that they would not allow the bill to be adopted under any circumstances. The opponents finally gained victory by having the discussion on the bill postponed for the September 1952 session of the Lok Sabha. Doctor Saheb was deeply disappointed, but he never lost fortitude. I too would keep building his confidence. There was still time. There would be seven or eight months of waiting. During this period, public opinion could be awakened; even the opponents could have a change of opinion. There was no reason for hope to be abandoned. Even if Saheb looked depressed, his resolve to get the bill passed in September remained firm.

A campaign began of speeches, protests and advertisements that let loose a veritable storm of criticism against the government and against Saheb. Protesters were hired to agitate in front of the Parliament. A gang of protesters once broke into our bungalow and began shouting slogans and had to be chased out by the security guards. Letters too arrived threatening death, but Saheb stood firm.

Unshakeable Willpower

When Saheb used to feel depressed by the political developments relating to the Hindu Code Bill, I would try to pull him towards activities related to religion. I would tell him that we should now focus our attention on dhamma [the Prakrit word for religion] and get into religious activities instead of political activities. He would always be very enthusiastic about working for dhamma. His slogan: 'I shall make India Buddhist' was an indication of his unshakeable willpower.

In a letter to Bhaurao, he writes [translated from Marathi]:

New Delhi
3-4-1951

My dear Bhaurao,

I have received all your letters and I am replying to them all. I have begun taking better care of myself.

> I would sometimes wonder why I should want to live for a longer time, but having taken the work of Lord Buddha and Buddhism in hand, I now have to live longer. My desire today is that I should live for a longer period. You too would have noticed that considering my age, a new vitality has arrived in my health.

The Winds of the 1952 Elections

As per the Constitution, the first general elections of 1952 were coming close; from that perspective, all the political parties were busy drawing up their battle plans. There was a lot of talk about forming electoral alliances. From the many conversations that took place between us during meals, walks and while sitting on the lawns, it was clear that an alliance with the Congress, the Jana Sangh, the Hindu Mahasabha, the Communists and such other parties would not fit within the principles that Saheb upheld. It was finally decided that there should be an alliance with the Socialist Party and that the SCF should support the leaders of the Peasants and Workers' Party, namely, Keshavrao Jedhe, Shankarrao Morey and Bhausaheb Raut.

The Election Symbol of SCF

Having decided to fight the first general elections in alliance with other parties, Saheb had a huge load of work related to the elections, such as discussions and consultations, canvassing for the party, making lists of candidates, choosing the candidates and so on. All these activities would leave him exhausted.

There being no way out except to take him away from Delhi, I planned a programme with the help of his secretary to take him to Ranikhet [in present-day Uttarakhand] for a much-needed rest. There is a reason why Ranikhet holds a special place in the memory. It was there, while resting in the Ranikhet guest house, that we selected an elephant as the election symbol for the SCF and later for the Republican Party.

What happened was as follows. The chief secretary of the Government of Bombay had called a meeting of the representatives of all political parties in the context of the first general elections that were due soon. As the secretary of the SCF, P.N. Rajbhoj would attend the meeting. He had sent a letter to Saheb asking him what he should say at the meeting regarding the election symbol of the party. In Saheb's opinion, the election symbol had to be easily noticeable and easy to remember because a vast majority of the electorate were ignorant and illiterate. It would have to be either a thing or an animal. Once we had decided on an animal, the next question was which animal it should be. As we were discussing the possibility of a tiger, lion, elephant, horse, camel, bullock, cow, etc., I said, 'Let's pick the elephant because it is easy to recall and it is completely different from the others. Also, the elephant occupies a special place in Buddhism.' The reason why I thought of the elephant was that I had seen a number of sculptures of the elephant in the Buddhist caves of Ajanta and Ellora. I also remembered the pictorial story of the bodhisattva elephant painted in an Ajanta cave. Saheb had an elephant in mind too. My suggestion of an elephant was the outcome of the lessons I had learnt from Saheb on Buddhism.

Nehru's Letter

Saheb had been keen to have the Hindu Code Bill discussed in the Parliament and passed. He wrote a passionate letter to Nehru on 10 August 1951, an important excerpt of which is given below:

> My dear Pandit Nehru,
>
> My health is causing anxiety to me and my doctors, and before I put myself into the hands of doctors, I am anxious that the Hindu

Code Bill should be disposed of. I therefore request you for a higher priority by taking it up in Parliament for consideration on August 16, so that it would be completed by September 1. The Prime Minister knows that I attach greater importance to that measure and will be prepared to undergo any strain on my health to get the Bill through.

Yours sincerely,
Bhimrao R. Ambedkar

Prime Minister Nehru responded to him on the very same day as follows:

Dear Dr Ambedkar,

You should take things easy and as there is opposition inside and outside to the Hindu Code Bill, the Cabinet has decided that it should be taken up at the beginning of September, 1951.

Yours sincerely,
Jawaharlal Nehru

[. . .]*

Hindu Code Bill Again

Doctor Saheb had written to Prime Minister Nehru and got him to prioritize the Hindu Code Bill and to present it to the House on 16 August. Nehru requested the Congress Parliamentary Committee to immediately approve the bill. But since this would be the last session of the Parliament, and more importantly, since a majority of the Congress people were against the bill, it was decided that it would not be taken up for consideration till the new Lok Sabha came into being. As a result, the Congress allowed its legislators to vote according to their conscience.

The bill was not taken up for consideration in the first week of September. Before any bill is tabled, it needs to be placed on the agenda and that is done through the office of the Speaker. But a lot of people were making strenuous efforts to ensure that the bill was not placed on the agenda. The Speaker, of course, has the authority to intervene and give precedence to an important bill, but the Congress bigwigs were taking every step with a firm eye on the impending elections. They were more interested in winning the elections and retaining power than in adopting the bill and bringing about equality in Hindu society.

The Congress Parliamentary Committee decided that the section on marriage and divorce would be taken up for consideration on 17 September, and if the sections related to property were comfortable to handle, they could be taken up too. Accordingly, Saheb agreed to Nehru's suggestion of considering marriage and divorce as an independent piece because he was determined to keep the Hindu Code Bill alive and kicking. But the Congress whips had deliberately not brought in constraints of time, nor had they exerted any pressure upon their members. As a result, the Congress members intentionally dragged their feet on everything and made pointless speeches so that they could eat up as much time as possible. The strategy of the Congress was to somehow exhaust the time of the session so the bill would then have to be taken up by the next Parliament.

In the earlier session, the members had wasted time in purposeless speeches and obstructionist strategies. In the later session too four days were wasted in a similar manner. Only four sections could be taken up for discussion till 22 September; the section on marriage and divorce too could not be discussed fully because of the paucity of time. It was in these unfortunate circumstances that the bill was finally abandoned. Doctor Saheb, who had made this bill his life's mission, had to suffer unbearable disappointment. N.V. Gadgil,

Pandit Kunzru and a few other members delivered speeches in support of the bill, but they didn't amount to anything.

The people who brought the maximum pressure against the passing of the Hindu Code Bill were mostly the Marwari and Gujarati capitalists. Had the bill been passed, then a wife and a married daughter would have received an equal share in the property.

All kinds of obstacles were thrown in the way. What connection could the Muslims have with the Hindu Code Bill? Yet there was a member of the House named Azizuddin Ahmad who was opposing the bill and wasting the House's time. When several members did raise the question as to what connection Ahmad could possibly have with the bill, the Speaker Ananthasayanam responded, 'Even if Mr Ahmad is a Muslim, he has the right to speak on every bill.'

Before I finish this unit on the Hindu Code Bill, I present here the opinion that Saheb expressed. This will also help form a clearer picture of the nature of the bill. He said in an interview [translated from Marathi]:

> 'Critics say that this Bill makes a mockery of the sacredness of the Hindu religion and is destructive of the joint Hindu family. But this accusation is an illusion. If seen from the perspective of the destruction of the joint family, even under the present laws, members of a joint family can even now demand separation. The Hindu Code Bill does not bring anything new into the dispensation.'

Reply to the Debate on the Hindu Code Bill

Replying to the discussion on the Hindu Code Bill, Doctor Saheb said:[35]

'If you want to maintain the Hindu system, Hindu culture, the Hindu society, do not hesitate to repair where repair is necessary. This Bill asks for nothing more than repairing those parts of the Hindu system which are [sic] almost become dilapidated.

'In the matter of marriage, effort has been made to satisfy people belonging to the old school of thought as well as the new school of thought. Orthodox people have been permitted to arrange for marriages as per their religion between brides and grooms from the same varna. The reformists have been given the freedom of looking into their own conscience and marrying outside their community if they so feel.

'The practice of divorce is prevalent even now among 90% of the Hindus. The custom of divorce among the 'shudra' who constitute 90% of the Hindu community is definitely prevalent. It's only among 10% of the Hindus that the custom of divorce does not exist. My question to you, therefore, is: will you impose the custom of 10% of the people upon 90% of the people?[36]

'You will find that the shastras have always allowed divorce. Some absurd practices have now broken the rules made by the shastras for making married relationships happy, trampled them underfoot and overridden them.[37]

'Looking at the experience of other people in the world among whom divorce is practiced, it is clear that the right to divorce is a healthy one.

'It is not binding either upon the government or the House to seek the opinion of the people on every bill or to publicise it.[38]

'The second thing is that a deliberate provision has been made for the implementation of this bill to be limited to the provinces. Speaking only for the provinces, the bill was presented thrice for testing the opinion of the people. I don't think anything can be gained by presenting the bill for the fourth time. Whenever the time comes for implementing this bill in the princely states, I can assure you that the opinion of the people of the princely states will be considered.[39]

'The Select Committee has added two new sections to the main bill that deal with marital rights and divorce.'

Aspects of the Hindu Code Bill

a. Divorce and women's rights

The smritis have given women the right to divorce under certain circumstances. The new bill had made some provisions for the return of these rights to women; while doing so, divorce had not been made a whit easier. The constraints related to it had been kept very strict. Divorce would be given only under the most unavoidable circumstances.

The bill was doing nothing new in the matter of giving inheritance rights to women. Even in the old Hindu laws, a woman related to the deceased, even if she is not a daughter, has been given inheritance rights. However, the woman's inheritance right comes into effect only as a last resort. The Yagnavalkya Smriti gives daughters the right to inherit 25 per cent of the property of the father/mother. It was the Privy Council, by ruling that custom would override law, that had taken away the daughter's inheritance right. The Hindu Code Bill only provided that the right given by the Yagnavalkya Smriti be restored to her.

b. Monogamy

The Hindu Code Bill had proposed the imposition of monogamy upon Hindu men. But this was based upon ancient traditions too. As of then, marriage between people belonging to the same lineage or *sapinda* [consanguinity of a certain order] was not allowed. That restriction had been loosened a little bit; but critics who said that this bill allowed close blood relatives to marry—the offspring of two brothers, for example—were wrong. The bill did not allow this freedom.

c. The law of adoption

The Select Committee said that when the father became incompetent because of converting to another religion, the right to give a child up for adoption should lie only with the mother.[40] Along the same lines, the bill provided that if a Hindu widow converted to another religion, her right to offer her child for adoption should be taken away from her.[41]

Since there were so many varieties of procedures for adoption, a few changes had been suggested there. The Select Committee had provided that no other procedure would be permitted except the one mentioned in the code.[42]

The Select Committee had recommended two changes in this regard. The right that the father had of being the natural guardian would be taken away from him in the event of the father taking *sanyas* [abandoning the world] or converting to another religion. Since the fundamental purpose of this bill was to unify the Hindus, this condition was thought necessary.[43]

d. Daughter's rights

The Select Committee had made important changes in the rights of the daughter. The original bill had recommended that the daughter should inherit half of what the son inherited. But in the interest of equity and for keeping women as successors, the bill now provided that the daughter's share should be equal to that of the son's share.[44]

e. Joint family system

Some persons had wondered whether the joint family system that existed under the Mitakshara laws would be destroyed by this code.

The code provided that independent shares would exist in the names of this member of the household or that. It was not a very revolutionary move. Everybody had wanted to live independently by then. Therefore, even if joint authority had been taken away from the joint household, the institution of the joint family would have remained. This meant that the Mitakshara law would then be substituted by the Dayabhaga laws.

f. Women's inheritance

The matter of women's inheritance of estate was complex. There are two different sets of inheritance: (1) stridhan property; and (2) widow's property. The estate that a woman gets out of her inheritance right from her husband is her widow's estate. The decision of the Select Committee on this matter was that since a woman was considered competent and intelligent enough to sell and dispose of her stridhan property, she must be held competent with respect to the disposal of her widow's property also. This was why the Committee had made the rule that a woman should possess absolute ownership right over her property.

However brief it may be, I have tried to give you complete information on the Hindu Code Bill. The reason is that some people even now carry misunderstandings in their minds, while there are some who have no idea what the controversial bill contained. I have tried to present here all the elements and information with supportive evidence so that the misunderstandings are cleared and the facts are placed before the public. Obviously, I have been a witness to this entire history.

Selfless Dr Ambedkar

Despite being the leader of the SCF, Saheb had joined Nehru's Council of Ministers as the law minister mainly out of a sense of duty in participating in the reconstruction of an independent India. Another sterling purpose was to make an effort to secure constitutional protection and provide for the rights of the millions of his untouchable brothers in the future Constitution of the country. Thus, although he was a member of the Council of Ministers, if the situation demanded, he never hesitated to offer constructive criticism to the Congress. He had no desire for power and, as a consequence, he never felt helpless. I cannot resist the temptation of presenting two examples in this regard.

The first example relates to the lecture he delivered in Lucknow in 1948. While counselling the workers of the Uttar Pradesh SCF in a well-attended meeting at Lucknow, he said:

> 'I have joined the Central Government, not the Congress Party. The Congress Party is a house on fire. It is smouldering. If the Party gets destroyed in a year or two, I shall not be surprised.
>
> 'Political power is the key to the progress of a community. Therefore the Dalit community should come together and capture political power by establishing a third front.'

Quite naturally, when the Congress leaders read this speech in the newspapers, they were upset. Pandit Nehru too wrote to Saheb expressing his personal regret and raising questions about the violation of the principle of joint ministerial responsibility by criticizing the Congress Party. Nehru was so peeved by the speech that he expressed his displeasure to Sardar Patel too. Doctor Saheb responded by writing a detailed letter to Nehru under copy to Sardar Patel.

Doctor Saheb published a leaflet explaining the substance of the speech and wrote to Nehru, saying:

> 'I agree that such a speech, as reported, may create in the public mind such impression as you have referred to in your letter.

> But I hope that the statement I have issued will remove such implications. If, however, you still feel embarrassed by my speech and that, vis-à-vis the Congress Party, your position has become indefensible, I feel the proper remedy for relieving you of your embarrassment is for me to offer you my resignation of my office as Law Minister of the Government of India. You perhaps know that to me, politics has never been a game, it is a mission. I have spent all my life and sacrificed all my personal prospects to help the Scheduled Castes in their betterment. I am grateful to you for your invitation to join your Cabinet and I am conscious that the acceptance of the invitation carries with it certain limitations. But whatever limitations have to be accepted, I can never surrender my right to advise my people [on] what is the best course for them to follow.'

The second example is of the unjust arrests that the central province government had made of some workers of the SCF. In that regard, Saheb wrote to Revaram Kawade of Nagpur:

> 'I heard of the arrest of our workers by the C.P. Government. I am most annoyed at their action. We must not tolerate this. The Federation is neither dead nor bound to the Congress. My joining the Congress Government does not mean that I have joined the Congress. You must not, therefore, hesitate to protest against the action of the C.P. Government.'

Thus, his resignation from the post of law minister was completely in character.

Resignation from the Post of Law Minister

Doctor Saheb had stayed on in the Council of Ministers only in the tenacious hope that he would be able to carry the Hindu Code Bill

Sharada Kabir (later Savita Ambedkar).

Dr Sharada Kabir with her MBBS degree.

Dr Ambedkar with Ramabai, his first wife, at Rajgraha, his residence in Mumbai. From left to right: Yeshwant (son), Dr Ambedkar, Ramabai (wife), Laxmibai (wife of his elder brother, Anand), Mukundrao (nephew) and Tobby (their dog).

Dr Ambedkar and Savita Ambedkar photographed on the day of their wedding, 15 April 1948.

At the house of C. Rajagopalachari, the last governor-general of India, 28 July 1948.

Holidaying in Mussoorie, during the last week of June 1949.

Handing over the draft of the Constitution of India to the chairman of the Constituent Assembly, Dr Rajendra Prasad, at the Central Hall of Parliament, 25 November 1949.

In Haridwar for a holiday, June 1949. Brahmachari (Prabhu Datt) is also in the picture.

Holidaying in Srinagar, Kashmir, 2 October 1949.

At Colombo Airport, 25 May 1950. The couple had gone to attend the Buddhist Conference held in Kandy, Ceylon.

At a felicitation programme in Mumbai on 18 November 1951, Dr Ambedkar invited eighty-five-year-old Rao Bahadur Bole, a senior colleague, to sit on his lap since there were only two chairs.

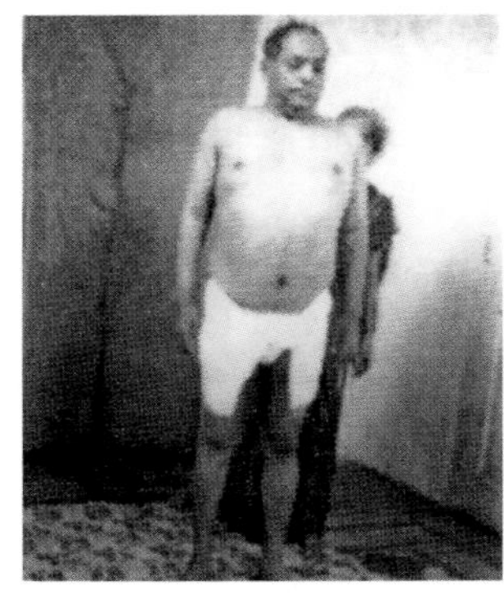

Dr Ambedkar doing yoga in his 26 Alipore Road bungalow, 23 September 1954. Savita can be seen behind him.

With the office bearers and workers of the Scheduled Castes Federation, 16 December 1954. Balu Kabir, Savita's brother, and K.V. Savaadkar are also in the picture.

Historic picture of Dr Ambedkar and Savita Ambedkar taking the deeksha of Buddhism on 14 October 1956, at the Deeksha Bhoomi, Nagpur, at the hands of Bhante Mahasthavir Chandramani.

Babasaheb Ambedkar and Savita Ambedkar in the company of his followers. Standing behind them: Barrister Khobragade, Bhaurao Gaikwad, Nanak Chand Rattu, B.H. Varale and others, 17 October 1956, Chandrapur.

This is regarded as the last picture of Dr Ambedkar. He was returning from the World Buddhist Conference in Kathmandu, Nepal. Picture taken at Sarnath Airport on 26 November 1956. Left to right: Bhante M. Sangharatna Nayak Ther, Bhante Dr Sudhatissa, Dr Ambedkar, Mai Ambedkar and Bhante Dharmarakshit.

Dr Ambedkar delivering the historic address 'The Buddha and Karl Marx' during the World Buddhist Conference in Kathmandu, Nepal, 20 November 1956. Seen here: Dr Ambedkar (at the mic), Maisaheb Ambedkar (behind him) and Mai's brother, Balu, to her left. Sitting: Bhante Chandramani and the King of Nepal, Mahamahendra Vikramdev.

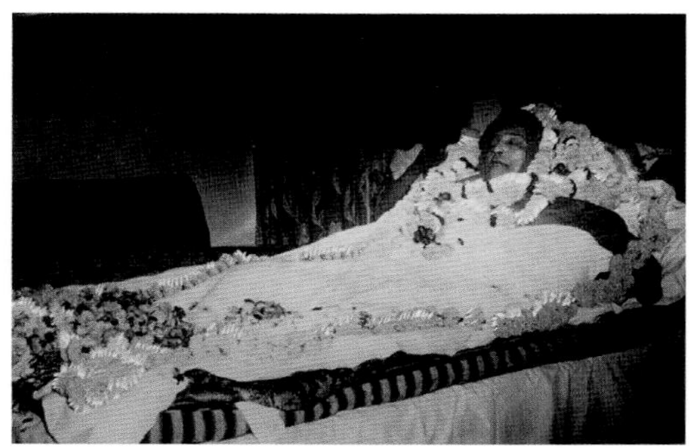

Babasaheb's body laid out at 26 Alipore Road, New Delhi, 6 December 1956.

Yeshwant and Mai meeting after a long gap at the house of Mai's brother-in-law, Bhuleskar, in Shivaji Park, through the efforts of Bawiskar (1970–71).

Protest against the effort to delete 'Riddles in Hinduism' from Volume 4 of *Babasaheb Ambedkar's Writings and Speeches*, due to be published by the then Government of Maharashtra. The picture is of 5 February 1988. Seen in the picture: Maisaheb Ambedkar, Prakash Ambedkar (to her left), mdeo Dhasal, R.S. Gavai, Ramdas thavale, Avinash Mahatekar, Arjun Dangale and others.

With Prime Minister Rajiv Gandhi in New Delhi in 1989.

With Vijay Surwade at his house.

Receiving the Bharat Ratna on behalf of her husband from President R. Venkataraman on 14 April 1990.

Honorary doctorate conferred upon Savita Ambedkar by the Dr Babasaheb Ambedkar Open University, Hyderabad, 26 August 1994. The chancellor of the university and the governor of Andhra Pradesh, M. Krishnakant, presented the degree.

The two persons who helped her write her autobiography: Vijay Surwade and Devchand Ambade, 23 August 1994.

Free meals are served every year at Chaitya Bhoomi, Dadar, Mumbai, on 6 December. This picture is of Suryavanshi Hall, 6 December 1994. Left to right: Vijay Surwade, Devchand Ambade, Hari Narke, Maisaheb and Vasant Moon.

Unveiling of Dr Ambedkar's bust at Columbia University, USA, 24 October 1995. Mai was the chief guest for the function.

Garlanding the statue of Dr Ambedkar at Chaitya Bhoomi, Dadar, on 6 December 1998. She performed this every year without fail.

To
Dr. S. Kabir
with the best wishes of the Author for a happy new year.
B.R. Ambedkar
2/1/48

Note from Dr Ambedkar to his fiancée.

Letter from Dr Ambedkar to his fiancée, Sharada Kabir, written on 21 February 1948.

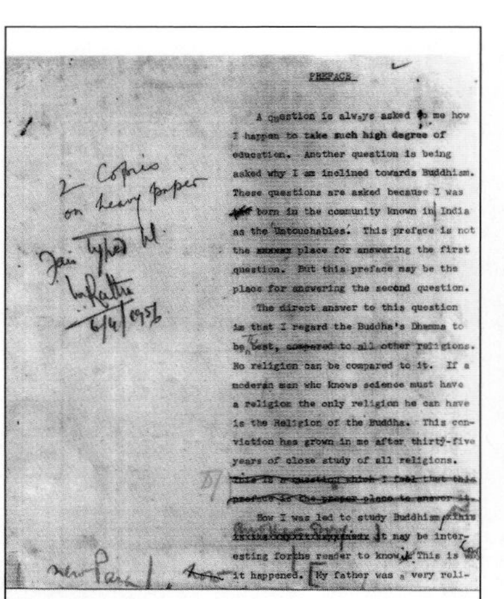

PREFACE

A question is always asked to me how I happen to take such high degree of education. Another question is being asked why I am inclined towards Buddhism. These questions are asked because I was born in the community known in India as the 'Untouchables'. This preface is not the place for answering the first question. But this preface may be the place for answering the second question.

The direct answer to this question is that I regard the Buddha's Dhamma to be best, compared to all other religions. No religion can be compared to it. If a modern man who knows science must have a religion the only religion he can have is the Religion of the Buddha. This conviction has grown in me after thirty-five years of close study of all religions.

~~This is a question which I feel that this preface is the proper place to answer it.~~

How I was led to study Buddhism it may be interesting for the reader to know. This is how it happened. My father was a very reli-

2 Copies on heavy paper

Fair typed by Rattu 6/4/1956

new Para

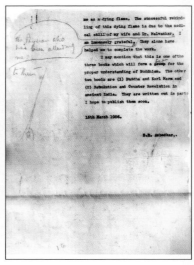

First page of the typed manuscript of the preface written for *The Buddha and His Dhamma*. Typed by Rattu and corrections made in Dr Ambedkar's hand on 6 April 1956.

me as a dying flame. The successful rekindling of this dying flame is due to the medical skill of my wife and Dr. Malvankar. I am immensely grateful to them. They alone have helped me to complete the work.

I may mention that this is one of the three books which will form a set for the proper understanding of Buddhism. The other two books are (1) Buddha and Karl Marx and (2) Revolution and Counter Revolution in ancient India. They are written out in parts. I hope to publish them soon.

15th March 1956.

B.R. Ambedkar.

the Physician who has been attending me

Last page of the same document, with corrections done on 6 April 1956.

through before the last session of the Lok Sabha ended. During our discussions, he would always say, 'I have to unseat Manu along with his prejudicial laws. The Hindu Code Bill is a live, vibrant goal for me, and I believe that establishing equality is as important to me as the Constitution was.' Therefore, when the bill was set aside, he had no interest in staying on in the Council of Ministers, and he submitted his resignation on 27 September 1951.

The five reasons that Saheb gave for his resignation are given below:

1. When handing him the responsibility of law minister, the prime minister had given Dr Ambedkar the assurance that the Planning Department would also be given to him. Not only was the Planning Department not given, but he was not appointed to any committee of the Council of Ministers either.
2. The government was indifferent to the question of the untouchables and issues related to the untouchables were always given secondary status.
3. Prime Minister Nehru's policy on Kashmir was wrong. (Saheb's opinion was that the enormous expenditure on the army that the government was incurring on keeping Kashmir in India would be better invested in the development of the country. Kashmir should be divided, with the Hindu and Buddhist majority areas coming to India and the Muslim majority areas going to Pakistan. Making this division would not only save the enormous expenditure being incurred on the army, but it would avert future conflicts on the matter of Kashmir and friendship would result.)
4. Because of Prime Minister Nehru's faulty foreign policy, India would end up with more enemy nations than friendly nations.
5. The fifth point of dissension was the Hindu Code Bill. Pandit Nehru had made loud declarations regarding getting the Hindu Code Bill passed, but he hadn't lived up to his word. He just

didn't show the enthusiasm and the determination he should have to get the bill passed.

Around that time, a convenient rumour had begun circulating in the Congress circles that Dr Ambedkar had submitted his resignation on the grounds of ill health. Reacting to this accusation, he declared, 'I am the last man to abandon my duty because of illness.'[45]

Focus of Attention on the Scheduled Castes Federation

In 1952, the winds had begun to blow for the first-ever general elections. The main parties that were in existence then were the Congress, the Communists, the Socialists, the Hindu Mahasabha, the Jana Sangh, the Bahujan Samajwadi[,] Shetkari Kamgar Paksh, our own Scheduled Castes Federation and a few others. The search had begun for party alliances from the perspective of the imminent elections. We had decided to focus our attention on our party organization for the purpose. S.K. Patil, the president of the Bombay Pradesh Congress Committee, had written to Saheb to discuss the prospects of a political alliance. But that was when Saheb was the law minister, which was why the Mumbai Congress supremo Sadoba Patil and others had thought they could form an alliance with the SCF. But after Saheb submitted his resignation, no further progress was made. The Hindu Mahasabha and the Jana Sangh being communal, there was no possibility of giving them a thought. There was no question of cooperating with the Communists either. Finally, Saheb decided to form an alliance with the Socialist Party for the limited purpose of the elections. Similarly, support had been announced for Keshavrao Jedhe and others of the Shetkari Kamgar Paksh.

Saheb himself prepared the manifesto of the Scheduled Castes Federation after consultation and contemplating on it day and night. Copies of the manifesto had been printed in Delhi. From the perspective of our movement, this manifesto has extraordinary importance.

Our Election Tour of the Punjab

The office-bearers of the Punjab SCF had been insisting that Doctor Saheb should tour the Punjab province and offer counsel to our people in view of the coming general elections. The fact was that Saheb's health was not good at all. I tried to explain to the office-bearers that Saheb's condition had been deteriorating by the day and the long tour and addressing crowds would cause extreme strain on his constitution. But the workers remained importunate. They said that the news of his tour had sent a wave of enthusiasm in the Punjab and his refusal would deeply disappoint the people. Saheb finally had to give his assent, and he told them to prepare a schedule for the tour.

As per the scheduled programme, we did a hurricane tour of Jalandhar and Ramdaspur on 27 October 1951, Ludhiana on the 28th and Patiala on the 29th. We were welcomed with great fervour everywhere. The meetings were attended by hundreds of thousands of people who would bring the sky down with their vociferous cheers.

Saheb told them about the goals and policies of the SCF and explained to them how bringing about the victory of the party candidates by huge margins was closely related to the welfare of the entire Dalit community. He exhorted them to put their seal upon the SCF symbol and elect the Federation candidate. I too offered them counsel at a few places. After finishing with the Punjab tour, we returned to Delhi.

Discussions with the Socialists

After we had returned from our Punjab tour, the president of the Bombay State Socialist Party, Harris,[46] came to visit us at our bungalow on 31 October 1951 in the company of his colleagues

S.M. Joshi and M.V. Donde to discuss the issue of an electoral alliance. I was present at the sitting too.

After a long discussion a few days later with socialist leader Jayaprakash Narayan, Saheb agreed to have an electoral alliance for the coming elections. The discussion with Jayaprakash Narayan lasted for a good hour and a half to two hours.

Grand Felicitation in Mumbai

It was for the first time since Saheb had resigned from his post as law minister that we were going to Mumbai. We alighted at the Bori Bunder railway station on Sunday, 18 November 1951. Saheb's eyes had recently been operated upon. Arches had been erected at the Bori Bunder station to welcome us. The Scheduled Castes Federation and the Socialist Party had organized a joint function to welcome us. We had travelled to Mumbai by the Punjab Mail. As soon as the train entered Bori Bunder station, the mammoth gathering broke out into slogans of 'Dr Ambedkar zindabad' [long live Dr Ambedkar] and 'Dr Ambedkar ki jai' [victory to Dr Ambedkar]. The first person to come up to our coach was the socialist leader Ashok Mehta. He shook hands with Saheb and requested us to disembark. Among the others present were Rao Bahadur S.K. Bole, Mukundrao Ambedkar, the principal of Siddharth College Karnik, Principal Patankar, my brother Balu Kabir, leaders of the SCF and the Samajwadi Party, and thousands of followers. A small welcome programme had been organized in the space between platforms 8 and 9 where we were offered garlands of flowers on behalf of several taluka branches and organizations.

Since it was a very small and formal function, chairs had been placed for just the two of us. Rao Bahadur S.K. Bole had been a senior colleague of Saheb from the very beginning; since arrangements for only two chairs had been made at the place of the meeting, Saheb called Rao Bahadur Bole to him and got his eighty-five-year-old senior colleague to sit on his lap. This event provoked a burst of laughter from Saheb, Bole himself and me. The rest of the crowd broke out laughing too. The photojournalists caught this rare moment perfectly with their cameras. Every one of the newspapers published this picture the next day along with details of this funny incident. (I have included this picture in this book.)

Felicitation by the Bombay Province SCF

The Bombay Province SCF had organized a huge programme to welcome us on the evening of 22 November 1951, at the Bhoiwada ground in Parel, Mumbai, under the chairmanship of R.G. Kharat.

The meeting began with J.G. Bhatankar offering garlands to Saheb and myself. Saheb was also presented with a purse. Saheb came down strongly on the goals and policies of the Congress. Saheb said that since the Dalits were merely 8 per cent, they would not be able to fight the elections without help from others. That was the reason for the electoral alliance with the Socialist Party. But the SCF would continue its work independently of removing the injustice and persecution perpetuated upon the Dalits.

Applauding the Samata Sainik Dal[47] [Soldiers for Equality], he expressed the hope that their help would be of great value in the forthcoming elections. Finally, he made a fervent appeal to his followers that they should vote for the candidates of the Federation and the Samajwadi Party.

After reaching Mumbai, we started our canvassing meetings. The first meeting took place at Chaupati and the second was organized jointly by the SCF and the Socialist Party. Shankarrao Morey of the Brahmanetar [non-Brahmin] party was present for this meeting. Then happened a humongous meeting at Nare Park. In the meeting held at Shivaji Park, Dadar, on 25 November 1951, Saheb publicly exhorted Prime Minister Nehru to join hands with the Socialist Party and with people like him. The meeting at Shivaji Park, which was attended by well over 3,00,000 people, had been jointly organized by the SCF and the Socialist Party.

The First General Elections of 1952

The first general election to the Lok Sabha and the assemblies took place in January 1952. Doctor Saheb stood from the reserved Lok Sabha constituency of North Bombay. The Congress had marked it as a prestigious seat and made preparations accordingly. Prime Minister Nehru himself was keeping a sharp eye on the constituency. S.K. Patil and Dange of the Communist Party had arrived at an agreement. What we had heard then was that Nehru, S.K. Patil and Dange had decided that they would do all that was required, use whatever strategy suited the occasion, but they were determined not to let Dr Ambedkar win. Patil and Dange had organized their forces with this goal in mind. Since it was a reserved seat, they were required to field a Dalit candidate and the non-Mahar community, particularly the chamars, hoped that the Congress would support them. Therefore, it was impossible for the Congress to find a suitable candidate except from among the chamars. The Congress found a person named Narayanrao Kajrolkar of the chamar community to put up against Dr Ambedkar.

When the dust and smoke of the electoral battle kicked up, we were living in Delhi, and it was not possible for Saheb to ensconce himself in Mumbai. He was also required to speak at election meetings across the country. His health had been slipping anyway, and these election meetings and the associated tours were only worsening matters for him.

The Defeat of the Constitution-Maker

The Congress placed its reputation at stake for these elections. S.K. Patil and Dange played all the tricks they had in their bag.

What therefore happened was inevitable—the Constitution-making Doctor Saheb was defeated. It was a terrible psychological blow for Saheb. An inconsequential person like Kajrolkar, who did not even possess ordinary strength or ability, managed to defeat no less a person than the creator of India's Constitution. While Saheb polled 1,23,576 votes, Kajrolkar got 1,37,950 votes and this was how the Congress finally won the contest.

It was proved that there was no place in the Congress for colossal scholarship, calibre or abilities. We were all very sure and Saheb was convinced too that not only would he win the elections, but he would also be a part of the future Council of Ministers; Nehru would be compelled to exploit Saheb's intellectual ability and experience for the sake of the country's bright future. But it was the Congress's manipulation that brought about the defeat of the maker of the Indian Constitution. A saraswat communist like Dange also participated in it. The poverty and ignorance of the Dalits too played its part here. When the election results were announced, we were in Delhi. This horrendous defeat in the elections had an extremely harmful impact on his already debilitated health. My big question was: what to do next? I had lavished such care upon him, guarded him like a fragile treasure, revived in him the desire to live and strive; and now this defeat had undone it all. Melancholy, disappointment, depression and disability returned. He began despairing of life. I would read out to him excerpts from the Tripitaka [the sacred Buddhist scriptures]. For putting him to sleep, I would recite to him the *sutta* [the teachings of Lord Buddha].

The Duplicity of Kajrolkar

The Congress had first asked Buvaji Songaonkar to stand against Saheb, but he had humbly turned down the offer of standing against Dr Ambedkar. That was when Kajrolkar had been told to stand for that seat.

In his interviews, meetings and speeches, Kajrolkar would always declare, 'I consider Dr Ambedkar as my god.' What I have to say is that if he really considered Ambedkar as his god, instead of standing against his god, he could have turned down the offer like Songaonkar did. But Kajrolkar was a denizen of the Congress world. How could he have left the company of power and selfishness by turning the offer down? He pushed his god aside and gave preference to the Party's diktat. The question that arises is this: is the god bigger or is the Party's order bigger? Is there any reconciliation between what this man says and what he does?

In trying to establish that he had a great deed to his credit, Kajrolkar says that he was instrumental in getting Dr Ambedkar elected to the Constituent Assembly. One look at the related documents will reveal that this statement is an outright lie and made only for the sake of gathering credit. An examination of the high-level correspondence and a look at other references will show where the truth lies. The excerpts from biographer C.B. Khairmode's *Biography of Dr B.R. Ambedkar*, Volume 8, pages 198–200; *Sardar Patel's Correspondence*, edited by Durga Das, Volume 5; the letter written on 30 June 1947 by Dr Rajendra Prasad, the president of the Constituent Assembly, to the then chief minister of Bombay State, Balasaheb Kher:

> ('Apart from any other consideration, we have found Dr Ambedkar's work both in the Constituent Assembly and in the various Committees to which he was appointed of such an order as to require that we should not be deprived of his services. As you know, he was elected from Bengal and after the division of the province he has ceased to be a member of the Constituent Assembly. I am anxious that he should attend the next session of the Constituent Assembly from the 14th July and it is, therefore, necessary that he should be elected immediately.');

Sardar Patel's letter written to Mavalankar:

> ('Dr Ambedkar's election requires early action and as there is only one vacancy at present, we have asked him to send his Form today. He has not been elected from Bengal and all the people here felt that his attitude has changed and he has been a useful member in the Committee');

another letter that Patel wrote to Mavalankar on 3 July 1947; the letter that Vallabhbhai wrote to S.K. Patil on 3 July 1947:

> ('Dr Ambedkar's nomination has been sent to P.M. I hope there would be no contest and he would be returned unopposed so that he could come here on 14th');

the letter that Patel wrote on 3 May 1948 to C.P. Ramaswami:

> ('Ambedkar, I assure you, we shall try to keep with us as long as possible. He may say things in order to defend his position. But I fully realize that he is and can be useful to the country');

if all these documents and other related correspondence are read, it can be clearly seen that Dr Rajendra Prasad, Sardar Patel and Nehru had already decided on Dr Ambedkar's name for the Constituent Assembly. The references to the documents given above in this regard show no trace of Kajrolkar, not so much as a mention of his name. There is just one single truth in this entire matter: when at the request of the Congress bigwigs, Saheb had filled the nomination form, Kajrolkar had signed as a proposer. An interesting fact that needs to be kept in mind is that he started spreading this canard only after Dr Ambedkar had passed away.

When Kajrolkar's candidature to stand against Dr Ambedkar had been announced, a newspaper had published an extremely telling, highly suggestive, perfectly apt and factual cartoon. It showed Dr Ambedkar standing huge and tall, while near his foot, barely reaching up to the heel of his shoe, stood Kajrolkar. The cartoonist of the time has drawn a perfect caricature of Kajrolkar, hence I don't see any need of writing any further on this subject.

When the election results were announced, we were in Delhi. We had gone to Mumbai in the first week of February. It was perhaps for a meeting of the People's Education Society that we had gone to Mumbai, as far as I can vaguely remember. We were there for three or four days. One day, Narayanrao Kajrolkar came to Siddharth College to meet Saheb. He could have been carrying a sense of guilt because he looked quite abashed when he came in front of Saheb. But as soon as Saheb saw Kajrolkar, he called out to him with great warmth and invited him over. Kajrolkar stepped forward, and he placed his head on Saheb's feet. Saheb lifted him up with both hands, got him to sit by his side, graciously congratulated him on his being elected and made courteous inquiries about him. He went even beyond this and invited him to keep meeting us in Delhi too. Any time he needed advice or any other kind of help, the doors of Saheb's bungalow were forever open for his own people. After that, Kajrolkar would always come to visit us in Delhi and Saheb would always give him all kinds of assistance and guidance. Not for a second did Saheb harbour any feeling of hatred or malice. He never looked at Kajrolkar as a competitor.

The Axe Handles among the Untouchables

It has to be said with great regret that in Dr Ambedkar's movement, the Harijan, mahar and other factions remained divided.

The mahars, the Harijans among the mahars, the chamars, the mangs and many other people joined Saheb's movement, but they could not anchor themselves in the movement, the reason being that they found self-service dearer and far more valuable than service of the community. They fell prey to the trivial lures that the party in power dangled before them and consequently got thrown out of the Dalit movement of social upliftment and were annihilated.

History has altogether forgotten the names of those who did not stay true to the revolutionary crusade of Doctor Saheb. The British used the policy of 'smash and thrash' to create rifts among the Indian people so as to rule over them; sadly, there were too many factions among Indians as well, which adversely affected Dr Ambedkar's movement.

The historical fact, however, is that the communities that flung themselves into the movement body and soul and resources were the majority community of the mahars in Maharashtra; the untouchables of Gujarat, Uttar Pradesh, Bihar, Punjab, Bengal and the southern states of Tamil Nadu, Karnataka and Andhra; and from among the caste Hindus, the C.K.P. [*kayastha*], the saraswat and some other Brahmin groups. There is no doubt that if all the untouchables had come together in a big way, the scene across the country would have been entirely different. Personal interest and selfishness had no place in the Doctor's movement; therefore, those who had drifted close with exactly that purpose in mind would have found it impossible to stay on.

26 Alipore Road, Delhi

When Saheb was inducted into Lord Wavell's Executive Council as labour minister in 1942, he lived in a government bungalow at 22 Prithviraj Road. Later, when he was the law minister in Nehru's Council of Ministers, he was given the government bungalow at 1, Hardinge Avenue. This was the bungalow where my marriage with Saheb was solemnized. Later, in September 1951, Saheb submitted his resignation from the post of law minister, because of which we finally left the government bungalow at 1, Hardinge Avenue by November end. Although Saheb had submitted his resignation in

September, as a mark of courtesy he had agreed to continue working in the ministry till he had finished the work of issuing notices on the bills that he had been working on, and so on. I think he stayed on in the Council of Ministers till the Dussehra holidays. It was only right that he should leave the government bungalow at 1 Hardinge Avenue after he had resigned as minister.

After that, we went to live at 26 Alipore Road in Civil Lines. It was a general conception among people that the bungalow belonged to Doctor Saheb, but the fact is that there was not a single bungalow in Delhi that belonged to him. Even in 26 Alipore Road we lived on rent. It belonged to the Maharaja of Sirohi. A brief history of how it was vacated after Saheb's passing away will be given in the appropriate place. We stayed in the bungalow from the time of Saheb's resignation till the day of his death.

My Desperate Efforts

The unexpected defeat in the elections had broken Saheb very badly. Doing something for the upliftment and development of his destitute people, particularly his brethren in the villages, was a passion with him, and for that it was necessary for him to be in the Parliament. All of this was severely hitting his health. On top of all that was the question: what should he be doing now? It was imperative to get him out of his mental shock. After a lot of thought, I wrote a desperate letter to Chitre, of which the important excerpt is given below:

> 'Doctor Saheb's partymen should do for [the] doctor what Congressmen were doing for Morarji Desai . . . Politics is the doctor's very existence, the best tonic for his mental and physical health and that Parliamentary work he enjoyed [the] most . . . I daresay he will start running about if (and a very big if though) he was to be the Prime Minister of India. That is the desire of his and let us pray someday it will be fulfilled. Though he has borne

well the present defeat, political events in the past have affected his health curve. He had planned so many things to be done when he returned to [the] Parliament, which was the one place for a man of the Doctor's height and stature. It is here that your role as a trusted lieutenant comes in. I am confident that you will move in the matter and there would be no disappointment.'

As I wrote to Chitre, so I wrote to my brother Balu, describing to him Saheb's mental state. Here is the letter:

'You say that [people] all over are stunned at the result of the election. Well, who is to be blamed? In spite of showing so much discontent, if the people have yielded to money consideration, nobody can help such demoralized [sic] people and their country. We have been told some 20 lac [sic] rupees have been spent by our enemies to defeat Dr Saheb. This is very likely true. In addition to this, there is always the communal bias against Dr Saheb. There is no value for [a] genius like him. Under these circumstances, why this farce of election? The long and short of all this, we are not yet prepared for democracy. That is not in our blood. Our P.M. (J. N.) never wanted anybody of the height and stature of Dr Saheb. So with the help of Patil he has succeeded. Politics and Parliament have been the very life of Dr Saheb. I only hope he doesn't take this to heart so as [to] spoil his health. No doubt, he is bearing it well; however, it is impossible for a person who has done so much in the Parliament for the country to swallow this incident. He is bound to remember of [sic] the old times and feel unhappy. Just see the ungratefulness of the Bombay people, to be lead [sic] away by the malicious propaganda of *[a certain person]. He is responsible for the greater part of the mischief.[48] I am sorry to say that Bombay has proved a city of caste-minded people and goondas. Bombay's results are all maneuvered by purchase and transport of ballot-papers from one polling booth to another. Now the only other

> possibility is to try further. If one can get actual evidence in the casting of votes, an election petition could be filed.
>
> '2. If persons like Gaikwad and his colleagues create an occasion by making some of their elected member to resign and thus enforce re-election, [sic] this is [a] real trial of their affection and respect of [sic] their Revered leader. Let us see how far they rise. Congress is doing that for Morarji, why shouldn't we do that? I want you to speak to people like Kharat and Bhatankar, so that they may convey to the proper source. Of course, Dr Saheb would never suggest this himself. It is they who must do such thing[s]. Isn't the Congress doing this? What is the use of [a] hundred people like Rajbhoj coming in [to the Parliament] unless one of them willingly vacates his seat for their able leader. You set this ball rolling and let us see. Go and tell Dr Malvankar that I want him to speak this to Chitre and find his reaction to this.
>
> '3. Elections to this Upper House, after seeing this disappointing result for [the] Parliament, Dr Saheb is not bold for this either. But we have to think of this also. So this is the position.
>
> 'Delhi is terribly cold. We are both O.K.'

So, this was how I was doing all that I could from my end and trying to hold Saheb together. My efforts brought him some fortitude. He was a fighter; so, although he was himself quite broken, he would admonish his colleagues that elections, after all, were a gamble and therefore there should be no despondency. As before, we should work for our party with greater energy and enthusiasm. He wrote to R.D. Bhandare on 14 January 1952:

> 'I am sorry for your defeat as you are for mine. But elections are gambles. Nobody can be sure of the result. All that one can do is to do his best. I think in your case, as in mine, the best was done. The results have not been bad, we were near success. We must

> not loose [sic] courage and keep alive the spirit of our people; that alone will lead to success.'

On 18 January 1952, Saheb wrote to D.G. Jadhav:

> 'You know the result of my election. We must learn to bear it with courage. What else can we do?'

Dr Ambedkar in the Rajya Sabha

The Bombay State of those times sent seventeen seats to the Rajya Sabha. In conformity with my letter to them, Chitre, Jadhav and Bhaurao Gaikwad began efforts to arrange that Saheb should get elected unopposed to the Rajya Sabha. I too began pressing him to agree to stand for the Rajya Sabha. Once he had given his acceptance, his application was filed in the middle of March. Fortunately, he was elected to the Rajya Sabha from Bombay State. Members of the opposition also gave their votes to Saheb. Saheb had sent requests to some opposition members and even met them personally to request their votes.

The Congress Gathers Credit

After Saheb had resigned as law minister, Haribhau Pataskar was appointed to that post. He held Saheb in deep respect. The responsibility of breaking the Hindu Code Bill into sections and getting them passed had fallen upon him. Accordingly, he would visit our 26 Alipore Road house every evening to seek Saheb's guidance. Saheb would advise him on what questions to anticipate and what answers he should provide to those potential questions.

The orthodox Hindus did not oppose the passing of the broken-down sections because they were delighted that their personal code was being shepherded not by an untouchable, but by a sanctity-wielding Brahmin. The surprising thing here is that President Dr Rajendra Prasad, who had taken such a contrary position, signed without a murmur. This gives us a picture of how sharp the caste system and caste discrimination are in this country. This was how the Congress gathered all the credit for the Hindu Code Bill.

Development Plan for Marathwada

Marathwada is an extremely backward region and the state of the untouchables there had best not be asked. Saheb believed that if the region were developed, the untouchables would develop too. Towards this goal, he had prepared several plans, and he was working for their implementation too. Marathwada should have an independent university; a bridge should be built at Kaigaon Tokey [sic] over the river Godavari to connect Marathwada to Pune; the Manmad–Aurangabad railway line should be converted to broad gauge to increase travel and commerce; a shorter road should be created for going to Mumbai instead of the circuitous one via Manmad and Nashik; the name of Aurangabad should be changed to Pushpnagar; cloth mills should be established with the cooperation of the country's labourers; a radio station should be started there; these and many such plans were revolving in his mind. It can be seen today that the government as well as the people were in conformity with the importance of these plans as so many of them have now taken physical shape. There are some, however, that have not yet come into existence despite their importance being accepted.

Recognition by Columbia University

The Indian universities have honoured so many people by conferring 'Doctorates' upon them, but not a single university has thought it fit to suitably acknowledge Saheb's scholarship, his enormous learning, and the historical deeds he has performed. This only reveals the orthodox nature of the country's universities. Of course, their recognition of him would not have made any difference to his intellectual attainments; on the contrary, it would have been the universities that would have felt themselves honoured by appreciating his achievements. The only exception here is the Osmania University of Hyderabad.

It was Columbia University, located thousands of miles away, that appreciated the value of Saheb's scholarship and his deeds. During its bicentennial celebration, it decided to confer upon Dr Ambedkar the honorary degree of Doctor of Laws and invited him for the occasion. For accepting this honour, it was necessary to travel to America. We reached Mumbai for that purpose on 31 May 1952. Siddharth College organized a programme that evening at the Cricket Club of India to offer him their good wishes. During that occasion, Patankar, the principal of the college, said [translated from Marathi]:

> 'The Indian University has not shown the good sense to honour the principal architect of the Constitution of India. That a foreign university should take the initiative for honouring Dr Ambedkar is strange.'

Responding to the felicitation, Saheb said [translated from Marathi]:

> 'I have never been a traitor to my country. I have always held the welfare of the country close to my heart. During the Round Table Conference, from the perspective of the welfare of the country, I was a hundred miles ahead of Gandhiji.'

The Columbia University convocation was held in New York on 5 June 1952, and the honorary degree of Doctor of Laws was conferred upon Doctor Saheb. The citation in the degree eulogized him in the following words:

'. . . Member of the Legislative Council, a framer of the Constitution, member of the Cabinet and of the Council of State, one of India's leading citizens – great social reformer and a valiant upholder of human rights.'

Saheb never went anywhere without taking me along. I moved around with him like a veritable shadow. Readers, therefore, would be surprised to know that he did not take me with him to New York. The reason is very simple: our financial status did not allow us this indulgence. Also, the constraints of acquiring foreign currency rose as obstacles.

I Get Appreciated

Doctor Saheb returned to Mumbai from New York on Saturday, 14 June 1952. The one thing that I particularly want to mention is this: when he left for New York, he had carried with him a short history of his health record, as well as of all the treatments he was undergoing. In New York, he showed this health record to a few specialist doctors and sought their opinion. I feel proud to state here that the expert doctors there were fully appreciative of the diagnosis as well as the treatment he was being given. They declared that it couldn't have been any better. Not stopping at that, they wanted to know the name of the doctor who was taking care of him. When he told them that his own wife was the doctor, those American doctors made very affectionate inquiries about me. Doctor Saheb himself told me of this conversation on his return.

We returned to Mumbai again. At a meeting organized by the SC Improvement Trust at Siddharth College on 17 August 1952, Saheb said [translated from Marathi]:

'I have done as much as was possible for a man to do in a single era for the upliftment of the untouchables . . . I say this not with pride

> but with confidence that whatever work I have done for you in the past 25 years, no other person has ever done so much anywhere during the same period of time, and this is a fact.
>
> 'Instead of merely hailing my name, it would be so much better that you struggle for things that in my view are of great value.'

It was in this speech that he stated the need for a community temple hall and implored the workers and assembled audience to begin collecting funds for such a building. The job of maintaining an account of the building fund was performed by an extremely trustworthy and intimate colleague of Saheb's from very early times named Shantaram Upsham (Guruji). Upsham Guruji had been in the movement with Saheb from the very earliest days. Saheb had been so impressed by his probity and sincerity that he had appointed him treasurer of almost all the institutions he established.

Historic Address at the Poona Law Library

A new wing of the Poona Law Library was inaugurated at the hands of Saheb on 23 December 1952. On this occasion, he delivered an impactful and thought-provoking address on the factors that are necessary for running a successful democracy. The definition that he gave of democracy was this: a system of governance that brings about a revolutionary transformation in the economic and social life of the people without bloodshed. I don't think that anyone has given a more comprehensive and perfect definition of democracy. The address remained a topic of discussion for many days in newspapers and various organizations. This exhaustive address on democracy is extremely valuable. I was asked to distribute prizes on this occasion. From Pune, we went to Kolhapur.

Rajaram College Golden Jubilee

On 24 December 1952, we attended the social gathering of Rajaram College in its golden jubilee year as chief guests. We drove towards Kolhapur and saw that from Karad right up to Kolhapur, people had gathered on the road like ants to welcome us in every single village we passed. Arches had been erected at the entry points of the villages. In every single village, women stood with aarti platters for the felicitation rituals. As soon as our car stopped, women would pour pots of water in front of us and swirl the platters round our faces. Flowers were tossed at us from all four sides. Arrangements for our stay were made at the Government Circuit House. After Saheb's address to the students delivering counsel, meritorious students were given prizes and certificates at my hands.

Kolhapur had a special attraction for Saheb on account of the work on social equality done by Rajarshi Shahu Chhatrapati. He enjoyed a very close relationship with a number of people in Kolhapur. He had decided to buy himself some land in Panhala and had already had a talk with Dattoba Pawar on this topic. He wanted to build a bungalow there so he could relax in its cool air, but this desire of his remained unfulfilled.

After the function at the college was over, Saheb took me to the house of an old, retired teacher. The wizened old man, bedridden on account of old age and illness, was overcome by this visit of Saheb's to his house. Despite having risen very high in life, Saheb never discriminated, nor did he ever abandon his humanity.

Love for Physical Exercise

While we were in the Kolhapur Circuit House, several wrestlers came to meet us. It appeared that Saheb had known a few of these wrestlers from much earlier times. Counselling those wrestlers, he said, 'Sandow wrestlers are always so fit, but the bellies of some of you have begun to sag! This means that there is some fault in your exercise system. You must do your exercises along modern methodologies.' Someone piped in, 'Baba, do you also do exercises?' At which Saheb pushed up his right sleeve and responded proudly, 'I do yogasanas every day.' Saheb loved the sport of wrestling. During the days of his youth, he had watched a number of renowned wrestlers in action at the Khasbag grounds of Kolhapur.

Felicitation by Osmania University

There was only one university in the entire country that had the good sense to honour Doctor Saheb for writing the Constitution of India, and that was Osmania University of Hyderabad. It conferred upon him the honorary degree of Doctor of Literature on 12 January 1952 in a ceremony organized during the convocation. By conferring upon him this honour, the university has gained credit for itself.

The citation in the degree conferred by Osmania University reads as follows:

OSMANIA UNIVERSITY

The Degree of
Doctor of Literature
Honoris Causa
has been conferred at the convocation upon
Dr Bhimrao R. Ambedkar
in recognition of his eminent position and attainments

Hyderabad – Deccan B. Ramkrishnarao
January 12, 1953 Chancellor

Dr Ambedkar's Health—My Role as Watchdog

There would be perennial fluctuations in Saheb's state of health. My job was cut out: administering medicines on time, giving him insulin shots, regulating his diet, giving him nutritious food, ensuring regular exercises, adequate rest, a proper night's sleep. I would bend over backwards to give him all the care he needed. Since I was a doctor, sometimes I would have to take some flak from others to make sure that everything was in order.

I exerted myself to the fullest to bring a system into his daily routine and prepare a detailed timetable for him. If the occasion demanded, I would even endure disparagement and put up with bitterness to ensure that he stayed in good physical and mental health. Throughout his life he carried the burden of immense quantities of work. He would fall ill off and on. Diabetes and rheumatism had exhausted him. Finally, tiring of these constant aches and pains, he had simply stopped bothering about his health. He wrote to one of his colleagues:

> 'One must learn to endure what cannot be cured. Everything that comes into being perishes. You must come forward to take over the responsibility of the community.'

Excerpts from the letters he wrote to Bhaurao Gaikwad will give a good idea of his mental status and his despair regarding the state of his health. In one letter he writes:[49]

> 'Since my return from Bombay my health has deteriorated considerably . . . But I suppose there is no escape now.'

In another letter to Bhaurao Gaikwad he writes:[50]

> 'My health is what it is. It is a cause of sorrow for all of you. I have ceased to worry for I don't think I can do anything to regain my old self. As the Buddha has said everything that comes into being perishes. You must learn to take it in that light. More important than worrying about my health is to think of taking over my

responsibilities which you must be soon ready to take over. I am sure I will not last long.'

For the sake of ensuring some rest for Saheb and giving him peace of mind, I had placed certain restrictions on the people who came to meet him. That would obviously upset some people, but there was no remedy for it. I had to ensure the maintenance of Saheb's health, even if it meant creating bitterness. Most of the leaders and followers, when they came to meet him, would bring along some work with them. They would come without bothering about the time and sit with him for hours, which left me with no choice but to send them back. It was quite obvious that they came to him seeking the resolution of their questions, anxieties, complaints, afflictions, injustices and atrocities. But without bothering about the state of Saheb's health, these leaders and followers would sit for hours laying out their grievances. This naturally made Saheb quite restless and ill at ease. Saheb was a patient himself, and when somebody came along with a plea, listening to it would unsettle him. Crippled in body, he would fret and fume, but the others wouldn't know of it. Therefore, at the cost of inviting resentment, I had to step forward and be firm.

When Saheb became really unwell, Dr Malvankar would sometimes be called over. Occasionally, Saheb himself would call him over, while at other times the advice would be given over the phone. Here's a letter that Saheb wrote to Jadhav on 24 February 1953:

'It is [a] long time ago that I got your letter. It has not been possible for me to reply [to] you earlier. In the first place, I have been unwell. Dr Malvankar had to be called here. He is still here attending to me.'

He writes further to Jadhav:

'I am feeling better though I am not able to walk freely.'

Buddha Jayanti at Mumbai

We were present for the Buddha's birth anniversary that was organized at Nare Park in Mumbai by the SCF on 27 May 1953. Saheb spoke on the Buddha's life and philosophy.

On 27 May we visited the Chembur area where the Untouchables Sanghatana Mandal gave Saheb a purse of Rs 1001 for the building fund. On this occasion, Saheb spoke to his followers about their clothing and manner of dressing. The dress should be such that it does not reveal caste. Even if the dress is simple, it should be clean and appropriate, he said.

We visited the Ravali Camp in Mumbai on 2 June, where we were given Rs 1001 towards the building fund.

We were stationed in Aurangabad in the July and August of 1953. Although he wasn't keeping good health, the hustle-bustle of the college's development went on. He wrote to Ghanshyam Talvatkar on 6 August 1953 in an emotionally charged state:

> 'I was glad to receive your letter of the 26th July. My hand has been giving me pain. That is why I have not been able to send you a reply . . . Soon some[one] must come forward to take my place. It is only then that the institutions I have created will last.'

The Ward Committee of the SCF in Aurangabad invited us for high tea on 9 August 1953, where Saheb said:

> 'If the government tries to take back the land from the untouchables, then, instead of depending on applications and pleas, turn brave and, instead of going empty-stomach, take occupation of barren lands.'

My Illness

During that time, a student named Vitthal Bayaji Kadam was studying in the London School of Economics. Saheb had helped him quite a lot. He would offer him frequent guidance, encourage him through letters, give him advice and ask him to dispatch books from London that were not available in India. He had also got him to type out and dispatch the essays that Saheb had written during his stay in London. He would also write to Kadam expressing his thoughts and even personal matters. Saheb writes to him on 23 October 1953 regarding the state of health of both of us:

> 'My progress has been very slow. What is bad [is] that my wife has become a sick person.'

A knot had formed inside my chest. Doctors in Delhi and Mumbai had examined it and suspected that it could be malignant. Saheb was deeply perturbed. It would be necessary to get the related tests and investigations done at the Tata Cancer [sic] Hospital. Accordingly, Doctor Saheb himself took me to the Tata Hospital and the necessary investigations were done. The doctors there suggested that I would need to be operated upon. We were also advised to sleep separately.

Saheb was on pins and needles all the time. He would constantly tell me, 'Sharu, if something untoward happens to you, what will happen to me? Who will then look after me? I'll take you to America. We'll get you treated there.' Tears would flow down his cheeks. I would keep up his spirits by saying that nothing was going to happen to me.

As per the doctor's advice, we would sleep separately. One night I woke up suddenly and noticed that the lights in Saheb's bedroom were on. Wondering what could have happened, I got up and walked up to his room and peeped in. What I saw there shattered me: Saheb had stuffed his face into a pillow and was crying. When I went up to him and caressed him, he lost all restraint and began crying incontinently. We held each other tight and began crying together. 'Sharu,' he sobbed, 'if something happens to you, what will happen to me? Who will look after me?' With that, he began crying even more. I tried to put courage into him and said, 'Don't worry, I'm going to be all right. Only, you don't lose heart.'

In due course, the Tata Hospital reports arrived that declared the doctors' fears as misplaced. The reports were favourable. The knot disappeared by itself after some medication.

Presence in the Rajya Sabha

Saheb was a member of the Rajya Sabha, but because of uncertain health he would not attend the House regularly. The chairman of the Rajya Sabha, Dr Sarvepalli Radhakrishnan, held Saheb in great esteem. Whenever an important discussion was to take place or whenever he felt the need for Saheb's presence, he would phone him and request him to be present. He would go even beyond and send someone to bring Saheb over.

Heart Attack

In the November of 1953, Saheb and I were going from Delhi to Mumbai by the Frontier Mail. We reached the station, and as we were alighting from the car, his fingers got slammed in the door. We, however, went ahead and got into the train. It was wintertime and the weather was very cold. His fingers began to hurt awfully because of the cold.

The train was moving fast. I inquired to find that the next station would be Ratlam. Saheb had begun to run a high fever. His fingers being caught in the door had been merely a pretext. The fever began mounting and Saheb began to babble, 'Sharu, I want to go.' This babble continued without a break. Although I was a doctor, I couldn't make much out of it. I gave him a Codopyrin pill and placed a cold wet cloth upon his forehead. I am sure he had lost awareness. He would just go on with his 'Sharu, I want to go.' After a while, his temperature came down a little, but his refrain of 'Sharu, I want to go. Let me go', continued. I began to panic. I didn't know what to do. Ratlam station had still not arrived. I couldn't decide whether we should continue on to Mumbai or get down at Ratlam and return to Delhi. After some time, his fever broke, and I decided to go straight to Mumbai. Saheb recovered consciousness. When I gave him the details, he also became worried.

We disembarked at Bombay Central Station. Kamalakant Chitre and some other people from the Society had come to receive us. Saheb did not appear to be in a clear frame of mind. Chitre was quite an experienced person, and he was quite senior too; therefore, I took him aside and told him about what had happened during the journey. I also told him about his unconscious mumbling of 'Sharu, I want to go.'

Chitre turned quite grave on hearing this and said, 'These are not good signs. We have to take special care of him.'

I suggested to him, 'Should we keep Saheb in a good nursing home?'

To which Chitre responded, 'Instead of that, let's keep a special nurse for him.'

Our staying arrangement had been made at the Mirabel Hotel near Liberty Cinema. We drove straight to Mirabel Hotel from Bombay Central station.

After we reached the hotel, Saheb began having breathing problems. Chitre immediately made arrangements for a nurse. Despite being in such a serious state, Saheb continued chatting with the people around him. He had ensconced himself in the couch outside the room and was continuing to talk. Despite our requests that he should go to sleep, he refused to stay quiet. Just then, the nurse arrived. She held him by the forearm and said, 'Dr Ambedkar, you have talked enough. You have to rest now.'

To which he replied, 'No, sister, I am all right now.'

But the sister held him firmly and tried to raise him, saying, 'No, you need rest now.'

We held him by both forearms and virtually lifted him up and laid him on the bed. But he was just not able to sleep peacefully.

His breathing problem had worsened. My anxiety increased too, and I told Chitre about my unease. He said, 'Don't worry. We will keep a round-the-clock nurse and call over a renowned doctor.'

Chitre called up Dr Malvankar and the famed cardiologist Dr Tulpule and requested them to come to Mirabel Hotel. Dr Tulpule was Saheb's special doctor. Even earlier, he had examined Saheb for breathing problems and high blood pressure, and had been treating him. When Dr Tulpule arrived, I went into an inner room and hid there. The reason was that he had been my class teacher when I was doing my MBBS at Grant Medical. I felt very abashed at the thought of meeting him. Saheb was so senior to me in age, and I looked so much smaller in his presence, because of which I felt very shy to come before Dr Tulpule.

Dr Tulpule examined Saheb and advised that he be put on oxygen immediately. Nasal tubes were quickly brought and inserted through the nose. Dr Tulpule gave instructions on medicine and care and left.

Saheb's state didn't look good. He would look around here and there, signal to me to come closer, and when I came, he would tell me, 'Sit here.' Once I had sat down, he would start with his earlier refrain of 'Sharu, I want to go. Let me go.' His statement had begun to intrigue me. For a while I thought that he wanted to go back to Delhi and would pacify him by saying, 'Don't say that. Just lie down and rest. As soon as you feel better, we have to go anyway.' When Chitre said that he didn't like the symptoms at all, I became extremely worried.

After he had been supplied with oxygen for four or five hours, he finally stopped his refrain and went into a very deep sleep. After he had been kept on oxygen for twenty-four hours, the doctors attending to him said that he had suffered a mild heart attack. Very fortunately, a great catastrophe had been averted. My spine tingles at the thought of what could have happened if I had got down with Saheb at Ratlam and tried to take him back to Delhi.

While we were still at Mirabel Hotel, the celebrated biographer Dhananjay Keer came over, tracking Saheb down. Doctor Saheb's nasal tubes had just been removed and he was lying on the bed. Keer was in the process of writing Doctor Saheb's biography. It was through Bhaskarrao Bhosle of All India Radio that Keer had contacted Saheb to get his approval and interview him for the book. Saheb had given him permission and Keer was quite close to finishing Saheb's biography in English.

After making inquiries about his health, Keer began talking about the biography. Then he asked Saheb the question, 'Had Gandhi signed the statement given to Prime Minister Ramsay MacDonald for the resolution of the "untouchables" issue?' Saheb sat up immediately and said, 'I'm telling you, Gandhiji had signed that statement. What else could he have done except sign?' Saheb began talking animatedly, which got me worried. I signalled to Keer to wind up the conversation, to which he complied.

When Saheb started feeling better, we shifted him to Jairaj House in Colaba. He had become awfully weak, so much so that he had to be carried on a chair to the first floor where we had our room.

This illness had become a life and death struggle for him, but fortunately, we were able to tide over the crisis. He himself had become sceptical about his chances of survival. This can be seen from the letter he wrote to Vitthal Kadam in London on 19 April 1954. Saheb writes:

> 'I am sorry to not acknowledge promptly the receipt of books sent by you and the two letters that followed their dispatch. I have been so terribly ill since November last and often times all hopes of my survival were given up. But thanks to Buddha, I pulled through. I was taken to Bombay and was in bed till the middle of March.'

Assault on Our Marital Life

It is important to talk here about an event in 1953 that made a horrific assault on our marital life. We had gone to Simla for our honeymoon after our marriage. I have always been in the habit of getting up early, but during those early months he would not let me get out of bed. On the contrary, he would pull the quilt over both of us and quote a saying in Sanskrit, which meant: 'Idleness is a great friend of the human body.' During those days I got to know about many aspects of his sense of humour.

When he expressed the desire of having a daughter, I suggested to him that we could adopt my sister's daughter. But his opinion was that instead of adopting, we would create our own daughter. Unfortunately, this desire of his could not be fulfilled. Actually, the seed of our love was growing in my womb in 1953. He would always say that it would be a daughter and we would argue about what we should name her.

During this period, we went to Kashmir on the special invitation of Sheikh Abdullah, the chief minister of Kashmir. He had made arrangements for our stay in a special guest house. He had also invited us over for a very special dinner. Saheb had discussions with Sheikh Abdullah about Kashmir. One afternoon, I felt dizzy and vomited a few times. My state perturbed Saheb, and we immediately took a flight for Delhi. In the aircraft, my stomach began rumbling. Saheb took me straight to the hospital from the Delhi airport. The doctors examined me and gave me medicines, but this incident had delivered a terrible assault on our marital life: I had had a miscarriage. It was a big wound inflicted on our minds. The mishap depressed him immensely, to the extent that he lost interest in married life.

After this event, I again began pressing him to adopt a daughter because I thought it important to pull the thorn out of his heart. Finally, he too got around to the idea. We had planned to adopt my sister's daughter, but this plan of ours never reached fruition.

Acharya Atre's Movie on Mahatma Phule

Saheb regarded the Buddha, Kabir and Phule as his gurus. The great doyen of literature Acharya Atre had decided to make a film on

Mahatma Jyotiba Phule and had invited Saheb for the launch of the shooting. Saheb was not keeping very well, but since it was a movie on Mahatma Phule and because he enjoyed a very close relationship with Atre, he could not turn the invitation down. The launching of the shooting was done at the hands of Saheb at Famous Studios, Mumbai, on 31 January 1954.

Some of the most respected names of those times had gathered for the programme: the producer-director Acharya Atre, Baburao Pendharkar doing the role of Phule, Sulochanabai playing his wife Savitribai, Periyar Ramasamy Naicker, Senapati Bapat, Shahir Amar Shaikh, the two of us, other members of the cast and a number of guests. Those present held Saheb in affection and they expressed their concern over the poor state of his health. In fact, so bad was it that he was finding it difficult to speak. He could not even wind up his speech properly.

Once the film was ready, Atre also invited us for its premiere. Saheb was completely overwhelmed when he saw the movie. As he saw it, he remembered Mahatma Phule's work and sacrifice and wept. After the movie was over, he patted Pendharkar on the back for his excellent performance and congratulated Atre too. Not satisfied with this, he wrote a letter to Atre on 20 November 1955, lavishing praises on him and wishing the movie success. The movie won some state awards.

In Lonavala for Rest

I planned a trip to Lonavala in March 1954 so Saheb could get some much-needed rest. Staying on in Mumbai would have meant a night-and-day, endless stream of colleagues and workers coming to meet him for some work or the other. We set off from Mumbai by car to spend some time in a bungalow that belonged to his very dear friend A.B. Nair who owned the English daily *Free Press Journal.* When Saheb had had his heart attack in 1953, it was in Nair's bungalow at

Juhu that we had stayed for about a month's rest. They would often get into intimate, heart-to-heart conversations.

Although we had gone there for rest, there would never be a break in his reading and writing. Also, however secret we tried to keep our movements, the news of his stay would spread like wildfire, people would arrive in swarms, empty-stomach, or with just a piece of bhakari and some chutney tied in a piece of cloth and sit patiently for hours for the good fortune of getting a darshan of Saheb. When he heard that his brothers were waiting for him, eager to merely look at him, he would go out and meet them with affection and inquire about them solicitously, even offer them guidance. Having got their darshan of him, these faithful, loyal people would return with a sense of gratification. Many of them would have tears of joy in their eyes for the great good fortune of having seen him in person.

One day an economist came to visit us; I don't remember his name. They sat chatting after finishing their tea. The cook entered to inform Saheb that a huge crowd of people was waiting outside for his darshan. Saheb instantly took the economist out with him to the veranda. When Saheb saluted them by bringing his palms together, the hands of the people automatically came together too, and all of them touched their heads to the ground to show their reverence for their liberator. Pointing at the fulfilled, poverty-stricken multitude, he told the economist, 'Look, these are my people. My people are ignorant and poor, but they are loyal.' Saheb then called two or three people closer and asked them to open the little bundles that they carried. They had bhakari, chutney and onions. Deeply moved, he showed the items to the economist and said, 'See what my people eat.' His eyes turned moist. The economist noticed Saheb's charged state and took his leave. Saheb looked extremely grave and grieved. He told the cook to distribute all the food that had been cooked to the people. All the chapatis, vegetables, rice and curries were distributed among the people. Neither Saheb nor the rest of us had dinner that evening.

Vitthal of Pandharpur? No, the Buddha!

During our stay at Lonavala, Saheb had taken in hand the writing of a research essay on [God] Vitthal of Pandharpur. He had written a few pages of the essay. The purpose of this essay was to prove that the statue of Vitthal was originally a statue of the Buddha. His opinion was that the word 'pundalik' was a corruption of the original Pali word 'pundarik', and he had collected a lot of evidence to support his claim. Saheb had written the introduction of this essay whose English title was 'Who is Pandurang?'. Saheb could not complete this essay. The original handwritten piece would have been carried away along with other documents by the People's Education Society when they took over our library.

Bhandara Lok Sabha By-Election

At the insistence of workers and colleagues, Saheb decided to stand for the by-election to the reserved seat in the Lok Sabha that was to take place in May. He filled up his nomination form and began canvassing. During his election meetings, Saheb would come down heavily on Nehru's leadership, the manner in which the government worked and on Nehru's foreign policy. He would also tell the audience that the government had a stepmotherly attitude towards the untouchables.

The Congress had chosen Bhaurao Borkar, a Harijan of the mahar community, to stand against Saheb. Saheb was sure of winning this by-election. Our election meetings everywhere were attended by hundreds of thousands of people. But what had to happen happened. While it is true that Saheb polled 1,32,000 votes, Borkar of the Congress won the election by a margin of 8,381 votes.

I am convinced that a great personality like Saheb was defeated because of the following reasons: the envious pulls and pushes among the mahar caste and sub-castes; the internecine feeling of high-and-low; the machinations of ambitious people; the negative votes of the upper-caste voters in a reserved seat; insufficient funds and internal differences, among many others. The sub-castes played a vital role in these elections. I know for sure that hundreds of thousands of people would come for our meetings wearing blue caps;[51] the same people, instigated only by the spirit of sub-caste and inter-personal envy, would put on Gandhi caps and attend the Congress meetings. The ignorant, brainless people vented their ire against local sub-caste politics, discrimination and internal disagreements, but the consequence had to be borne by Saheb. The sculptor of the Constitution of the country had to face electoral defeat in two consecutive elections. What can that mean? The big tragedy is that Saheb's defeat was nothing less than the defeat of progressive and egalitarian concepts in the country.

The Ungratefulness of [This Sub-caste among the Mahars]*

We later learnt that there is a sub-caste of the mahars in Vidarbha.* After marking their attendance in Saheb's meetings, this sub-caste cast their votes for the Congress and stabbed Saheb in the back. It is a matter of great misfortune and shame and humiliation that they did not leave much undone to defeat, in an act of treachery, their very own liberator.

As all this information trickled in, Saheb had become extremely depressed. I was at my wits' end on what I should do. It was with the greatest difficulty that he had finally digested the first defeat in elections. What would happen after this second defeat?

Saheb had been sceptical too. He had written to Chitre:

> 'Reports from other sources reaching here speak of my being eliminated in the election. This is not impossible and I am quite prepared for it.'

Saheb had turned extremely melancholic, therefore it was important to take him out of this atmosphere. By a stroke of luck, around the same time, he had been invited to attend a conference in Rangoon to celebrate the birth anniversary of Lord Buddha. I succeeded in persuading Saheb to attend this conference and decided to go there before the election results were declared.

Congress Games

It was the Congress that had earlier got Saheb elected to the Constituent Assembly unopposed. It had then gone on to place upon him the national responsibility of writing the Constitution and of the Ministry of Law. Therefore, it should have displayed the largeness of heart to re-invite the sculptor of the Constitution with due honour. Likewise, the people of Mumbai too should have shown the breadth of vision to elect him. For the sake of the welfare of the nation, if not for anything else, Nehru should have left the way open for Saheb to be elected to the Lok Sabha. But quite to the contrary, the Congress shook hands with a person like Dange and applied all its strength and got into all kinds of machinations to defeat Saheb, which proves that the Congress cared more for the party than for the welfare of the country. The same tradition seems to be in operation right up till today with 'India is Indira'. This is the great tragedy of our democracy.

The Buddha's Birth Anniversary in Rangoon

With the purpose of distracting Saheb's mind, I took the initiative of taking him to Rangoon. We found out the results of the Bhandara by-election in Rangoon.

We departed by a BOAC flight from Delhi at 5.10 a.m. on 16 May 1954 and landed at the Rangoon airport at 3.30 p.m. Our stay had been arranged in an excellent hotel. The people who came to visit us would rake up the topic of the election, and a few correspondents too would riddle him with questions on his defeat. Shutting them up was a difficult task, but I had to do it in view of Saheb's state of health.

We were present for the inauguration of the Buddha Sasana Council on 17 May 1954. There were some programmes in the afternoon too, but since it was raining all afternoon, we stayed in the hotel.

Saheb suddenly began to feel uncomfortable on the 18th and he began running a fever too. Since he was feeling extremely exhausted, we could not attend any of the functions or even the sessions of the Sasana Council. Saheb lay completely listless, causing me a lot of consternation. I immediately called over some expert physicians who examined him and advised complete rest.

On the 19th we were informed that our staying arrangements had been shifted to a luxurious government guest house[52] and we moved there accordingly.

We were present for the convocation ceremony that was held in the Presidential Palace. There is a government organization that trains bhikshus, and those who successfully complete the curriculum are awarded a certificate. Those learned bhikshus who have excelled in the curriculum are awarded the degree of Agga Maha Pandita by the government. This degree was conferred upon eight bhikshus on the day we were present.

On 21 May 1954, we set off for a town called Pegu fifty miles to the north. A cavalcade of fifty cars carrying the representatives of many nations was travelling to see this place. At the head and in the rear of the cavalcade were the vehicles of armed soldiers, a special arrangement that had been made by the government for the security of the representatives from across the world.

On the morning of 23 May 1954, we were flown to Mandalay. A fleet of eight aircraft carried about 200 people that included a number of bhikshus, the representatives of various countries, the officials of the Buddha Sasana Council, government officials, security men and others. As the weather was cloudy and stormy, the pilot lost his way. After floundering around for an hour, we flew in the right direction. But because it was heavily cloudy and there was fog everywhere, everything looked hazy. In the evening we returned to our guest house.

On 25 May we were invited for lunch by U Chan Htoon, the attorney general and the chief secretary of the Buddha Sasana Council, at his residence Themis Court No. 1, Church Road, Rangoon. That was where we formally met several important members of the Buddha Sasana Council. The chairman of the council asked Saheb a number of questions and shared his doubts about the dissemination of Buddhism. In response, Saheb quoted excerpts from the Milind Panha and explained to him the difficulties that lay in the dissemination of the dhamma.

Saheb's Important Suggestions

For the purpose of disseminating Buddhism across the world, Saheb suggested the establishment of the International Buddhist Mission and laid out the goals for this organization. They are as follows:

1. The youth should be given appropriate education.
2. The Burmese government should help in the opening of schools and colleges in India. It is through them that dissemination of the dhamma will take place along with education. Through the collection of fees, these institutions will become self-reliant and there will be no need for help from the Burmese government. The Dalit and backward class students should be offered scholarships along with free education. It is through discourses on dhamma and the prayer sessions in these institutions that people will appreciate its importance and become automatically attracted towards Buddhism.

3. Monasteries should be constructed in the important cities of India. The Dalits and the backward communities (including communities like fishermen and oil crushers) that form 89 per cent of the country's population have already expressed their eagerness to embrace Buddhism.
4. People who submit high quality theses on Buddhism should be given motivational prizes.
5. Preachers should be trained for proselytizing in missionary mode.

On 27 and 28 May, U Chan Htoon invited us for tea, during which extensive discussions took place. He looked extremely enthusiastic. We learnt that U Chan Htoon had completely immersed himself in dhamma work. He had persuaded the Burmese government to make laws that required the government to bear some of the financial burden of the Buddha Sasana Council. Provision had been made in the country's budget for religious activities. All of this was obviously the result of U Chan Htoon's labour and acumen. We were delighted at having met a person who had so totally committed himself to Buddhism, and we felt that our tour of Burma was successful.

We were very keen to hear the address of the prime minister of Burma, U Nu. Doctor Saheb had been deeply impressed by the progress that Burma had made after its independence. He had liked the plan of the Burmese government of nationalizing land. 'This is a real socialistic plan,' he had commented. He requested a copy of the proposed Land Nationalization Act and the Burmese Constitution.

U Chan Htoon asserted that the number of plans that Saheb had presented as also the book he was in the process of writing should be published at the earliest and translated into different languages. He also gave the assurance that he would get the Buddha Sasana Council to help in the publication of the book. He added, 'Whether the Sasana Council agrees or not, I shall see that we get your book (*Bible of Buddhism*) published.' Saheb felt deeply gratified.

U Chan Htoon put forward the proposal that batches of Indian youngsters should be sent to Burma for periods extending from three to six months. During this period, the youngsters would observe the working of the Buddha Sasana Sabha. The Sabha, on its side, would train them in the matter of Buddhism and its propagation, make them efficient campaigners of Buddhism and send them back to India. The entire expenditure for this exercise would be borne by the Burmese government. Saheb happily accepted this proposal. The discussion then turned to the subject of Bhikshu Sangha. Saheb said, 'It has now become necessary to establish new sanghas as they had existed in ancient times. The Japanese system of sangha looks good and is worth implementing.'

On 29 May, U Chan Htoon arranged our meeting with Prime Minister U Nu. We had met U Nu before, but on that day we experienced for ourselves his affectionate nature. It was sharply evident that U Nu, who possessed an attractive personality, had completely given himself over to Buddhism. We also learnt that despite being the prime minister, U Nu devoted six hours daily to religious work, which included prayers, meditation, reading, etc. Saheb and he had detailed discussions on how Buddhism could be spread in India.

On 30 May 1954, we went to see the Mass Education Centre and Rehabilitation Brigade. We were given a security officer from the Foreign Office as a guide. The work of this organization is in the nature of a service where instructions are given on how community development can be brought about through mass awakening. Countless workers have thrown themselves enthusiastically into this work without expecting anything in return. The Burmese are a very hospitable people and are forever ready to extend a helping hand to others. There is no doubt that this is due to the indoctrination of Buddhism.

During our few days of stay in Burma, we collected a number of rare legends and books written in Pali and other languages that would be useful for the books Saheb planned to write on the Buddha. A large number of books were procured from a variety of Buddhist viharas. We observed minutely and in person the Buddhist traditions and rituals followed in those viharas. We wound up our tour of Burma and returned to India in the first week of June. Saheb's health had remained in a debilitated state.

'Let's Do Social Work instead of Political Work!'

Saheb had been deeply disappointed by his defeats in the 1952 and 1954 elections for the Lok Sabha. He had lost interest in politics, but it was important to stay in politics for the sake of the Dalits and the impoverished masses. Saheb was in a quandary. On one side stood the strong Congress Party, the party in power, and on the other side was the absence of unity among the Dalits; such being the situation, satisfaction and success in politics appeared impossible to achieve.

To wean Saheb away from politics and for the sake of his mental health and contentment, I would always tell him, 'Instead of doing political work, let's just do social work. As per the announcement you have made, let's take the work of Buddhism in hand.' This was my perpetual insistence with him. Saheb would often rage against the Congress.* That was the reason why I would try to induce him to work for society and for religion. His acceptance of invitations to Buddhist conferences, his announcement that he would write books on religion and his pledge to spend the rest of his life in religious work were the result of those inducements. It is of course true that he had decided to get into all these activities many years ago, but I humbly beg to submit here that I was to some extent responsible for helping him give concrete shape to these things by supporting him and insisting on his taking them in hand immediately.

Invitation from Japan

Dr Felix Valyi of Tokyo, Japan, had assured Saheb that he would help him in every possible way for the propagation of Buddhism. The Society of International Cultural Relations, recognized by the Government of Japan, had requested Saheb to read his thesis, titled 'The Roots of Indian Philosophy', which compared Jainism and Buddhism, at the Round Table Conference to be organized in Tokyo. Felix Valyi wrote to Saheb, 'It is very important that you participate in this Round Table Conference. You are famous in Japan as an Indian Buddhist leader and your international fame will bring international importance for our effort.'

He further said that Saheb's book *The Buddha and His Gospel* was an example of his enlightening and awe-inspiring work, and that it should be translated into the Japanese language. He sought Saheb's permission to talk to publishers in Japan to get the book published.

It was not possible for us to accept Dr Valyi's invitation on account of Saheb's ill health. He was also busy writing his book and mulling over the thought of religious conversion. Importantly, we had already accepted the invitation to be present at the conference in Rangoon celebrating the Buddha's birth anniversary.

Buddhist Seminary at Bangalore

Saheb had in mind the establishment of a Buddhist seminary at Bangalore with the help of Dr Felix Valyi and the Society of International Cultural Relations. In this context, when Saheb met the Maharaja of Mysore on 8 July 1954, the maharaja had gifted to us a piece of land. The plan for the proposed institution was that bhikshus should be trained in the dhamma and the propagation of the dhamma as preachers along the lines of the Christian missionaries; there should be a well-provided, well-stocked, grand library for studies on the dhamma; there should be staying arrangements for foreign researchers and scholars coming to conduct their studies; Saheb had these and many other plans. Correspondence was happening on this subject with Dr Valyi and the consulate general of Japan. Saheb wrote on 4 June 1954 to F. Hyanshi, the consulate general of Japan:

> 'I am sorry to say that the proposal for the establishment of an Institute at Bangalore has not taken any shape. I think it will take some time. I have not been able to put myself in contact with the Maharaja of Mysore on account of my illness.'

Later, the Maharaja of Mysore did give us the land as a gift, but no construction could take place because of financial reasons. A lot of time was spent in correspondence with the Japanese organizations. Later, because of other engagements such as Buddhist conferences, the religious conversion programme, book-writing and because of ill health, Saheb could not give much attention in that direction. Later, not long after, he passed away. There's no way now to know what happened to that piece of land, but I hear that it has been taken over by unauthorized hutments.

Doctor Saheb's Health Deteriorates

Saheb's health had taken a downward turn in Rangoon; after returning to Delhi, it showed no signs of improving; it just kept deteriorating. The governing body of the People's Education Society was slated to meet in the second week of June, but despite being the president, Saheb was in no state to be present. He wrote to his colleague Balwant Varale:

> 'I have your letters. I have just returned from Rangoon much poorer in health. I am afraid I won't be able to attend your

meetings. You had better ask Jadhav to come and preside over the meeting.'

He also wrote to Vitthal Kadam, saying [translated from Marathi]:

'I have not been keeping good health since returning from Rangoon. I shall be taken to Bombay for treatment.'

In the last week of June, I took Saheb to Mumbai for a complete investigation. Dr Malvankar and Dr Tulpule examined him and began treatment.

On 7 July 1954, we went from Mumbai to the Nilgiris where Saheb delivered a lecture at the Military Staff College on the Constitution of India. From there we returned to Delhi on the 15th or 16th.

Despondent Dr Ambedkar

Saheb could never get over his defeats in the elections. His letter to Jadhav of 1 August 1954 is quite revealing:

'What was I before [the] election[s]? What am I now? It is not that sorrow does not enter my mind. I ask the question: have I [a] future? Sometimes I get a negative answer. But these are momentary thoughts. They never disturb the peace of my mind.'

His physical and mental state had become very worrisome, but his willpower remained strong. He would function only on the strength of his extraordinary willpower.

Vitthal Kadam would ask in his letters about Saheb's health and mine, to whom he wrote on 6 August 1954:

'Mai is keeping well. I am pulling on.'

Saheb's Expectations and Desires

While Saheb was a student in England, he had a lady friend whose name was FX. She worked in the Secretariat of the Parliament. Because of her he was able to witness how the Parliament in England functioned. The influence of parliamentary democracy there had left a deep impression on his mind. It is no surprise, therefore, that he fell in love with parliamentary democracy. It was only in England that real parliamentary democracy could be witnessed because the democratic tradition is very old there; this was the ideal that Saheb always carried in his mind's eye.

Saheb always expected me to be present in the Visitors' Gallery on the day he was to make an address in the Parliament. On the day that he was due to speak, when leaving home, he would tell me to stay ready. He would send the car for me with the driver. It was also his insistence that I should wear a sari of his choice. His other expectation and desire was that I should sit at a place in the Visitors' Gallery where he could see me. As he talked, he would turn his eyes in my direction off and on. If he did not find me in the expected place, he would feel upset; with my sitting there, he would feel content. I feel that this desire to have me sit in the Visitors' Gallery was perhaps picked up from Churchill's example; Churchill too would tell his wife to sit in the Visitors' Gallery of the Parliament.

Affectionate Anger

Let me recount a memory of Saheb's anger. He was due to deliver an address in the Parliament once, and he told me to come along. I put on a sari and got ready, but it was not the sari he had told me to wear. He was very upset, and he said, 'You just don't understand what you should be wearing.' As he was leaving, he said, 'You don't come.' I told the driver, 'Come back after dropping Saheb. I too have to come.' Saheb got into the car in a huff and left for the Parliament.

As per my instructions, the driver returned to pick me up. I was ready and waiting, dressed in the sari that Saheb had recommended. I reached the Parliament and sat in my usual place. Saheb got up to speak and turned his eyes upwards as was his wont. When he saw me sitting there wearing the sari of his choice, he kept staring at me in surprise. He had never thought that I would go to the Parliament that day. When he saw me, his anger evaporated. After he had finished with his work in the Parliament, we returned home together. Such was his anger of love.

He took a minute interest in everything related to me. He had expectations about what I should wear and what I should do. Till as long as he was alive, I found great fulfilment in wearing the saris of his choice. His selection was sharp and perfect. He knew better than me what suited me best. He did not like me to wear saris with wide borders; his preference was for narrow ones. If I ever pulled out a sari with a wide border, he would say, 'Aga, you just don't understand. Do such saris suit you? A sari border should be thin and light and delicate looking!'

Diamond Jubilee Celebrations

In the last week of October [26–28], the SCF had organized a gala conference under the presidentship of Saheb at the Purandare Stadium [Mumbai]. Saheb said in the conference [translated from Marathi]:

> 'The citadel of the SCF has been raised on the sentiments of the untouchable people. My desire is that this citadel should never fall down.
>
> 'We should decide our goals like the moustaches of the Marwaris. Depending on their goals, their moustaches are either turned upwards or downwards. That is how our goals should be decided too. Keep this in mind.'

On the evening of 28 October 1954, Saheb was presented with a purse of Rs 1,18,000 on behalf of the SCF. The function was celebrated in the presence of hundreds of thousands of people. Actually, Saheb had completed sixty years on 14 April 1954, but this diamond jubilee celebration was organized on 28 October 1954. A committee called the 'Dr Ambedkar Diamond Jubilee Celebration Committee' had been formed for the purpose. Responding to his felicitation, Saheb said, 'The diamond jubilee is only a pretext. This money is yours, that I have collected for the building fund.'

Saheb recounted a number of episodes from his childhood. The memory of his father, mother and his father's sister made him emotional. He said, 'Not one of the persons who brought me up is alive today. If they had been around to see the honour being bestowed upon me, they would have been delighted.'

In the course of his address, he declared that he held the Buddha, Kabir and Phule as his gurus, and knowledge, humility and integrity as his most revered godheads.

Dr Ambedkar: One among the Six Intellectuals of the World

On 14 November 1954, we were present at the students' get-together at Hyderabad. Advising the students to educate themselves and do constructive work, Saheb said, 'The Brahmins in this country had this notion that they alone could acquire knowledge. But this is altogether false. A certain European has said that there are six intellectuals in the world and Dr Ambedkar is one of them.'

Rangoon Buddhism Conference

The Burmese government had sent a special invitation to Saheb for participating in the third conference of the World Fellowship of Buddhists to be held in Rangoon, and we had decided to accept the invitation. Accordingly, on 1 December 1954, Saheb, I and a loyal colleague of Saheb's named Kashinath Vishram Savaadkar took the Pan American flight to Rangoon. Whenever he travelled, Saheb always carried with him books he would need for his writing and stationery, and he personally took care of this. Before setting off on his travels, he would carefully gather the needed books and keep them aside.

Savaadkar's seat in the aircraft was quite far away from us; on top of that he was flying for the first time. Saheb and I walked up to his seat to check whether all was going well with him to find the gentleman fast asleep. I shook him awake and said, 'Savaadkar, Saheb has come.' When he got up with a start, Saheb said to him, 'Arré, have you got enough coverings? Otherwise, you may take my blanket.'

We disembarked at 1 a.m. at Rangoon airport, where we found some government officials waiting to receive us. Arrangements for our stay had been made at the magnificent Kawn Bawza Hotel.[53]

Community Buddha *vandana* [prayer] was organized on 3 December 1954, at 7.30 a.m. at the Chattha Sangayana cave [the World Peace Temple] in the presence of the prime minister of Burma U Nu, but we could not attend because of Saheb's ill health. The two of us visited the Kaba Aye pagoda in the evening. We entered the pagoda, went down on our knees before a colossal statue of Lord Buddha and bent down to pay our humble obeisance to the Lord.

On the 4th, the Buddha Sasana had organized speeches in the hall of the Upper Goyana Hostel by a few select representatives who had come to attend the conference from around the world. The Maha Thero [Pali honorific for a senior *bhikku*] sat in the central chair of the hall. Saheb got up at around 11 a.m. to deliver his address. After explaining to the audience the decline of Buddhism in India, he expressed regret at the dismal pace at which Buddhism was spreading. He went on to say [translated from Marathi]:[54]

> 'When I was in the Parliament, I had made arrangements for the resurrection of Buddhism. I am the sculptor of the Constitution of India. For one, I provided incentives in the Constitution for learning the Pali language. For another, when I showed the first instruction of Pali "Dhammachakra Pravartan" etched on the front part of the Rashtrapati Bhawan to the President of Burma [sic] Dr G.P. Malalasekera, he was astounded. The third thing is that the Ashok chakra on the national flag of India has gained recognition as the symbol of the Government of India. While I was doing this, I had made such a matchless and logical presentation in the Parliament that neither the Hindus nor the Musalmans nor the Christians nor members belonging to other faiths had raised any serious objection.'

Doctor Saheb then informed them about the colleges and the plan for constructing Buddha viharas at different places. The representatives of twenty-eight countries of the world listened to this forty-five-minute thought-provoking speech with rapt attention. Finally, Saheb criticized the donation system and the unnecessary expenditure on various festivals practised by the Burmese government and the Burmese people.

After the speeches were over, we returned in the evening to our hotel. Saheb was sitting in the hall engrossed in conversation with the representatives of other countries when Savaadkar came up to Saheb and told him, 'Baba, the bearded gentleman who had come to meet you in Mumbai, I saw him here.'

Saheb replied, 'Oh yes! That's Ramasamy Naicker. Go, tell him that I've asked him to come.'

Savaadkar ran out and brought along Ramasamy Naicker with him. We had an hour-long chat with him. Finally, Saheb said to him, 'You should give up anti-Brahminism and start propagating the religion of Lord Buddha.'

We then went out and visited the book shops. Saheb picked up some useful books available there. A few bhikshus whom he knew, including Anand Kausalyayan and Kashyap, came to meet him there [Rangoon].

We flew from Rangoon to Mandalay in a special aircraft on 8 December 1954. The Burmese government had specially arranged this aircraft for us to ensure our security. There had been incidents of railway trains becoming the targets of bombs and robberies. At Mandalay we stayed as guests of Dr Sohni. We saw a few Buddha viharas in Mandalay. Some of the viharas were gargantuan, measuring up to 500 feet in height; some of the Buddha statues were 150 feet tall too.

After returning to Rangoon, we stayed at the house of Saheb's friend, Dinanath. This Dinanath was a close associate of Netaji Subhash Chandra Bose and was a frontline manager of Subhash Babu's Burma affairs. He was a native of Punjab, but he had taken Burmese citizenship and settled in Rangoon. Saheb and he enjoyed a very close relationship.

Savaadkar had gone by train to Mandalay with the other representatives. When he came to meet us at Dinanath's house, we took him in too. There was a group of Dalits from the southern part of India who were traders in Rangoon. They came in a group to meet us at Dinanath's house. They had organized a big programme that very day to which they invited us. They gave both of us a formal welcome, in the course of which they presented to Saheb a scroll of a formal address placed in a silver casket. We later learnt that this casket was originally created for Marshal Tito. After the meeting, we were taken for dinner to a grand hotel. Dinanath accompanied us for this programme. On 18 December 1954, we returned to Delhi by a BOAC flight. A few days later we went to Mumbai because Saheb had agreed to install a statue of Lord Buddha in a Buddha vihara at Dehu near Pune.

Our Conversion

An important and historically relevant matter needs to be recorded here. Saheb's followers are a far cry, even among the people who came in close association with him, very few people would know that much before we went to attend the third World Fellowship of Buddhists in Rangoon, both Saheb and I had personally taken the deeksha and been initiated into Buddhism.

I don't remember the exact date [2 May 1950], but we had both embraced Buddhism well before we went to the Buddhist conference. I told Saheb, 'We have taken the work of Buddhism in hand and invitations at the global level have begun coming. We will be present at Buddhist conferences, therefore we must get initiated into Buddhism and participate as Buddhists.' Saheb was convinced and accordingly, we decided to convert to Buddhism.

One day at 6 a.m., we pulled out our car and presented ourselves at the Buddha vihara in the Birla Temple complex in Delhi. There, at the hands of Bhante Aryavansh, the two of us took the *trisharana* and *panchsheel* and embraced Buddhism. Only a very few people know about this. I remember Mahasthavir Bhadant Anand Kausalyayan referring to this historical event during his interview at Akashvani.

Dehu Road Buddha Vihara

A Buddha vihara had been constructed on Dehu Road, which falls on the Mumbai–Pune highway. Saheb had committed himself to installing a Buddha statue in this vihara. We had brought a Buddha statue from Rangoon specifically for installing in that vihara. Actually, we had brought two identical statues. From among many statues, Saheb had chosen one with the eyes open and the posture of delivering a sermon. Saheb did not subscribe to the statue of the Buddha sitting in meditation with his eyes closed. He would say, 'All through his life, Lord Buddha roamed every nook and corner of the country with his eyes open. It was with open eyes that he observed the sorrows of the world and his roamings were literally on foot. He never used any vehicle or any other means for his travels.' One of these two statues we had placed in a glass case in our bungalow at

26, Alipore Road. It was in front of this statue that we would recite our Buddha vandana morning and evening. This statue from our bungalow is as of now in Pune and will be placed in the planned Dr Ambedkar Memorial Vihara. It was the other one of the two that we gifted to the vihara at Dehu Road.

A function had been organized at Dehu Road on 25 December 1954, and we had set off from Mumbai by car. We had with us my brother Vasant Kabir, who was an engineer, and a foreign Buddhist bhikshu. I don't remember the bhikshu's name, but I think he was Burmese. As soon as our car entered the premises of the vihara, we were hailed by the hundreds of thousands of people gathered there. Turning to the bhikshu sitting next to him, Saheb said, 'Look, these are my people. For my sake they have come travelling long distances. They are poor, but extremely loyal.'

We held the Lord's sparkling white statue in our hands and entered the vihara. Saheb then installed the statue. The sound of the trisharana emerging from hundreds of thousands of mouths reverberated in the sky.

On that occasion, Saheb said, 'The honour of installing the Buddha's statue after 1200 years belongs to us people of the Dalit community; this is an extremely important occasion, and this shall certainly be recorded in history. It's from this small Buddhist temple that the religious revolution shall begin.'

It was on this occasion that he announced his intention of writing on the Buddha and his religious philosophy.

Immersed in Religious Work

Saheb intensified his involvement in religious work, with the result that his attention was diverted a little bit from politics and some enthusiasm was created in him. It was in the flush of this enthusiasm that, for the purpose of religious propagation, he established contact with Devipriya Walisinha of the Mahabodhi Society in Calcutta,

Mahasthavir Chandramani, Bhante Sangharakshita, Bhante Anand Kausalyayan, Felix Valyi of Japan and many other notable Buddhists, and began discussions with them for a religious conversion function, for proselytizing and for propagating the faith. Both of us had been swept away by religious work. Keeping in mind the superstitions and the social circumstances prevailing in India, Saheb had chalked out a unique deeksha ritual. The twenty-two pledges[55] taken at the time of the deeksha were a part of the same ritual. Saheb's opinion was that if a new movement of Buddhism had to be started in India, then it would have to be done in the Christian style. As there is baptism among Christians followed by confirmation of initiation by a priest, the followers of Buddhism should also follow the same pattern, meaning that [conversion to] Buddhism should also have two rites.

'I have decided that our conversion (that of myself and my wife) will take place at Sarnath,' Saheb had written to Dr Walisinha, but that was not how it actually happened.

Here's a letter that Saheb wrote to Vitthal Kadam in London on 6 February 1955, marking the intensity of our engagement with Buddhism:

> 'I am keeping well. My wife is also keeping well. We have both been engaged very deeply in our Buddhist work. The Maharaja of Mysore has given us five acres of land situated in Bangalore for an Institution.'

Constitution of the SCF

Saheb was busy drafting the constitution of the Scheduled Castes Federation towards the end of February 1955. Till then, the constitution of the SCF was not in written form. Believing that the party should have a written constitution, he had drafted it as per his perspective and sent copies of it to Bhaurao Gaikwad, Rajabhau Khobragade, N. Shivaraj, Hardas Avale and other prominent members with the request that if they had any comments to make, they should send them within a month. After taking the comments of the members into consideration, we gave the constitution of the SCF its final shape and got it printed in Delhi.

Ill Health Again

In the first week of March [1955], Saheb's health dipped again. Even in that state, he would attend the Rajya Sabha sessions off and on. The planned writing and reading of books would also carry on. When his health sank, Dr Malvankar had to be called over. He examined Saheb and prescribed some medicines; but not being able to arrive at a proper diagnosis, he advised us to go to Mumbai to get Saheb investigated thoroughly.

On 15 March 1955, Saheb wrote to D.G. Jadhav:

> 'I have received your letter long ago and I had wanted to send you a reply, but before I could do so, I was struck down quite suddenly by a terrific illness which put a complete stop to my activities.
>
> 'Dr Malvankar had to be called. He too was unable to diagnose the malady but he was able to give relief. It is only for the last few days that I am walking about.'

Despite being unwell, he attended the Rajya Sabha on 18 March. While the address was in progress, he began feeling uncomfortable. He began sweating profusely and he sat down. Dr Radhakrishnan, the chairman of the Rajya Sabha, noticed this. He called the security staff in and told them to escort Saheb to an empty room. They took him to an outer room, seated him in an armchair and unbuttoned his jacket and shirt. Radhakrishnan phoned me up, and I rushed to the Rajya Sabha hall to find Radhakrishnan standing next to Saheb. His sweating had reduced. Dr Radhakrishnan gave us two security guards and told them to escort us to the bungalow.

I took Saheb to our bungalow and requested Dr Malvankar to come over urgently too. The doctor advised a few days of complete rest for Saheb and suggested that we should go to Mumbai for a proper investigation and left.

Saheb wrote to Bhaurao Gaikwad on 22 March 1955 [translated from Marathi]:

> 'I was going to reply to you immediately, but I suddenly fell [ill] and couldn't do any work. We had called Dr Malvankar over from Bombay. He's just returned. As he was leaving, he told me emphatically that I should not do any intellectual work for some time. Till now I was not an obedient patient, but I have now decided that I will not do any work till I am well. My physical strength has reduced further because of the tension of delivering the address at the Rajya Sabha on the 18th. As of now, therefore, I am bedridden . . . There is just one reason for writing this letter, and that is because I had been feeling that I should get some activity going with regard to a land for the mahars, but now it has become impossible. After I finish with my medical examination, I shall soon come to Bombay. Dr Malvankar has also advised me to come over to Bombay. He will also make suitable investigations to find out why I had this sudden bout of illness.'

We went to Mumbai and got the necessary tests done. After examining him, both Dr Malvankar and Dr Tulpule advised complete rest.

'Get Ready for *Dhamma Deeksha*!'

A function to felicitate U Yan Tan, justice of the Supreme Court of Burma, had been organized at Siddharth College on 3 April 1955. We were invited as the chief guests of the function. Speaking on this occasion, Dr Ambedkar emphasized the need for religion and identified dictatorship and the policy and culture of discrimination as the two enemies of democracy. Declaring that equality could never flourish in Hinduism, he finally said, 'I am giving all my untouchable friends the right that if they want to liberate themselves and establish equality, they should stay ready to take the deeksha of Buddhism.' After finishing this programme, we returned to Delhi.

Secret Oxygen Intake

Saheb's health continued to fluctuate after our return from Mumbai. Once in a while he would visit the Rajya Sabha. With the swings in the state of his health continuing, we returned to Mumbai. Saheb had dental problems too. Some of his teeth had begun to shake and a few molars had turned carious, raising the fear of pyorrhoea. Finally, the doctor advised that the teeth be pulled out; accordingly, we went to a dentist in the St George Dental Hospital at Bori Bunder and had the teeth extracted. From May onwards his health began slipping rapidly. Actually, his health had turned delicate since he had had the heart attack in 1953, but we were pulling the cart along somehow.

Further on, he would begin to pant even while breathing. When this breathing problem began, the cardiologist Dr Tulpule advised that we should keep an oxygen cylinder at home along with the tubes and the rest of the equipment required for artificial respiration. We had therefore got all this equipment organized at our bungalow. Any time that Saheb felt uncomfortable, he would be given a few inhalations. A little later on, he was required to be given oxygen regularly twice a week; but because of instructions from Saheb, this was kept a secret. He would say, 'My people are ignorant. If they hear that I am being given oxygen, their morale will be shaken.'

Quite naturally, this was known only to the closest of Saheb's associates. Our cook Sudama, Shankaranand Shastri, Sohanlal Shastri, Nanak Chand Rattu, D.G. Jadhav and Bhaurao Gaikwad knew all the details. After a round of oxygen inhalation, Saheb would feel a little energized.

As a modern therapy, we would give him electric baths for his neuritis and joint aches. Delhi gets to be very cold, and his joint aches turned quite severe, which made life for Saheb very painful; so much so that we would heat up bricks and foment his limbs to the extent that we could; that would at least make him feel cared for. The pain would sometimes be so extreme that he couldn't sleep through the night. When the cold turned severe, we would run a heater in his bedroom. Sometimes we would also apply machines to give his body some heat. During such times, our cook Sudama and Saheb's typist Nanak Chand Rattu would be of help.

Even a Drop of Alcohol Forbidden

Like his father, Dr Ambedkar too had no addictions at all. Despite living in Western countries, he had never touched a drop of liquor. Doctor Saheb was an embodiment of integrity, high character, purity and gentlemanliness. The doctors had suggested that he should take a spoonful of brandy during the winter and a little bit of beer during the summer as medicines, but the thought of consuming alcohol was intolerable for him. He told me in clear terms, 'I don't care what happens to me, but I shall not take a drop of alcohol.' But after all that, it was necessary to administer it as medicine; therefore, I had got Rattu to fetch a bottle of brandy. Since he was not going to take it directly, we strategized: we tried to conceal a spoonful of brandy in Coca Cola or lemon juice and slip it to him, but he would immediately smell it and wave it violently away from his mouth, often spilling the drink. Finally, we gave up this ruse. Saheb never touched a drop of liquor in his life.

His health was slipping with every passing day. The tiniest of exertions would make him breathless. He had become so lean that his clothes had begun to hang loose on him. We were required to call over our Muslim tailor and get his clothes altered.

The swings continued. Saheb writes to Vitthal Kadam on 8 June 1955:

> '. . . The last quarter of the last year and the first quarter of this year have been bad for me. I have been more often ill than well. That is why I have not been able to write to you. My work had also to be suspended. I have just resumed it.'

On 5 July 1955, he again wrote to Kadam:

> 'I have just got out of my illness.'

Perpetual Worry

Despite his health being poor, his reading and writing continued unabated. However much we protested, his response would always be: 'Just this little bit', or 'Just a line or two of writing to do'. The visible-invisible impact of all this work kept happening. He would be in rigors when he read in the newspapers about the injustices and atrocities perpetrated upon the Dalits and be livid at the indifference of the government. Freedom had been gained, the Constitution had been implemented, but the atrocities on the Dalits had not waned a whit. Saheb had therefore risen in rebellion and begun mulling over the possibility of writing a well-corroborated paper for the United Nations Organization with the tentative title of 'A Case for the Untouchables'. He had gathered a number of newspaper cuttings reporting on these injustices and atrocities.

Activities Related to Educational Work

We went to Mumbai in the August of 1955 to get Saheb's health investigated. Our stay then was on the first floor of Jairaj House in Colaba. The People's Education Society was always scraping and scrounging to meet the expenditure of running its colleges. Doctor Saheb gave as much importance to character and moral conduct as he gave to education. He believed that the characterless among the capitalists gathered their wealth through illegitimate means and by exploiting the poor. He did not want this kind of money to be used for the sacrosanct purpose of imparting education, or in return for christening sacred buildings like educational institutions in their names.

For collecting funds for our educational enterprises, we had prepared a request leaflet. At the request of Doctor Saheb, Prime Minister Nehru had sent a message. Saheb had modified it by adding a paragraph outlining the goals and deeds of the People's Education Society and requested him to send a fresh message. He wrote to Nehru:

> 'I am writing this from Bombay. I had hoped to see you personally and get your message rectified. But my doctors have prohibited me from undertaking any journey as I am unable to stand fatigue.'

We had gone to Aurangabad in October both for rest and for some work related to Milind College. Principal Chitnis had established a students' Bodhi Mandal. Varale's son Bhalchandra was the secretary of this mandal. This mandal decided to invite Saheb to deliver a lecture on Buddhism. But since Saheb was not keeping well, he turned down the invitation, making the boy feel very disappointed. Actually, Saheb had quite a lot of affection for Bhalchandra and admired him for his enterprise. I too had a lot of regard for him. Hence, I told Saheb, 'Aho, this boy has come to you with such a lot of hope. Say yes to him. Why disappoint him?' Saheb finally gave his assent. Principal Chitnis had also come with Bhalchandra.

A few days later, Bhalchandra came and said, 'Baba, you are delivering an address tomorrow. I have come to remind you.' Saheb told him, 'I am not feeling well. I won't be able to come.' I told him to go and to return the next day. 'If Saheb feels well enough, we will take him along.'

When Bhalchandra came the next day, Saheb snapped at him, 'I had already told you that I am not keeping well! I won't be able to deliver a lecture. Why have you come back?' Bhalchandra was quite crestfallen. I then intervened and said, 'Aho, you have already committed yourself to delivering a lecture. He has gone and made all the arrangements. He's bought bouquets and garlands. Go and speak there for a little while. Don't disappoint the poor boy.' Saheb then turned to me and said, 'Look, I can't go for the lecture. You pay him for the bouquets and garlands if you want to and finish off the nuisance.' But finally, we brought him round and took him to deliver his lecture. He talked on *dwesh-moolak* [vicious] and *prem-moolak* [loving] anger that occur in the Dhammapada. It was in this meeting that he christened the extensive precincts of the college as 'Nagasena Vana'.

There was a professor named B.G. Gokhale who later went to America as a professor. He was quite learned in Buddhism. Saheb wrote to him on 4 November 1955, asking for his help in academic matters for the People's Education Society, in which he also talked about his health:

> 'I have received your letter of October 20, 1955 which has been forwarded to me at Aurangabad, where I have come in search of health.'

Love for Moral Conduct and Character

Saheb gave great importance to moral conduct, integrity and character. Let me relate to you a memory in this regard from Aurangabad. We were staying on the upper floor of the Railway Hotel. By a matter of chance, [a matinee idol of those times]* had arrived there and was staying on the ground floor. My brother Balu and Bhalchandra Varale had gone for some shopping; when they returned, they ran into him and brought him up to meet Saheb. The actor wanted to offer help for the educational institution. Saheb told him that he had a dislike for people of the cinema world on account of their morality and character. The film star defended his profession and said that not all people were like that. Saheb rendered him speechless by recounting to him the scandals of a number of actors and actresses. The actor looked extremely uncomfortable. He told Saheb, 'I am not in agreement with you.' At which Saheb retorted, 'Because I speak the truth and truth is bitter.' On hearing this acerbic retort, the movie star got up in a huff and left. For a few moments, the atmosphere was quite tense.

Breaking this silence, my brother Balu told him, 'You should not have been so brusque with him. Our institutions could have received thousands of rupees from him as donation. He wanted to help.'

Saheb flared up at this and said, 'What are you saying? Money that has been acquired by corrupt means after selling one's integrity and character I have never accepted and shall never accept. I don't care if my institutions close down, but I shall not conduct the sacred work of the acquisition of knowledge through money earned by immoral means.'

There is the other example of Saheb literally driving away the famous theatre man Patthe Bapurao by telling him, 'I don't want so much as a shell from a person who makes his money by getting untouchable women to dance on the stage.' A number of capitalists had expressed their readiness to help on condition that the institutions be named after them, but Saheb never accepted money that was earned by illegal means.

Theatrical Performance of *Yuga Yatra*

The staging of *Yuga Yatra*, a play written by Professor Chitnis, was organized by the Bodhi Mandal on 20 November 1955. It was wintertime and Saheb feared that he would fall ill by staying out in the cold. I intervened and said, 'We will watch the play for twenty-odd minutes and return.' Bhalchandra Varale said, 'Baba, I shall arrange for your seating where you will not have any problem of cold.' Accordingly, he arranged for our seating in an enclosed room. Chitnis had delineated the miserable state of the untouchables starting from the Ramayana era up to Dr Ambedkar's times. The play began at 9.30 p.m. We had gone for twenty or twenty-five minutes, but the play was so gripping that we had no consciousness of either the cold wind or the lateness of the hour. We stayed on right till the end. Saheb lavished genuine praise upon the actors as well as upon Chitnis. At the initiative of Bhalchandra, we posed for a group photograph with the entire team.

Saheb had so loved the play that when the historical event of religious conversion took place in Nagpur on 14 October 1956, the play was performed on the dhamma deeksha stage as per Saheb's desire.

Sacred Text on Buddhism

Saheb believed that the Buddhists of India should have a religious book along the lines of the Bible among the Christians. Accordingly, in 1951, he had taken in hand the mammoth task of writing a book on the Buddha's life and philosophy. He had brought this historic book to near completion by the early days of 1956. He had undertaken an in-depth study of whatever Pali books he could get from across the world and books written by foreigners and Indians on the Buddha's life and philosophy. This book was typed out by Nanak Chand Rattu and Parkash Chand. He made considerable alterations to his original manuscript, wrote out new chapters and rearranged the sequence because he wanted it to be a flawless document. He had first thought of the title 'Bible of Buddhism' for the book, but he got a few limited copies printed for private distribution under the title *The Buddha and His Gospel*, which he dispatched to Hindu and Buddhist scholars in India and abroad, as well as to renowned universities, for their comments. But the response was not as much as was expected. Since his health had been failing rapidly, he had wanted the book to be published as early as possible. He wrote to his colleague Shantaram Shankar Rege, the librarian at Siddharth College, 'I am in a hurry.'

He then added a few more chapters to *The Buddha and His Gospel*, changed the title to *The Buddha and His Dhamma* and handed over the responsibility for its printing to the librarian of Siddharth College, S.S. Rege. Saheb would constantly instruct Rege on what the shape of the book should be, what kind of paper, how many lines on each page, what posture of Lord Buddha's hand on each page, what typeface, what cover, what binding—in short, every little minute thing about this incomparable book.

Later, we got busy with the work of religious conversion and his attention was diverted from the book. The biggest tragedy, of course, was that this book could not be published during his lifetime. It was after his passing away that the People's Education Society got the book published on 19 November 1957. Saheb had written the preface of this priceless book on 15 March 1956, which he had revised on 6 April 1956. Again, on the eve of his passing away, that is on 5 December, he had made some corrections and improvements with his own hands. But this preface was not printed in the book. He has given me credit for the help and participation he received from me in the writing of this book.[56] The reason this preface was prevented from being printed by some self-interested persons is quite obvious: the credit given to me by Saheb would have harmed their political interests if it were to reach the public. I have included that entire preface for the readers at an appropriate place in this book.

Pure and Selfless Public Character

Yeshwant, alias Bhaiyya, lived in Mumbai and worked as a salaried employee of the Buddha Bhushan Printing Press. Shantaram Anaji Upsham worked as the treasurer of almost all of Saheb's institutions. We would often get complaints that Yeshwant interfered in all the dealings of the organization. Finally, Saheb wrote to Yeshwant in disgust on 26 February 1956. Without even bothering to address his only son as 'My dear Yeshwant', he got straight into the letter:

> This is to inform you that I have received several communications from Mr. Upsham that you are not allowing him to conduct his duty as Accountant and Cashier of the Boudha Bhushan Printing Press. You seem to be under the impression that by these tactics, you will be getting possession of the press. I am writing to warn you that [the] press is public property – neither yours nor mine and it is not possible to allow a public account to be misappropriated by an [sic] public individual.
>
> Your conduct has been utterly disgraceful. You have misappropriated several hundred rupees and although many concessions have been given to you, you have not cleared yourself. I write this final letter to tell you that you had better hand over charge to Upsham and not disturb him in performing out [sic] his duties. If I don't hear from you that you have acted in accordance with my last and final direction which I am giving you, I shall not hesitate to turn you out of the press and also to prosecute [you] for the defaultication [sic] of this warning.
>
> I am coming to Bombay in the last week of February and I want to have this matter cleared up before my arrival. The blame for the consequences will be entirely yours. I take no responsibility for the maintenance of you or your family. You have received more than your share. I am sending a copy of this letter to Upsham.
>
> Yours,
>
> B. R. Ambedkar[57]

Training School of Politics

Saheb opened a training school in July 1953 named 'Training School of Politics' under the supervision of the librarian [of Siddharth

College] S.S. Rege, with the following goals: to give currency to democratic concepts, to explain to the public the importance of democracy, to provide well-trained candidates to political parties, to keep the Lok Sabha and the state assemblies well supplied with deserving, well-trained, expert people's representatives for giving appropriate direction to political activities and to apprise the people's representatives of their rights and responsibilities. A number of renowned personalities from various walks of life came to the school to offer guidance to the students. Saheb himself had wanted to deliver a few lectures, but he couldn't manage it because of work pressure. Saheb was the founder–director of this school and he had appointed S.S. Rege as the secretary.

Last Meeting in Mumbai

On 1 May 1956, Saheb delivered an emotionally charged address in the Rajya Sabha on the organization of the states on a linguistic basis. After that we went to Mumbai. The Mumbai workers had organized a Buddha birth anniversary celebration programme under the presidentship of the then premier [as the chief minister was then called] of the Bombay State, Balasaheb Kher. We were not sure whether we would be able to attend the meeting because we were due to leave for Delhi, but since we could not manage a reservation right up to 12 May, the workers insisted on having us come over. Once the word got around that Saheb would attend the meeting, Nare Park filled up to overflowing. This turned out to be the last public speech Saheb would deliver in Mumbai. He first explained the importance of self-respect, and after making a well-supported comparison of Hinduism and Buddhism, emphatically declared that the two were not the same. Savarkar had written an article in the *Kesari* titled 'Buddhachya Aatataayi Ahimsecha Shirachchhed' [roughly translated as the 'Decapitation of the Buddha's Impetuous Non-violence']. In that context, Saheb said [translated from Marathi]:

> 'I just don't understand what Savarkar is trying to say. He should express his position in clear words, I am capable of answering him . . . Not Savarkar alone, anybody who has any question to ask on Buddhism should ask me openly; I have the daring to answer them.
>
> '. . . The vast bhikshu organization that Bhagwan Buddha had, 75 per cent of them were Brahmins, does Savarkar know that? He shouldn't forget that pundits like Sāriputta and Moggallāna were Brahmins. I have to ask Savarkar the question: who were the Peshwas? Were they bhikshus? So, how did the Englishmen snatch away their kingdom? Therefore, one should not place much trust in such irresponsible people. Some people say that Savarkar spewed poison, but I say that he spewed out the hell that resides in his stomach.'[58]

After analysing the decline of Buddhism, Saheb said, 'When the Buddhism wave arrives, it shall never return.'

Colossal Book-Writing

Alongside handling with great competence such variegated responsibilities as the work for the upliftment of the Dalits, political leadership, work for the establishment of equality, the work done towards the construction of a nation, Saheb created a colossal treasure house of published and unpublished books that leaves one stupefied. His health had steadily been deteriorating, but there was never a break in his unremitting reading and writing. His book-writing continued till the very last moment of his life. Among his unpublished books, *The Buddha and His Dhamma* was on the way to being published, but unfortunately it couldn't get published during his lifetime. Also, the preface he wrote for that excellent book could not be included in the book, which is a matter of great surprise and great shame.

His love for books is well known. There were no facilities like xeroxing and microfilming during those times; therefore, if he didn't have a rare book in his collection, he was quite prepared to literally write it out by hand or type it out. This was how he made copies of a few of Mahatma Phule's books, I remember. He had got some books from the British Library typed and sent over from London. His devotion to and craving for knowledge was so intense that once a book landed in his hands, he would forget the world and focus night and day on reading it and making notes on it. There would be a number of subjects floating in his head. Once a subject or an issue struck his fancy, that would be it—the outline of a book would be readied immediately. Then there would be the shifting and shuffling of chapters and the table of contents. It wasn't as if the writing would begin from the first chapter; it could begin from any chapter. Once the rough draft was ready, there would be corrections, changes, the inter-change of chapters. This would go on over and over again till the day the printing actually began.

Saheb did almost all his writing in English; thus, he could place the question of the untouchables on the world platform and draw the attention of the greatest thinkers of the world towards their issues. Since the language of governmental administration in subservient India and of its rulers was English, it became possible to present the grievances and the various difficulties of the untouchables to the government, thus compelling it to pay attention to their problems. Along with mastery in English, he enjoyed complete proficiency in Marathi. To bring awareness among his illiterate people, he would deliver his lectures, hold his discussions and deliver his presidential addresses in meetings and conferences in Marathi and thus forge public opinion. Beyond this, the letter writer and essayist Ambedkar one sees in the editorials and lighter articles in *Mook Nayak*, *Bahishkrut Bharat* and *Janata* leaves one amazed. He would freely intersperse his writings with sayings, idioms, fables and traditional folklore to ensure that his points came out clearly. One can experience satire, sarcasm, defiance, logic, argumentation and many such skills in every one of his words.

However bad his health, whatever bother with the eyes, his reading and writing never came to a halt. His mandate was that there should always be a stool or a table in the right corner of every room with a writing pad, a pen and a pencil kept on it. If ever a new issue, a fresh thought struck him at any given moment, particularly in the odd hours of the night, he should be able to grope his way to the writing pad and scribble out the thought (often without even seeing the page), so he could put the thought to use the next day. He would often say that a thought just flashes in one's head at any given moment. There is no saying whether it will ever return, so it is best to jot it down immediately so that it can be deliberated upon later. This was how his book writing proceeded.

A number of his unpublished books were all written and ready; some just had a skeleton of chapters; yet others had some chapters ready, some were half-written, and some were not written at all. A mere look at the list of titles of these unpublished books gives an idea of the range of his thoughts and brings to mind the chain of books. Some of the unpublished books and their chapters that I can remember are these:

1. Philosophy in [sic] Hinduism
2. India and Communism
3. Symbols of Hinduism
4. Essays on Bhagavat Geeta
5. Buddha or Karl Marx
6. Essays on Untouchability
7. The Case of the Untouchable
8. Riddles in Hinduism
9. Riddles in Indian Politics
10. Riddle of Gita
11. Riddle of Vishnu

12. [This number has been missed]
13. Riddle of Women
14. Essays on Castes
15. Revolution and Counter-revolution in Ancient India
16. What Brahmins Have Done to the Hindus? [sic]
17. Can I be a Hindu?
18. Waiting for a Visa (autobiography)

Some of these books are complete, some are half-done, while some have not been written at all. Some are independent books, some are chapters for some unnamed book, some others are essays that have emerged from the chain of thoughts. From the first thought to the second, from the second to the third, this was how his reading, thinking and writing would proceed. All of Saheb's handwritten manuscripts and other documents were under the charge of the Administrator-General, Mumbai. The government showed readiness to get all his writings published and my grandson [Prakash] and I gave our consent to it. Accordingly, four volumes have already been published and the fifth is on the way to being published.[59] All of the Ambedkarites, students of history, thinkers, researchers and I myself consider ourselves eternally indebted to the Government of Maharashtra for this praiseworthy initiative. I do want to publicly congratulate the Government of Maharashtra for this. The controversy kicked up by the Riddles[60] [in Hinduism] clearly demonstrates how Doctor Saheb's thoughts hold a mirror to facts and churn up public sentiment.

Saheb had expressed his intention of writing his autobiography in several meetings and interviews. He had even taken in hand the task of writing a draft. I think he had even handwritten some seventy or eighty pages of it under the title 'Waiting for a Visa'. Along with his autobiography, he had also wanted to write a biographical book on Gandhi. He would often say, 'I alone understand Gandhi well.' It was his desire to write a biographical book on Gandhiji's statements and deeds, but he hadn't begun this enterprise.

In the same way, he was very keen to write on Mahatma Jyotiba Phule. He had wanted to write a comprehensive biography of Phule that would include an evaluation of his revolutionary and historically significant deeds. He had gathered all the books written on Jyotiba for that purpose. Where copies were not available, he had got those books either copied by hand or typewritten. He had carried to Delhi several reference books borrowed from the Asiatic Library, Mumbai, and the Itihas Sanshodhak Mandal [Historical Research Institute] in Pune, of which he was a member. Likewise, Acharya Atre had collected artefacts, books, documents and other material for his movie *Mahatma Phule*. Saheb had called over from him all the material that would be useful for writing a biography, which Atre had sent over with great pleasure. But he couldn't get the Phule biography started either. If he had, Saheb would have created an authentic and well-supported presentation of Phule's work.

Dhamma Prachar Sabha, Delhi

The Delhi branch of the Bharatiya Bauddhajan Samiti [Indian Council of Buddhists] organized a Dhamma Prachar Sabha [Propagation Meeting] on 10 June 1956 on the extensive grounds of Ambedkar Bhavan, Delhi. We were present for the meeting. We had already started publicly propagating Buddhism; this meeting was a part of the same exercise. In his speech on this occasion, Saheb emphasized the importance of Buddhism and said that the ahimsa [non-violence] of Buddhism was based upon the acknowledgement of the need to kill and the readiness to kill.

He finally exhorted his audience to take the path of Buddhism to give their children a bright future and to live a life of self-respect.

The Buddha Prachar Samiti had organized a second meeting in Delhi on 24 June 1956 at which we were present as the chief guests. Saheb stated in his speech that Buddhism was realistic and was based on the principle of equality. The only religion that stood true in all aspects was Buddhism. He said that Buddhism should be embraced only if it appealed to the intellect, otherwise not.

Elphinstone College Function

Dr Ambedkar had passed his BA examination from Elphinstone College in 1912. To celebrate its centenary year, the organizers had invited the college's renowned alumni to participate in the lecture series organized for the occasion. It was proposed that these lectures would later be published in the form of a book. Accordingly, an invitation arrived from the then principal of the college, N.L. Ahmad. Responding to him on 26 August, Saheb told him that he would like to speak on the subject: 'What is Democracy and What are Its Prospects in India?' But he further wrote:

> 'I am not sure that I shall be able to address the gathering because of my ill-health; my eye-sight [sic] is also poor and I have been advised by my doctor not to put strain on my eyes. It may be that by the time the date arrives, my eye-sight [sic] may improve and I may be able to attend the function.'

[. . .]*

Affection for Party Workers

Doctor Saheb showered boundless love on his colleagues and workers and took motherly care of every one of them. This memory of August 1956 is worth mentioning. The present president of the People's Education Society, Ghanshyam Talvatkar, had come to us in Delhi along with a colleague. He had been called for a job in Akashvani. Since he was working at the Society, he had come to ask for Saheb's advice. A few months earlier, on 14 April 1956, Talvatkar had taken the help of his colleagues and edited a book called *Parimal*, dealing with Saheb's memories. When Talvatkar came, I said, 'Look, this gentleman has printed a book dealing with your memories.'

Saheb responded, 'Yes, I am going to write my memoirs.'

Talvatkar stayed with his friend for two or three days. When Saheb asked him whether he had seen Delhi, Talvatkar said he had not.

Saheb then told me, 'Let's show him Delhi.'

We then took Talvatkar out and showed him the Qutub Minar, the Red Fort, the Parliament House, the Rashtrapati Bhavan, and other sights. Each time I took him out, Saheb would sit in the car reading a book. Even during meals, he would pay particular attention to him and have him served well. He was always extremely alert to his workers getting their tea, food, etc. at the proper time. He would also personally take care of their sleeping arrangements.

The Historic Religious Conversion at Nagpur

Saheb's health had been sinking rapidly since June–July 1956. Walking was a far cry, he could not even sit without help. It was the city-dwellers who had benefitted the most from Saheb's efforts; but the untouchable people of the villages were ignorant and economically subservient.

Saheb would feel quite upset at seeing spite and envy among his main associates. I would try to divert him towards religion to the extent that I could. Saheb would say in exasperation, 'I have no faith in all these educated people. Once they are educated, once they get a place of authority, car, bungalow, a fair-skinned wife, they are done. They will go anywhere for greed; but my people from the villages are steadfast. From here on, I'll spend my life for the upliftment of these village people and for propagating religion.'

My urging with Saheb would continue: 'Let's do religion work.' Since he was fully aware of the state of his health, when he got into a conversation with his colleagues, he would say [translated from Marathi]:

> 'I have been delaying the religion question till now, but my health has been slipping away on a daily basis and I feel that my end is nearing. I have been pulling along exclusively on the strength of my willpower, but this willpower too has its limitations. Therefore I won't push back this religion question any further. Whoever wants to convert with me, I shall welcome them. If they don't want to come with me, they are free to go their way. Even if I don't have a single person to convert with me, my wife and I are changing our religion, that is certain.'

Those of his associates who were interested in politics were of the opinion that the religion conversion ceremony should be postponed because the 1957 elections were round the corner. The fear they carried was that after conversion, they would run into technical difficulties in standing from the constituencies reserved for the untouchables.

We had earlier decided that we would first go to Sarnath for our conversion and then hold a public ceremony in Mumbai, but we were still not being able to decide on a place acceptable to all. The leaders from Vidarbha and Mumbai wanted the event to happen in their area. Every one of them was trying to bring Saheb round to their line of persuasion. Saheb had told Wamanrao Godbole of Nagpur, the general secretary of the Bharatiya Bauddhajan Samiti, on 23 July 1956, that the conversion would happen in Mumbai. People like Bhandare of Mumbai and Bhaurao Gaikwad of Nashik wanted the conversion ceremony to be in Mumbai; while Godbole, Avale Babu, Khobragade and others wanted it to be in Nagpur. The solution we found for this dilemma was that the first public function of the conversion would happen in the area of the group that gathered the largest number of signatures. The leaders got busy accordingly, and since Wamanrao Godbole brought in the largest number of signatures in the least amount of time, Nagpur was finalized for the dhamma deeksha ceremony. Even otherwise, Saheb had a special attraction for Nagpur because, from the perspective of Buddhism, Nagpur had historical significance. The people of the Naga race had lived there, and these Nagas were Buddhists; hence the name Nagpur. Hence Saheb wrote to Godbole:

> 'I had declined to come to Nagpur for my conversion. On further consideration I have come to the conclusion that Nagpur is the best. I would, therefore, like you to come to Delhi so that we could discuss what arrangements we could make in order to make the ceremony successful.'

The question now was: at whose hands should the initiation happen? After discussing the matter with a number of people and some bhikshus, it was decided to take the deeksha at the hands of Mahasthavir Chandramani of Kushinara, as he was the senior-most in age. On behalf of both of us, therefore, Saheb wrote to revered Chandramani requesting him to be the priest for the occasion. He wrote to him on 24 September 1956:

> Revered Bhante,
>
> This is to inform you that I and my wife have decided to embrace Buddhism. The Ceremony is to take place at Nagpur on the 14th of October, 1956. The time of the ceremony is fixed in the morning between 9 and 11. It is our great wish that you should officiate at the ceremony. You being the oldest monk of India, we think it would be appropriate to have the Ceremony performed by you.
>
> We realize that your physical condition may make it difficult for you to go to Nagpur, but we can manage to provide the transport from Kushinara to Nagpur, either by air or by train, and all other arrangements for your living in Nagpur. We can send

someone to take you from Kushinara to Nagpur. Please let us know whether you can accept the invitation of ours.

Yours sincerely,
B. R. Ambedkar

A press-note was sent to the Press Trust of India announcing that the conversion would take place on Ashok *vijaya-dashami*, 14 October 1956. This news was flashed in newspapers all across the country. Saheb's health was not good at all. It was through the exercise of sheer willpower that, against all odds, he was determined to go through with the conversion. He had become so weak that even sitting for any length of time had become difficult.

We had kept the mode of our travel to Nagpur secret for security reasons. We had earlier decided to go by train, but later opted to go by air. Complete secrecy had been maintained about our arrival. Rattu was sent on 5 October 1956 to buy two air tickets for the 11th. Saheb also gave Rattu a letter to hand over to the airport official, reading:

> 'I propose to go to Nagpur by Air Service on the morning of 11th October, 1956. I am being accompanied by my wife and an attendant, whose services I need very much on account of my physical disability to walk.'

As planned, we alighted from the morning flight at the Nagpur airport. Varale, Kawade and Godbole were present to welcome us with bouquets and garlands. Godbole had arranged for our stay on the second floor of Shyam Hotel, to which we were taken directly from the airport. Two rooms had been reserved for us. We took our lunch there.

Although the news of our arrival had been kept confidential, it did leak out after we had arrived. Saheb got into a discussion with his colleagues, offering them advice. After finishing with our breakfast, we personally went to take a look at the pavilions and other arrangements made on the huge open grounds near the Chokhamela Hostel in Shraddhanandpeth. This fourteen-acre plot of land had become the Dhamma Deeksha Bhoomi [the Land of Religious Initiation].

I had stated earlier that a few political leaders had discussed the issue of postponing the deeksha ceremony till after the 1957 elections, and this had reached Saheb's ears. Therefore, he had called a meeting of the prominent workers on the evening of the 13th at Shyam Hotel and admonished all of them:

> 'I am most certainly going for this religion conversion. Those who are not inclined to convert are free to do what they want. I shall only understand from this that those who come with me and my people are mine.'

After such a clear and sharp admonition, who could have dared to go against him?

14 October dawned and we awoke at six o'clock. Saheb was not feeling well, and he was running a mild temperature. I took my bath, put on a white sari and got Saheb out of bed. I arranged for hot water for his bath. After he had bathed, Rattu and I got him dressed in a white silk *dhotar* and the sparkling white kurta and jacket we had got sewn in Delhi specially for the initiation ceremony. He wore his dhotar in the Bengali style, but because he was not used to it, it didn't sit properly; as a remedy, I got him to wear a leather belt to keep it in place.

The fourteen-acre Deeksha Bhoomi was jam-packed with men and women. Hundreds of thousands of people—young and old, men and women along with their children—had gathered enthusiastically at the Deeksha Bhoomi to receive their deeksha at the hands of their liberator. Mahasthavir Chandramani and Saheb were received at the car and escorted to the stage. When Saheb stood to make himself visible to his hundreds of thousands of followers, the sky reverberated with the sound of their applause. A bronze statue of Lord Buddha was placed on a table at the front of the stage. The chairs for seating us had been placed close by. Varale's daughter, Indumati, sang in her mellifluous voice a welcome song—*Aalaa Dalitaanchaa Bhagwan* [the god of the Dalits has arrived]—which had been penned by her father.

After that, the humongous assembly observed a minute's silence to pay tribute to Saheb's virtuous father—and my father-in-law—Subhedar Ramjirao. After the bhikshus who had arrived from Burma and Ceylon finished reciting their prayers to Lord Buddha, Mahasthavir Chandramani stepped forward, had us recite the trisharana and the panchsheel and gave us the deeksha of Buddhism. We lowered our heads before the statue of the Buddha with deep reverence and hailed the lord thrice. Saheb had never bowed his head before anybody in his entire life; now, for the first time, he humbly bowed at the feet of the Buddha. Devipriya Walisinha of the Mahabodhi Society garlanded us and gave us a statue of the Buddha as a gift. Saheb had taken a pledge at the Yevle Conference in 1935: 'I was born a Hindu, but I shall not die a Hindu.' He converted that historic vow into reality on 14 October at Nagpur by embracing Buddhism.

After that, Saheb got up to give the deeksha of the religion of the Buddha to the massive assemblage. He got them to recite the trisharana, the panchsheel and the twenty-two-point oath.[61] This, by my reckoning, was an event that had never happened before in all of human history, nor would it ever be replicated. This is the one single example of a single person initiating millions of his followers into a religion. What the founder of no other religion had done, Doctor Saheb caused to happen; it is only right that he is referred to as Bodhisattva [the Buddha in the making].

That evening, the Manohar Chitnis play *Yug Yatra* was performed on the very stage from where the dhamma deeksha was given. Hundreds of thousands of newly initiated Buddhists watched the play. This too constitutes a record in the staging of plays.

The conversion ceremony had finally happened, true, but the strain it caused on Saheb's health was enormous. He became totally enervated. He just lay down in a state of listlessness after returning to the hotel. The next day a colleague came along with Varale, placed his head at Saheb's feet and began crying incontinently, grieving because he could not be present to receive deeksha at the hands of Saheb. Saheb pacified him and got a rug spread on the floor of the room. He then had a few incense sticks and candles lit, got him to recite the trisharana and the panchsheel, had him take the twenty-two-point oath and initiated him. The man was altogether beholden.

The next morning, 15 October, a public meeting was held on the Deeksha Bhoomi. Saheb delivered his historic speech, again endorsing the finality of his conversion. The Nagpur Municipality felicitated him that evening and presented him with a Citation of Honour. During his response to the felicitation, Saheb seriously criticized Nehru's policies and personality.

Chandrapur Conversion Function

Saheb's colleague Barrister Rajabhau Khobragade had organized a conversion programme in Chandrapur on the 16th. He was importunate that we be present for the function. The strain of the Nagpur function had been so intense that Saheb was completely drained, but on account of the insistence of the workers and since it was a conversion event, we found it imperative to go. The travel from Nagpur to Chandrapur had to be done by car, which caused great inconvenience to Saheb. To top it all was extreme exhaustion and a bad car journey! His tooth had started to play up too, wearing him down further. We had Rattu, Khobragade, Bhaurao Gaikwad, Varale, Avale Babuji and others for company. The conversion programme was slated for 9 p.m. We carried Saheb to the site, but the stage was at quite a height, so Saheb had to be literally lifted up to the stage. Thousands of men and women of all ages were present along with their children to receive deeksha. They were lustily roaring the names of the Buddha and of Saheb. Despite his extreme weariness, Saheb got the crowd to recite the trisharana and the panchsheel and to take the oath. The enormous swarm of people was aching to hear some utterance from the mouth of their revered leader, but Saheb was far too gone in terms of enthusiasm and vitality to oblige. His ear had begun to ache too. We returned to the dak bungalow immediately after the function, and I administered medicine to him. I also put drops in his ear, but relief wouldn't arrive. Saheb had no dinner that evening, not even a cup of tea. He groaned and keened all night because of the pain in his ear. None of us could get a wink of sleep either. The next day we decided to take the train to Nagpur because the road journey the previous day had been horrendous.

Saheb had been battling against his health through sheer willpower on account of the extreme desire for the conversion. But now that the conversion had been put behind, the body had begun to pack up and its response had become tardy.

Contentment Post Conversion

After returning to Delhi, I requested Saheb to go for complete rest. To ensure that he stayed in bed, I placed restrictions on his sittings and meetings. Because of the tremendous strain he had suffered, he had become utterly fatigued, but the sense of gratification at having succeeded in living up to his pledge was audible in everything he said. For a few days I compelled him to take complete rest and some energy started returning to his limbs. We were utterly thrilled at the conversion programme turning out to be grander than we had anticipated. Two large albums of the pictures of the functions had been sent to us. A look at the pictures and another look at the tremendous response gave him great joy and satisfaction. He would say that he wanted to do many such conversion rallies across the country.

A letter arrived from Devipriya Walisinha, the secretary of the Mahabodhi Society, felicitating Saheb on the resounding success of the conversion function. Saheb responded to him with a lot of excitement:

> 'It certainly was a great event and the crowd [that] came forward for the conversion was beyond my expectation. Thank the Buddha, it all went well.
>
> 'I am glad you realize that having begun the task well, we have to look to its continual progress in the future. We have to consider ways and means for imparting knowledge of Buddhism to the masses who have accepted this Dhamma and will accept it on my word. We should, no doubt, train a large number of workers to teach the Dhamma to the people, but the best agents for carrying out the same are the Bhikkus. They could carry a great [deal] of prestige with them which no layman could do. [The] [o]nly difficulty with the Bhikkus is that they don't care to learn the language of the people. I am afraid the Sangha will have to modify its outlook and instead of becoming recluse, they should become like the Christian missionaries: social workers and social preachers . . .'

Kathmandu World Buddhist Council

We had focused all our attention on Buddhism. Our minds and bodies were completely engrossed in the Buddha. Since the conversion function at Nagpur, Saheb was driven by the desire to visit the Buddhist pilgrimage sites. He had been mesmerized by the character, the philosophy and the sacrifice of the Buddha.

Saheb's health had become feeble to the extent of being immediately visible, putting all of us into deep anxiety. There was nothing left now in Saheb's consciousness except the Buddha. He had lost interest in politics. The fourth General Conference of the World Fellowship of Buddhists was being organized in Kathmandu, Nepal, for which Saheb had received an invitation. Saheb's health was down in the dumps, but due to his obsessive attraction for Buddhist philosophy, he had become unyielding. I therefore suggested that we should consult Dr Malvankar. The doctor was called over. After he had examined him, it was finally decided that Malvankar would also come along with us. When Saheb informed his colleagues Varale and Principal Chitnis, they too agreed to accompany us. My brother Balu also came on board. It was decided that we would fly to Kathmandu via Patna. M. Jyoti, who was working for the Buddhist Parishad at Calcutta, was taking special care of us and had made arrangements for our tour. We were readying ourselves for our journey when an incident took place that tested us to the core.

Rajgraha Expansion—a Testing Event

Saheb had hired a contractor named Mavani for some expansion work on Rajgraha. A conflict arose over the payment of the enhanced amount; we didn't have the money to pay the enhanced amount. The contractor went to court and a court notice arrived. Saheb then asked a lawyer named Kale to fight the case for us and told him to file an application stating that he was not in a position to travel on account of bad health and would therefore not be able to present himself in court. Kale completed all the formalities and presented himself on the date of the hearing.

But the judge in whose court this case was to be heard was very likely a staunch Hindu fanatic, because he ordered that Rs 40,000 be immediately deposited. Not satisfied with that, he wanted to know why Ambedkar couldn't present himself in court for the date if he could travel to Nagpur for the conversion.

When the lawyer Kale informed us about the court's decision, we became awfully worried. We didn't know how and from where we could gather such a large amount. We began thinking seriously. It was not in Saheb's nature to go begging to anybody, but the money had to be deposited; there was neither any alternative nor much time allowed for it. Therefore, at the end of our discussion, we decided to ask for this money from a person named Puranchand who was an engineer in the public works department of the Government of India. Puranchand belonged to a scheduled caste and Saheb had procured justice for him. Despite his education being a little less, Saheb had got him appointed. It had so happened that when Saheb was a minister in the Viceroy's Executive Council, a crack had developed in the Taj Mahal at Agra, which this Puranchand had managed to seal. Despite having done such an important job, he was refused the job in the hope of which he had done the work. The engineers had simply pushed him aside, filed the papers and closed the case. When Saheb got to know of this, he called for the file, got the matter properly investigated and called Puranchand over to Delhi. After having satisfied himself, he took the man to meet the governor-general and explained the entire matter to him. He respected the man's work and got him appointed as a deputy engineer. The government went further and recommended his name for the title of Rao Bahadur.

Even after the decision to borrow money from Puranchand had been taken, Saheb was extremely hesitant. He was not able to get himself round to it. But since there was no remedy, we pulled the car out. Since we had not taken a driver with us, I was at the wheel. I brought the car to a halt in the lawn of the man's bungalow. Saheb couldn't gather the pluck to go into the bungalow to ask for the money. Therefore, while he sat in the car, I went in and brought Puranchand out. Saheb continued to sit in the car and showed him the court's letter and requested him to lend the money. After spending so many years in the public works department, Puranchand had become quite an indecorous person. He had also forgotten about the favours he had received. 'I don't have any money,' he said in Hindi, 'but I'll ask my daughter. If she has it, I shall have it sent to your bungalow.' We returned home deeply dejected.

The next day, Puranchand's daughter came with Rs 20,000. Puranchand had avoided coming himself, perhaps because he wanted us to believe that the money was really his daughter's. This money, however, would not be enough to resolve the problem. Another 20,000 was needed. After some thought, I suggested that we should ask Chitre, who was then the secretary of the People's Education Society. Saheb could hardly have got a colleague as selfless as Chitre. He had made a major contribution to the raising of the People's Education Society. We called him and apprised him about our need. Chitre announced that the Society would take the basement of Rajgraha for its use and gave Rs 20,000 from the Society's account. There really had been no other way out.

The money had to be sent to Mumbai for payment. Saheb's state of health being what it was, letting him travel alone was beyond consideration and an air ticket for the two of us was unaffordable. Finally, I decided that I should go alone and deposit the money. Saheb, however, was quite worried. 'How can you go alone? You've got a lot of money with you! How will you manage all that?' But I just firmed up my mind, reassured Saheb and set off. Saheb, of course, continued to worry. For one reason: this was the first time I was travelling alone with a lot of money; for another, there was the uncertainty about the Mumbai money. Would I get it at all? Would I be able to deposit it within the given time? Saheb simply couldn't sit still. His prestige and honour were at stake; no wonder, therefore, that he bid me goodbye with an extremely agitated heart.

My brother Balu and Chitre had come to the airport to receive me. Chitre had been able to organize the remaining money. The next day I went to the court, deposited the Rs 40,000 and thus defused the crisis that had come upon our reputation.

As soon as the court work was over, I took the first flight to Delhi. When I reached home, Saheb was sitting in the veranda waiting for me anxiously. As soon as he saw me, he got up from his chair and said, impatiently, 'Ah, Sharu, you've come. Everything went off well? Could you deposit the money at the court? Did you have any problems?'

I first sat him back in the chair and said, 'Stop worrying now. Everything went off well. Chitre had made arrangements for the money, and that we have now deposited. No worries now.'

Heaving a sigh of relief, he said 'Aga, I have been sitting in this chair right from the time you left. I couldn't sleep through the night, I was so worried about you.'

Saheb was looking very run-down. I called the servant and chastised him, 'Why didn't you put Saheb to sleep? Why didn't you serve him his meals?'

The servant responded, 'Mai, I did ask Saheb again and again about meals and sleep, tried so much to reason with him, but he refused to budge from his chair. He's been waiting for you from the moment you left. He sat here all through the night.'

I felt terribly overwrought at hearing this. I immediately made an egg dish, buttered some bread and served him tea. That was how I got him to finally eat something.

We had borrowed from Puranchand in the first week of November. Within a month's time, Saheb passed away, raising the question of how this money would be returned. Puranchand started badgering me because I was in Delhi then. When I asked Yeshwant for help, he refused outright. What was I to do now? Finally, Puranchand filed a case in the court. Willy-nilly, I had to hire a lawyer too. Plenty of arguments took place in the court. Puranchand's daughter gave witness in the court, saying, 'That money was mine, and I had given it into the hands of Dr Ambedkar.' A lot of questions and answers followed. Finally, the court decided that since the money had been physically handed over to Dr Ambedkar, it was given to him alone.

Now that he was no more, the wife couldn't be held answerable for the money. Thus, it was through this court decision that this bother of Puranchand got shaken off.

The Journey to Kathmandu

We had decided to go to the Buddhist Council at Kathmandu via Patna. On 12 November 1956, Saheb, Dr Malvankar and I landed at around 2 p.m. at the Patna airport. My brother Balu, Principal Chitnis and Varale had set off from Mumbai by train and were waiting at the Patna airport to receive us. Saheb's health was just not good, but he had become completely fixated on attending the conference. We had to carry him off the aircraft to the VIP section of the airport. Dr Malvankar gave him pills and injections to reduce his discomfort, after which we put him to sleep. He lay listless for an hour or so. When he came to on his own, I served him some biscuits and tea. That brought a semblance of life into him. By then, it was time for the Kathmandu flight. Dr Malvankar and I then helped him board the aircraft and soon we were off. All through the flight, I was in a state of nervousness. It was a long journey, and we were going to a foreign land. It was while these thoughts were storming through my mind that we landed at the Kathmandu airport. M. Jyoti and other important officials had come to the airport to receive us. We were welcomed with a band and a guard of honour under a pavilion erected at the airport. Our stay had been arranged in the magnificent old palace of the king of Nepal, which was called 'Sheetal Nivas'. We were driven there in a special car. That was where the other important leaders and representatives of various countries of the world were housed.

The World Conference was inaugurated on 14 November 1956, at the hands of the Nepal monarch King Mahendra. The king had got Saheb seated next to him with great courtesy and deference. This honour was not granted to any of the other world leaders present there, which shows the esteem Saheb had gained in the world of Buddhism. Mahasthivir Chandramani and I were also sitting next to the king. After the inauguration ceremony was over, we returned to Sheetal Nivas.

The conference began on the day after the inauguration, but since Saheb was not feeling well, we returned to our room in half an hour's time. His treatment continued for the entire day as he lay listless, frustrated on account of being unable to participate in the conference that he had wanted so much to attend.

On the third day, as he was feeling marginally better, we went to see a pagoda of the Chinese people three or four miles away. Saheb gathered information on the pagoda from the Chinese gentleman who looked after the administration there. Saheb's state was so bad that he couldn't even sit up by himself. He was feeling deeply upset at not being able to participate in the conference. He would fret and fume in helplessness, saying, 'Even if I had been slightly better, I would have been able to do so much work.'

At Kathmandu, we got to know that the *shimpi* [tailor] community was also regarded as untouchable there. A few leaders of the untouchables came to meet Saheb, requesting permission to felicitate him in their locality. His health, however, would allow no such indulgence. I found a way out by suggesting to Varale that this programme could be held on the grounds of the Sheetal Nivas. Accordingly, the next day a small tea party was arranged during which the felicitation programme was held.

Since Saheb had not been able to participate in the conference because of ill health, a special address of Saheb was arranged on the last day in the king of Nepal's new hall. The king, Bhante Chandramani and all the representatives of the world had gathered with excitement and enthusiasm to listen to Saheb. In this address, Saheb made a comparative analysis of the philosophies and values of the Buddha and Karl Marx. He established that whatever Karl Marx had said, the Buddha had not only stated 2500 years earlier but had also implemented it. This address is well remembered as 'The Buddha and Karl Marx'.

Tour of Buddhist Pilgrimage Sites

After the conference was over, we chalked out a Buddhist pilgrimage, particularly of those places where the Lord had lived and roamed. Accordingly, on the 20th we went to the historically important township of Lumbini, the birthplace of Lord Gautam Buddha. We flew from Kathmandu to a makeshift airstrip a few miles away from Lumbini and travelled the rest of the distance by road. But this bus travel once again did Saheb in, compelling us to take him to the guest house for rest. Some tea and medicines revived him a little bit and we left for our round. We saw the images of Lord Buddha and Mahamaya etched near a memorial. We bowed to these images in reverence.

We then went to the 2500-year-old Ashoka Pillar. Saheb actually swung his arms round the pillar and hugged it. He then bowed his head in reverence and began crying incontinently. The thought of the glorious work of the Buddha and Emperor Ashoka had overwhelmed him. After spending a few hours there, we returned to the airstrip and then back to Kathmandu.

The next day [21 November] we flew from Kathmandu to Patna. We were due to go to Bodh Gaya from Patna, but since there were a few hours to go before our train arrived, we accepted the invitation of the Governor of Bihar, Rangrao Divakar,[62] for a meal and went to the Raj Bhavan. We left Patna late in the afternoon by train and reached Bodh Gaya late in the evening. Our stay had been arranged in the VIP guest house at the railway station.

We got up the next morning [23 November], finished our morning ablutions and had our breakfast. After I had given Saheb his medicines, we set off for Bodh Gaya by a special car. The first thing we did on reaching there was to take a holy sighting of the Bodhi

Tree. It was under this Bodhi Tree that Lord Buddha had gained enlightenment. After that we went to the Buddha vihara, where Saheb went down on his knees and recited the *trivaara* before the statue of Lord Buddha. He then began reciting his prayers in a deep, grave voice. We joined him in the recitation. After the prayers were over, Saheb stood before the statue in a charged state, looking unblinkingly and with deep concentration at it for a long time. Tears were flowing unchecked down his cheeks. He had become extremely overwrought.

We reached the Bodh Gaya railway station, from where we left for Benares. The news of our arrival had preceded us, resulting in a massive crowd waiting for us roaring out the names of Saheb and the Buddha. Our stay had been arranged in a well-appointed bungalow. The next morning [24 November] we reached Sarnath. All the arrangements for our meals and for our stay had been made by the Bhikshu Sangh. The Dhammapal Sangharika had constructed a huge vihara there. Looking at the extreme physical debility of Saheb, the four-wheeled chair that Dhammapal Sangharika had used was made available to us by the Sangha Nayak [the head of the Sangh] there. It doesn't need telling that nobody other than the Dhammapal had ever sat in that chair. We got Saheb to sit in the chair and took him around everywhere. Saheb was deeply impressed by the rare artefacts from Ashoka's times that he saw in the museum there.

We stayed in Sarnath for three days during which we went to visit a Chinese Buddha temple. One day we went to the Benares market where I purchased a few Benares silk saris. We also saw the temples on the banks of Benares. When we saw the filth scattered everywhere and the polluted water of the river Ganga, we couldn't help feeling nauseated.

On 26 November, we went to Gorakhpur from where we were to travel to Kushinara. A Sikh friend of Saheb's was waiting to receive us at Gorakhpur. He took us to his spacious and well-appointed bungalow. After we had finished with tea and refreshments, he provided two cars for us in which we set off with him. Kushinara would be about forty or forty-five miles from Gorakhpur. On the way to Kushinara was a farmhouse of the Sikh friend. Our meal had been arranged at this farmhouse. Sardarji was extremely enthusiastic and efficient; we were amazed at his vivacity at such an advanced age.

After our meal, we resumed our journey to Kushinara. Mahasthivir Chandramani, who had initiated us into Buddhism, had arranged for our stay at the government dak bungalow. While at Kushinara, we were shown a hillock on which, it is believed, the last rites of Lord Buddha were performed. We also went and saw the spot where the Lord had laid down his body. A beautiful memorial vihara had been constructed there. Saheb's health was in a poor state, but he had gathered all his energy through sheer willpower and was moving around to offer his reverence to the land that had been sanctified by the presence of Lord Buddha. That vihara had just four or five steps, but they too had become impossible for him to climb. Varale, Chitnis and the rest of us were left with no choice but to leave him behind and take a round of the inner areas of the vihara. When we returned, Saheb badgered us with questions on what we had seen inside. There was a 20- to 25-foot-long statue of the Buddha carved in stone, resting on its right side, in a pose of quietus. When he heard the description of the statue from us, he became obsessed with the idea of seeing the statue with his own eyes, but he simply didn't have the energy left that day to climb those four or five steps. The next day, at the crack of dawn, he began importuning us for a visit to the memorial vihara, compelling us to take him back. He gathered all his strength to step inside. We held him from either side, helped him up the steps and managed to take him inside. A great glow of achievement lit up Saheb's face. He went down on his knees, said the trivaara prayer and then began reciting the trisharana and the panchsheel, in which we joined him. After the recitation was over, Saheb kept staring at the statue with all his powers of concentration. Tears were flowing in an unending stream down his cheeks. He was completely overwhelmed by being able to stand in a place that had been consecrated by the steps of Lord Gautam Buddha and the dam inside him had burst.

Saheb was in an utterly broken-down state of health, but he could withstand this pilgrimage only on account of his inextinguishable desire to visit these places. Saheb would get into a frenzy when contemplating the magnificence of Lord Buddha and His great deeds. He was also feeling deep inside himself that this would be his last visit. It was on account of this devotion that, despite the total collapse of his bodily strength, he had set off first for the Kathmandu Conference and then for this pilgrimage on his journey home.

On the day of our departure from Kushinara, we acceded to the request of Mahasthavir Chandramani and visited him at his vihara. He welcomed us there with great affection. We returned to Gorakhpur from Kushinara and left for Delhi on 30 November 1956. Nanak Chand Rattu was waiting with the car for us at the airport.

The Last Days

We returned to Delhi after attending the Buddhist Conference and visiting the Buddhist places of pilgrimage, but this trip had exhausted Saheb completely. His deterioration was visible even to the untrained eye. I have given in this book a picture of us taken at Sarnath on 24 November 1956. He didn't eat much after returning from our travels. Since he was completely drained, I rubbed oil into his head, reciting the Mangal Sutta and the Ratan Sutta all the while, till he went to sleep.

On 1 December 1956, when I went to wake him up at around 7.30, he was already awake. We had our tea together and then came and sat in the veranda of the bungalow. Balwant Varale and Principal Chitnis were staying with us then. They came to Saheb and sought his permission to leave, but Saheb asked them to stay on for another day.

By then breakfast was ready and Saheb got Varale and Chitnis to sit with him for breakfast and served them himself. It was a rule with Saheb that he would always have them sit with him for meals and serve them with great love and affection. While having breakfast, Saheb told Varale, 'The elections are due now and I desire to stand from Mumbai and Kolhapur.' He also advised Varale to stand from Belgaum for the Assembly seat. They had a long discussion on politics. Saheb said quite agitatedly, 'My village brethren have not received the fruits of my deeds. Something has to be done for them now. But I am completely drained out physically. There is no certainty of my life. I am living on willpower now. Let's see how long this willpower helps.'

In the afternoon too they were talking on the same topic. I then compelled him to sleep in the afternoon. At about 4 p.m., I took coffee for him and woke him up. We had our coffee together. All of us had our dinner together too.

For the Dalai Lama's Welcome

A programme to mark the 2500th year of the Buddha's passing away was due to be held at Bodh Gaya. The Dalai Lama, the spiritual leader of Tibet, had come to India to participate in the programme. The head of the Ashoka Buddha Vihara in Delhi [Mehrauli], Mahathero Dhammavar, had invited us for the programme organized at the Ashoka Vihara to welcome the Dalai Lama.

Since Varale and Chitnis were due to leave by the eight o'clock train on the morning of the 2nd, I had woken up a little early to arrange for their tea. After taking a round of the garden, when I went to wake up Saheb, I found that he had woken up and was sitting in the gallery [sic] of the bungalow. He had known that they were due to leave by the eight o'clock train and therefore Saheb, who could not get up without somebody's aid, had got up with the help of a stick and had walked all by himself to the veranda. Varale and Chitnis took their leave and departed.

After that, we attended the welcome ceremony for the Dalai Lama at Ashoka Vihara. As he was feeling very fatigued after returning from the function, I served him a little food and put him to sleep. To put him to sleep, I would rub oil into his scalp and recite the Mangal Sutta and the Ratan Sutta. He would get so absorbed in the listening that he would begin mumbling it to himself and go to sleep. My insistence was that he should sleep for at least an hour or two in the afternoon. I would pet him and cuddle him and sometimes even admonish him to sleep.

I woke him up in the evening, served him coffee and then we all went out and sat on the lawn. My father, my brother Balu and Dr Malvankar had still not returned to Mumbai. We sat chatting and laughing and having fun on the lawn outside the bungalow. A few followers then came to meet Saheb. Their discussion then began on the social situation and on politics. The chat went on till quite late.

When our cook Sudama informed us that dinner was ready, Saheb told him to bring the food out to the lawn where we were sitting, and we had our dinner there. Saheb's health was worsening day by day. I gave him his medicines and insisted on his going to bed early. I sat pressing his legs and in a little while he slipped into deep slumber.

As always, I got up early on 3 December and took my round of the garden around the bungalow. I went to our gardener's house and inquired about his state of health. After a little bit of roaming around I readied the tea tray and took it with me to wake Saheb up. He was not feeling well at all. He had his tea and then began his morning ablutions. I had to hold him and help him through this whole exercise. The table had been laid for breakfast, but Saheb had no desire for it. Dr Malvankar examined him and gave him his regular medicines. After some time he started feeling a little better, but he continued to look extremely fatigued. He took just the littlest bit of breakfast after which I gave him a jab of insulin. He then sat quite listlessly in the armchair in the veranda.

My brother Balu expressed his desire to take a few photographs and Saheb gave him his assent. He told Sudama to lay out a few chairs on the lawn, after which my brother took our photographs as well as the entire group in different poses. We then sat there chatting. During the conversation, I informed Saheb that our gardener (his name was Bhasmasoor and he belonged to the washermen community) was not keeping well and that he would often ask about him. Saheb sent for Nanak Chand, who was sitting inside typing, and, leaning upon his shoulder, he went to inquire after the gardener. After giving him words of encouragement, he returned and said, 'That poor gardener is afraid of death, but I am not afraid at all. It may come any time, I am waiting for it.'

Rattu then reminded Saheb of a chapter of *The Buddha and Karl Marx*, at which he leaned on Rattu and went to the library. I got busy making arrangements for our meal. Saheb examined the last few chapters of the book and gave them to Rattu for typing. Rattu left for his house on his bicycle. I brought Saheb over to the dining table and seated him. As always, we had our food together, after which we went out to the lawn for a bit of chatting. I then put Saheb to sleep early. Actually, he had wanted to read for a bit, but I compelled him to retire.

4 December

We had been out of Delhi for three weeks, and although we had returned on 30 November, Saheb had not been able to attend the Rajya Sabha because of his health. As a member of the Rajya Sabha, one is required to attend according to the rules. But his health was going from bad to worse with every passing day. But, after all that, on 4 December 1956, he insisted on going to the Rajya Sabha. Dr Malvankar examined him and gave him the sanction to go. I got him ready and after he had had his breakfast, he went to the Rajya Sabha. When he returned for lunch, he looked quite exhausted. We had been waiting for his return and sat down together for lunch. After lunch, I recited the Mangal Sutta and the Ratan Sutta and compelled him to sleep. That visit of Saheb to the Rajya Sabha turned out to be his last.

I served him coffee in the evening, and we sat on the lawn as always and chatted. He had become extremely debilitated. Just then, Rattu came. The Mumbai leadership had decided to hold a conversion programme on 16 December, and we had obviously decided to attend. The plan was to have another Nagpur type of programme where the public giving of deeksha would be done at the hands of Saheb. He was instructing Rattu about reserving train tickets for Mumbai for 14 December when I told him, 'You will not be able to undertake such a long journey. Instead, we two will go by air.' Saheb agreed to my suggestion. He had decided that my father, my brother Balu, Shyamrao Jadhav (whom Varale had kept as a helper for Saheb) and the rest of the people should leave for Mumbai on the night of 4 December; therefore, they set off for the station after their meal. Dr Malvankar was to take a flight the next day. Saheb and I would fly to Mumbai on the 14th and see the programme of the 16th through. Saheb told Rattu to make the air bookings accordingly.

After that, Saheb spent a long time writing, giving Rattu the material for him to type. Since it was very late, we told Rattu to sleep in the bungalow. After typing for some time, he went off to sleep.

5 December

I got up in the morning as usual and took a round of the garden. I went to the gardener's house, made inquiries about his health and had the black tea that his wife offered. At around half past eight I took the tea tray and woke up Saheb. We had tea together. When Rattu came to Saheb to take his leave, he was given tea too, after which he left for office.

I helped Saheb with his morning ablutions and took him to the dining table for breakfast. Saheb, Dr Malvankar and I had our breakfast together and then went out to the lawn for a chat. Saheb went through the newspapers, after which I gave him his medicines and his insulin jab. I then went in to look after the preparation of the meal while Saheb and Dr Malvankar continued with their conversation.

When I went at around noon to call Saheb for lunch, he was busy reading–writing in the library. The printing of *The Buddha and His Dhamma* was nearing completion in Mumbai under the supervision of Shantaram Rege, the librarian of Siddharth College, which was why Rege had been getting after Saheb to send the preface for the book. Saheb had actually written the preface in March, to which he had made some modifications on 6 April 1956, but it still had to be given a final reading. To ensure that the book was understood well, he had also brought the other two books, *Revolution and Counter-revolution* and *The Buddha and Karl Marx*, to near completion. He was very keen that these three books should be published as early as possible. One—*The Buddha and His Dhamma*—was, of course, ready. I went to the library to bring Saheb over and we had lunch together. After the meal, I arranged for him to sleep.

It had become my custom since I had moved to Delhi to personally go and buy all the household things that were needed, including food items; in other words, I did all the shopping. I would, of course, go alone. In any case, because of his health and his other engagements, Saheb would not be able to accompany me. When it was the buying of books, clothes and trinkets, Saheb would mostly come along. It would sometimes happen that I would go to Connaught Place and tell the bookseller to send over certain books for Saheb's selection. Saheb would never send back any of the books; he would, in fact, compliment me on my choice. I would do my shopping either when Saheb was in the Parliament or when he was taking his afternoon siesta.

I had to go to the market as usual to buy vegetables and some other household things. On that occasion, Dr Malvankar was with me. He had bought his ticket for the evening flight to Mumbai and wanted to buy a few things from the market; he therefore decided to come along with me. I couldn't take Saheb's leave before leaving for the market because he was sleeping. In any case, since it was a daily routine with us, it didn't matter. Accordingly, I left for the market at around half past two.

I bought the stuff that I needed while Dr Malvankar bought his things (mainly woollen clothes and some other fancy stuff). When we returned by half past five, I found Saheb in a huff. There was nothing unusual in Saheb's being angry. If he couldn't locate his book at the exact spot, if he couldn't locate a pen, he would bring the house down. If things didn't happen as per his desire or expectations, his temperature would shoot up instantly. His anger was like a passing thunderstorm. It was because of his fear of Saheb's temper that Yeshwant would not stay with us in Delhi. I so often entreated him to stay with us, but he would say, 'He gets irritated, so I feel afraid of him.' There were, of course, other reasons why he didn't stay in Delhi. Saheb's anger would always be momentary. The moment he located his book or his notebook or paper, the anger would vanish. I would always tell him, 'You are the incarnation of Jamdagni.'[63] He would laugh and say that his anger was the anger of love and it was momentary.

I understood that he would have got up early and wanted his coffee at my hands, or he could have been getting bored after having got up and wanted me around for company. Therefore, before carrying the stuff I had bought into the kitchen, I first peeped into his bedroom. He looked at me sharply and snapped, 'You took such a long time! I've been waiting for you for I don't know how long!' I pacified him and got busy with my work in the kitchen.

That evening, a Jain muni and a delegation of representatives arrived to meet him by appointment and sat in the drawing hall talking on the subjects of Buddhism and Jainism. When it got to be time for Dr Malvankar's flight, he collected his effects, took Saheb's leave and left for the airport. The discussion with the Jain muni and the delegation ended in due course and they left too.

In a little while, the singing of the Lord's prayer *Buddham Sharanam Gachchhaami* [I take refuge in Lord Buddha] floated out from the drawing hall in the peaceful, mellifluous voice of Saheb. Whenever he was in a peaceful and happy state of mind, he would sing this prayer and some couplets of Kabir.[64] When I peeped into the drawing hall, I saw Saheb sitting on the sofa with his eyes closed, drumming the beat with his fingers on the arms of the sofa, singing the prayer with complete concentration, throwing his heart and soul into the prayer, not letting a note go astray. He then asked Rattu to play the gramophone record of the prayer and began singing along with it in a loud voice. Wasn't this behaviour of his an indication of a happy and enthusiastic heart?

It was time for dinner. Since he liked his food served hot, I got busy in heating the food and sent Sudama to fetch Saheb. We sat together for our meal. He ate a little, humming the Buddha prayer all the while. I somehow got him to focus on his food and eat something.

He stayed on while I was finishing my own dinner. He soon started singing Kabir's couplet *Chalo Kabir Tera Bhavasagar Dera* [Move on Kabir, this is your temporary abode] with a lot of passion and musicality. He looked in a state of great joy and contentment. First the prayer and then the Kabir couplet: both suggested that he was in a happy and enthusiastic state of mind. Completely making himself one with the singing, he sang the couplet and walked to the bedroom, stick in one hand and a book in the other.

It was very important to send the preface of *The Buddha and His Dhamma* to Mumbai for printing. Saheb therefore told Rattu to keep on the table a copy of the preface as well as the letters he had written to S.M. Joshi, leader of the Samyukt Maharashtra Samiti, and Acharya Atre. I got busy in sorting out the kitchen issues.

Saheb went into the bedroom and got busy giving the preface its final shape. He made some corrections with his hand on the typewritten manuscript, acknowledged his indebtedness to me and to Dr Malvankar and recorded clearly and in grateful terms that the great work of completing that historical book had become possible only on account of my support. But it is unfortunate and shameful that while some self-seeking, mean leaders did get the book printed after Saheb's death, in the pursuit of their own political ambitions and for their selfish interests, they have not got the preface printed till date.[65] I had shown this hand-corrected preface to Prime Minister Nehru on 6 December 1956. Dr Bhadant Anand Kausalyayan has also mentioned in an interview that when he came to take a last look on 6 December, the ink hadn't dried on the corrected preface. This preface was handed over to the People's Education Society along with all the other documents and it is still in their possession. A typewritten additional copy is in Rattu's collection too. In the meantime, Advocate Bhagwan Das edited a booklet published by Dr L.R. Bali titled *Rare Prefaces Written by Dr Ambedkar*, but obviously, the corrections made by Saheb on the night of 5 December could not possibly appear in that book because there was just this one single copy that Saheb had asked that night to be placed on the table. It happens to be the biggest evidence for establishing the importance of my place in Saheb's life. Doctor Saheb gave this certificate to me on the night of 5 December 1956, that is, before he passed away.

As I had promised earlier, I am giving here the original preface of this priceless book, inclusive of all corrections, in its exact form. Readers and Ambedkarites should investigate why this preface is not being printed, demand answers and insist on its inclusion in the book. Without the inclusion of this preface written by Dr Ambedkar himself, the book cannot be considered as complete.

PREFACE[66]

> A question is always asked to me: how I happen[ed] to take such [a] high degree of education. Another question is being asked[:] why I am inclined towards Buddhism. These questions are asked because I was born in a community known in India as the 'Untouchables'.

This preface is not the place for answering the first question. But this preface may be the place for answering the second question.

The direct answer to this question is that I regard the Buddha's Dhamma to be the best. No religion can be compared to it. If a modern man who knows science must have a religion, the only religion he can have is the Religion of the Buddha. This conviction has grown in me after thirty-five years of close study of all Religions.

How I was led to study Buddhism is another story. It may be interesting for the readers to know. This is how it happened.

My father was a military officer, but at the same time a very religious person. He brought me up under a strict discipline. From my early age I found certain contradictions in my father's religious way of life. He was a Kabirpanthi, though his father was a Ramanandi. As such, he did not believe in Murti Puja (idol worship), and yet he performed Ganapati Puja. Of course for our sake, but I did not like it. He read the books of his Panth. At the same time, he compelled me and my elder brother to read every day, before going to bed a portion of [the] Mahabharata and Ramayana to my sisters and other persons who assembled at my father's house to hear the Katha. This went on for a long number of years.

The year I passed the English Fourth Standard Examination, my Community people wanted to celebrate the occasion by holding a public meeting to congratulate me. Compared to the state of education in other Communities, this was hardly an occasion for celebration. But it was felt by the organizers that as I was the first boy in my community to reach this stage, they thought that I had reached a great height. They went to my father to ask for his permission. My father flatly refused, saying [that] such a thing would inflate [the] boy. After all, he has only passed an examination and done nothing more. Those who wanted to celebrate the event were greatly disappointed. They, however, did not give way. They went to Dada Keluskar, a personal friend of my father, and asked him to intervene. He agreed. After a little argumentation, my father yielded, and the meeting was held. Dada Keluskar presided. He was a literary person of his time. At the end of his address he gave me, as a gift, a copy of his book on the life of the Buddha, which he had written for the Baroda Sayajirao Oriental Series. I read the book with great interest and was greatly impressed and moved by it.

I began to ask [myself] why my father did not introduce us to the Buddhist literature. After this, I was determined to ask my father this question. One day I did. I asked my father why he insisted upon our reading the Mahabharata and Ramayana, which recounted the greatness of the Brahmins and the Kshatriyas and repeated the stories of the degradation of the Shudras and the Untouchables. My father did not like the question. He merely said, "You must not ask such silly questions. You are only boys, you must do as you are told." My father was a Roman Patriarch, and exercised most extensive Patria Protestas [Potestas] over his children. I alone could take a little liberty with him, and that was because my mother had died in my childhood, leaving me to the care of my aunt.

So after some time, I asked again the same question. This time my father had evidently prepared himself for a reply. He said, "The reason why I ask you to read the Mahabharata and Ramayana is this: we belong to the Untouchables and you are likely to develop an inferiority complex, which is natural. The value of [the] Mahabharata and Ramayana lies in removing this inferiority complex. See Drona and Karna, they were small men, but to what heights they rose! Look at Valmiki, he was a *Koli*, but he became the author of [the] Ramayana. It is for removing this inferiority complex that I ask you to read the Mahabharata and Ramayana."

I could see that there was some force in my father's argument. But I was not satisfied. I told my father that I did not like any of the figures in [the] Mahabharata. I said, "I do not like Bhishma and Drona, nor Krishna. Bhishma and Drona were hypocrites. They said one thing and did quite the opposite. Krishna believed in frauds. His life is nothing but a series of frauds. Equal dislike I have for Rama. Examine his conduct in the Sarupnakha [sic] episode, in the Vali Sugriva episode, and his [. . .]* behavior towards Sita." My father was silent, and made no reply. He knew that there was a revolt.

This is how I turned to the Buddha, with the help of the book given to me by Dada Keluskar. It was not with an empty mind that I went to the Buddha at that early age. I had a background, and in reading the Buddhist Lore I could always compare and contrast. This is the origin of my interest in the Buddha and his Dhamma.

The urge to write this book has a different origin. In 1951, the Editor of the Mahabodhi Society's journal of Calcutta asked me to write an article for the Vaishak Number. In that article I argued that the Buddha's Religion was the only religion which a society awakened by science could accept and without which it would perish. I also pointed out that for the modern world Buddhism was the only religion which it must have to save itself. That Buddhism makes [a] slow advance is due to the fact that its literature is so vast that no one can read the whole of it. That it has no such thing as a Bible, as the Christians have, is its greatest handicap. On the publication of this article, I received many calls, written and oral, to write such a book. It is in response to these calls that I have undertaken the task.

To disarm all criticism, I would like to make it clear that I claim no originality for the book. It is a compilation and assembly plant. The material has been gathered from various books. I would particularly like to mention 'Ashavaghosha's Buddhavita' [Buddha Charita], whose poetry no one can excel. In the narrative of certain events I have borrowed his language.

The only originality that I can claim is the order of presentation of the topics, in which I have tried to introduce simplicity and clarity. There are certain matters which give headache[s] to the students of Buddhism. I have dealt with them in the Introduction.

It remains for me to express my gratitude to those who have been helpful to me. I am very grateful to Mr. Nanak Chand Rattu of Village Sakrulli and Mr. Parkash Chand of Village Nangal Khurd in the district of Hoshiarpur (Punjab) for the burden they have taken upon themselves to type out the manuscript. They have done it several times. Shri Nanak Chand Rattu took special pains and put in very hard labour in accomplishing this great task. He did the whole work of typing, etc. very willingly and without caring for his health and any sort of remuneration. Both Mr. Nanak Chand Rattu and Mr. Parkash Chand did their job as a token of their greatest love and affection towards me. Their labours can hardly be repaid. I am very much grateful to them.

When I took up the task of composing the book I was ill, and [I] am still ill. During these five years there were many ups and downs in my health. At some stages my condition had become so critical that doctors talked of me as a dying flame. The successful rekindling of this dying flame is due to the medical skill of my wife and Dr Malvankar, the physician who has been attending me. I am immensely grateful to them. They alone have helped me to complete the work.

I may mention that this is one of the three books which will form a set for the proper understanding of Buddhism. The other books are: (1) Buddha and Karl Marx; and (2) Revolution and Counter-Revolution in Ancient India. They are written out in parts. I hope to publish them soon.

B. R. Ambedkar
15th March, 1956[67]

The biographer Dhananjay Keer too has made reference to this unpublished preface of *The Buddha and His Dhamma* in his biography of Dr Ambedkar. Particularly, my information is that Keer actually saw this original preface and got a blue copy made of it. Dhananjay Keer writes about this unpublished preface[68] [translated from Marathi]:

> 'The world does not know about the gratitude that the writer inside Dr Ambedkar had expressed in the Preface of his book *The Buddha and His Dhamma*. Ambedkar had written: "During these five years, there were many ups and downs in my health. At some stages my condition had become so critical that doctors talked of me as a dying flame. The successful rekindling of this dying flame is due to the medical skill of my wife and Dr Malvankar, the physician who has been attending me. I am immensely grateful to them. They alone have helped me to complete the work." Why the Preface that was ready and particularly this part was not published is a mystery.'

Passing Away

Saheb would sit reading and writing till quite late in the night. Once he got into the groove, he would carry on right through the night. But on 5 December 1956, Saheb made some modifications to the preface to *The Buddha and His Dhamma*. He also gave a last look at the typed letters he was due to send to S.M. Joshi, Atre and the Burmese government and went to sleep that night earlier than usual, that is at around half past eleven. The night of 5 December turned out to be his last night. In his description of 5 December, the renowned biographer Dhananjay Keer writes[69] [translated from Marathi]:

> 'Neither Dr Ambedkar's wife who had been taking care of his life for the previous years nor their servant had the slightest inkling that death lay hiding behind Dr Ambedkar's bed.'

On 6 December, I got up early as usual. As per my habit, I took a round of the garden and went to our gardener and inquired about his health. I then finished with my morning activities, washed my face and went with the tea tray, as usual, to wake Saheb up. It would have been seven o'clock or half past seven. I found that one of his legs was resting upon a pillow. I called out to him twice or thrice, but when I got no response, I assumed that he was fast asleep. I then tried to shake him awake and . . . I then felt a big jolt. He had passed away in his sleep. There was nobody in the entire bungalow except me and Sudama. And for all that I was a doctor, I was, after all, a woman. I just didn't understand what I should do. I let out a loud wail and shouted for Sudama. I couldn't get a word out of my mouth. What should I do? Who should I call? My mind had turned numb. In that utterly confused and rattled state, I called Dr Malvankar to ask him for advice. He too was shocked. He tried to calm me down and suggested that I should give him an injection of Coramine. But quite a few hours would have gone by since he had passed away, therefore it was not possible to give him any injection. I then dispatched Sudama to get Nanak Chand Rattu over immediately.

Sudama took the car to bring Nanak Chand, who arrived in a little while, looking dazed. One look at him and all my restraint broke to pieces. I bawled out to him loudly, 'Rattu, Saheb has left us!' I couldn't say a word more; I simply collapsed on the sofa. Rattu also began wailing. A few moments slipped by thus. After that we gave Saheb's body a massage and tried artificial resuscitation. But that wasn't of any use. Saheb had left us forever. We then decided to spread the word about Saheb's death. I, being a woman, didn't know what to do. Nanak Chand, however, began making phone calls to our close acquaintances, to the government departments, to the PTI [Press Trust of India], the UNI [United News of India] and Akashvani to give them the sad news.

The news spread far and wide like wildfire. Thousands of his grief-stricken followers began making their way towards 26,

Alipore Road. By then, with the help of Sudama and Rattu, I had managed to place Saheb's body in the hall for the last darshan. Hundreds of thousands of distressed people had gathered for a last look at Saheb.

A decision was taken to perform Saheb's last rites in Mumbai. Some had been of the opinion that these last rites should be performed in Delhi or at Sarnath; but Mumbai had been his field of action, and we insisted that his last rites should happen there.

Ministers of Nehru's Council of Ministers, government officials, members of the Lok Sabha and the Rajya Sabha—all of them began lining up to take a last look at Saheb. Nehru himself came over; he consoled me and made a number of inquiries about his age, his health, his illness, how and when he had passed away and so on with great courtesy. I told him that he had had discussions with the Jain muni, taken an inadequate dinner and made corrections to the preface to his *The Buddha and His Dhamma* in his own hand. I showed him the sheets that carried the corrections. I even told him that he had finished with his work in life after finishing his role with his important book.

Babu Jagjivanram arrived and asked where the last rites would be performed. When I told him that it would be Mumbai, he assured me that he would give instructions for the body to be flown there. He also arranged for the aircraft to be hired at half the rate.

Saheb's body was kept out for the last darshan till 6 p.m. A truck was then arranged on which the garlanded body was placed and taken in procession down Delhi's important roads in the direction of the Safdarjung airport. Bhadant Anand Kausalyayan was in Delhi when Saheb passed away. I sent Rattu to call him over, and he then stayed with us. Bhadant Anand Kausalyayan, Sohanlal Shastri, Shankaranand, I and a few others sat around Saheb's body. The aircraft was due to leave at 10.30 p.m. By the time we reached Parliament House, hundreds of thousands of sorrowing people had begun to trail the truck. When the funeral procession reached Parliament House, it was already 10 p.m. We appealed to the grieving crowd that the aircraft was due to fly at 10.30 p.m., hence they should now return so the truck could move faster. On reaching the Safdarjung airport, the body was moved from the truck to the aircraft. A vast sea of humanity had gathered around the airport for a last look at their leader. When Saheb's body was flown to Mumbai, there were eleven or twelve of us in the aircraft, including our cook Sudama, Sohanlal Shastri, Shankaranand Shastri, Nanak Chand Rattu, Bhadant Anand Kausalyayan, T.B. Bhosale [engineer], Raisingh, Tuladas, I and a few others.

We landed at the Santacruz airport at about 3 a.m. and drove with Saheb's body to Rajgraha. People had been waiting in their thousands since the previous day for the arrival of Saheb's body. The street from the airport to Rajgraha was lined on both sides with hordes of grieving people. The crowd around Rajgraha ran into hundreds of thousands, their anguish breaking all restraints. Saheb's body was placed in the porch of Rajgraha for people to take a last look. People had been lining up for this last sighting since the previous day, tired and hungry and desolate.

The Sun of Knowledge Had Set

Saheb's body was placed for the public to see till 3 p.m. of 7 December. Hundreds of thousands of heartbroken people took a last, final look at their deliverer. The sea of humanity that had gathered around Rajgraha was so colossal that traffic was jammed all over Central Mumbai. At 3 p.m., Saheb's body was placed on a flower-laden truck, and the biggest funeral procession in the history of Mumbai began to move. The funeral procession went down Hindu Colony, Vincent Road [now Dr Ambedkar Road], Poyabawdi, Elphinstone Bridge, Sayani Road and Gokhale Road to reach the cremation ground at Dadar Chowpatty. The crowd that had gathered on Dadar Chowpatty was so huge that it appeared that even the sea had bowed its head and gone into ebb tide. The people were distraught with grief. Bhadant Anant Kausalyayan had collected a number of bhikshus to give him the Buddhist last rites. Saheb's body was placed on a funeral pyre of sandalwood. The Mumbai Police paid their homage by giving him the final guard of honour. At around 7 p.m., Yeshwant set the pyre alight, setting up a loud roar of lamentations.

The entire country was grief-stricken at Saheb's death. The Parliament, the Rajya Sabha, the State Assemblies, all the institutions across every region of the country, autonomous institutions, the renowned people of the world, judicial bodies and the newspapers—local and foreign—expressed their sorrow at the passing away of Saheb and paid him fulsome homage.

The Ordeals That Followed

On the day after the funeral, that is on 8 December, I was at my parents' house, sitting with my father, my brother Balu, my sisters and my sisters-in-law in a desolate frame of mind. There was no way that my tears would stop flowing. My head had turned numb. My sisters and sisters-in-law were consoling me; that was when Bhaurao Gaikwad arrived. Seeing the despair I was in, he began to commiserate with me. Balwant Varale arrived too. Bhaurao said, 'Maisaheb, please don't lose heart. After the passing away of Babasaheb, you are our guide. All of us together will try to get you elected to the Rajya Sabha in Babasaheb's place. You have no reason at all to worry or to fear. If you are at all feeling daunted, come with me to Nashik. I take guarantee of your security.'

After Bhaurao had gone, Varale pleaded with me, 'Maisaheb, please get together with Yeshwant and sort things out, but don't get into litigations.' After I had given him my assurance, he brought Yeshwant along with him. But it was difficult to know what was going on in his mind. He told my father, 'Let's collect the ashes. I have to go to Delhi.'

My father told him, 'The ashes will still be hot. How can the bones be collected in such a hurry?'

The bones were gathered on 10 December 1956. Yeshwant set off for Delhi that very evening. My sister's husband Bhuleskar [Pappa] said to me, 'We too should go to Delhi. The hurry in which Yeshwant left suggests that something is amiss.' Accordingly, we also left for Delhi.

We were not being able to fathom Yeshwant.

Finally, he made a claim that he was the sole heir, and all the property should go to him. And how much was Saheb's property, anyway? Rajgraha at Mumbai, a small plot in Delhi, another small plot at Talegaon with two small rooms on it!

The petition filed in Delhi came before Justice C.B. Kapoor. When Saheb was the law minister, Kapoor was working as joint secretary in the ministry. I had never known him personally, but he called me and Yeshwant over to his chamber. He advised that we should settle it between ourselves, but Yeshwant was in no mood to listen to anyone [. . .]* Justice Kapoor took Yeshwant seriously to task, but he was in no mood for settlement. Therefore, Justice Kapoor ordered the bungalow to be sealed and said that the heirs could approach the civil court to demand their share. Yeshwant would stay either with Shankaranand Shastri or with Sohanlal Shastri during those days.

As per the court's orders, the superintendent of the court came over the next day to seal the bungalow. The court employees got busy in sealing everything, bookshelves and steel almirahs included.

The Mystery of My Cupboard Key

When the gargantuan funeral procession had set off for the last rites, Yeshwant, Shankaranand, Bhaurao Gaikwad and I were on the truck with some others. Before leaving for the procession, I had given my purse to our cook Sudama for safekeeping. I had placed the wristwatch that Saheb had given me, earrings, a ring, the key of my Godrej almirah in the Delhi bungalow and a few other valuables in that purse. After the last rites were over, Sudama had given the purse back to me on return. Without bothering to check the contents, I had taken the purse and come home. But when I opened it to retrieve my watch, I was shocked to find that all my valuables, including the key, had vanished from it. Now, when the people from the court began sealing everything as per the orders of Sessions Judge C.P. Kapoor, they came to my almirah and demanded the key. I told them that it was my personal almirah. Yeshwant pulled the key out of his pocket and handed it over to the court people. My brother-in-law Bhuleskar and I opposed the sealing of that almirah because it had belonged to me since before my marriage and it contained my clothes, things of daily use and plenty of personal effects. Fortunately, my name (Dr Miss Sharada Kabir) had been done on it when the almirah had been bought. The court people also had to admit that it was my personal property since before my marriage and they handed it over to me instead of sealing it.

How and where the things from my purse that I had handed over to Sudama in Mumbai disappeared on the seventh day of December 1956, and how the key of my almirah arrived in Yeshwant's pocket was a mystery that bothered me for thirty-two years. Then, one day, in 1988, it got resolved on account of my intimate associate Vijay Surwade. Vijay Surwade is forever eager to collect everything connected with Dr Ambedkar, such as photographs, letters, memorabilia and all other kinds of information. It was in this connection that he got acquainted with Shankaranand. In 1988 Shankaranand happened to be in Mumbai, and he called Surwade over to the house of his son-in-law who lived in Mazgaon. During the conversation, Shankaranand talked about the key and the mystery was resolved. Yeshwant and Shankaranand himself had wanted to rifle through my almirah by somehow procuring the key and they had managed to recruit Sudama in the plot. It then happened by chance that I handed my purse to Sudama, and everything became easy. It was Sudama, therefore, who had whisked away everything that was inside my purse, and that was how Yeshwant had promptly brought the key out of his pocket when the court people had demanded it.

I thus got to know the history of the key that had disappeared from my purse. Later, I got to know from Nanak Chand that he had seen my wristwatch with Shankaranand. But what happened to my earrings and my ring remains a mystery.

After the sessions court had got the cupboards in the bungalow sealed, Yeshwant filed a petition in the civil court and requested the case to be shifted to Mumbai. The petition, therefore, landed in the court of Justice Koyaji. Koyaji had had occasions to come in contact with Dr Ambedkar, therefore he called the two of us over to his chamber. When Yeshwant again began with his old refrain, the judge told him in exasperated terms that Dr Ambedkar was a great person and he had always held him in awe and respect. Therefore, his name should not go to court and that we should sort things out between ourselves. This was how Justice Koyaji brought about a settlement.

Dr Ambedkar's Last Wish

It was Dr Ambedkar's keen desire that his heirs should not go to court and that was why he had prepared a will. He had wanted to register his will on coming to Mumbai. The signatures of the witnesses had still not been taken. But then, the Buddhist Conference happened, followed by the visit to the holy places and then he got busy writing

The Buddha and His Dhamma. The visit to Mumbai never happened. The incomplete will would have fallen into Yeshwant's hands, perhaps, or it could have been among the books that the People's Education Society brought over. When we were in Aurangabad once, Saheb had said in the presence of Varale, Chitnis and Bhaurao Gaikwad, 'After me, my wife and my son should not go to court. I have made a house for my son at Khar and have also taken a press for him. There's no need to do anything more for him. If I can make an arrangement for my wife to get Rs 200 per month, that should be enough. My last desire is that the rest of my estate should be used in the service of orphans.'

He had expressed his desire to name me custodian in his will. He had expressed the same desire when his closest friend Naval Bhathena had come to meet him a couple of months before his passing away. As a matter of fact, in his letter of 23 February, he had clearly written to Yeshwant, 'I cannot take responsibility for supporting you and your family. You have already got more than your share.' But even so, he went to court with the desire to take over the entire property. He thought nothing of respecting his father's wish of his heirs not going to court and that is truly unfortunate.

Intrigue of Political Leaders

After Saheb's passing away, the tug-of-war began among political leaders for the leader's post. So as to ensure that the leadership did not pass to me, they deliberately misled the simple and ignorant people by creating suspicions regarding Dr Ambedkar's death. To manufacture an atmosphere of mistrust in the entire community, suspicions were intentionally planted against me, and poison was purposefully spread against my name.

These people had held secret confabulations and hatched a conspiracy to ensure that I did not get the leadership. It was sad to see that these people who declared themselves as the heirs to Dr Ambedkar's legacy could sink to such levels of wickedness to further their political ambitions.

Political Conspiracy

After Dr Ambedkar's passing away, everybody was fired up with the desire to become a leader. But before they did so, they obviously found it more important to first create a distance between the heirs and the rest of the community. It would have been natural for the common people to line up behind Saheb's heirs and therefore they systematically kept Yeshwant and me separate. They went further and installed him as the president of the Buddhist Society of India and sent him from town to town propagating Buddhism. On the other side they created an atmosphere of suspicion around me. They wilfully spread poison regarding me and kept me away from the community. But, in due course, every one of these leaders went on to create their own little camps, threw slime at each other and destroyed the organization that Saheb had erected with such labour. The history of this disintegration is too fresh for me to recount here.

26, Alipore Road Becomes a Memory

We had moved into 26, Alipore Road after Saheb had resigned from the post of law minister. We had taken it on rent, but the owner [the Prince of Sirohi] had held such affection for Saheb that he had refused to accept rent. It was only when we had threatened to move out that he had finally agreed. It was around the same time as Saheb that the Maharaja of Sirohi passed away too and the ownership [of the bungalow] passed to his daughter. She had to put the bungalow on sale, therefore she got after me to vacate it. Since this bungalow had been sanctified by the presence of Saheb, it was my desire that it should not be sold or demolished. To push this matter, I met all those parliamentarians and leaders who regarded themselves as Ambedkar's political heirs; but nobody showed any desire along my lines.

The party went to court and the court issued *ex parte* summons for the vacation of the bungalow.* The manager of the lady showed me the court orders. What could I have done alone? I went to Bhaurao Gaikwad who was then a member of Parliament and told him what had happened, but he showed no enthusiasm. I then told him, 'Try to bring pressure and get at least the room where Saheb passed away, because it has historical importance.' But nobody listened to my appeal. Nobody was bothered even the tiniest whit.

In due course, the place that had been hallowed by Saheb's living and became a place of pilgrimage on account of his breathing his last there was demolished and a new structure was raised there. 26, Alipore Road is no longer in existence today and there is no place left to show where Saheb departed from the world. There is a plan now to make a memorial for Saheb at the place where he was born, but the historical spot where he took his last breath has been altogether lost to history.

Passing Away: Facts

After Saheb had passed away, selfish political leaders systematically sowed seeds of doubt in the minds of the people and spread poison against me in the community. The fact of the matter, however, is that when I had entered Saheb's life, his health had been deteriorating day by day. His body had been hollowed out by the numerous ailments that he had been suffering from. Later, when he had a heart attack in 1953, from then onwards his health began slipping down rapidly. All this can be very easily established with documentary evidence from an examination of his letters, his speeches and the remembrances of his colleagues. But the amazing thing remains that even after thirty-two years have gone by, the same storm is sought to be created, deliberately and calculatedly, to spread poison against me among the illiterate community.

The letters of Saheb's colleagues, friends, followers and workers demonstrate one thing forcefully: they would all inquire very solicitously about his health. Add to that Saheb's reference to his health in almost every one of his own letters. It is clear that from 1934 onwards, he was always down with one ailment or the other. He was later struck by serious afflictions like neuritis, diabetes, rheumatism, breathing problems and heart ailments. I have already established this by producing Dr Ambedkar's letters to his friends and colleagues.

Information on his health and his passing away can equally well be gathered from the memoirs of his close associates and other contemporary people. Saheb himself had sensed that his last hours had arrived and had said that he was carrying on only on the strength of his willpower. Let's therefore first find references in Saheb's own letters and documents related to this issue. I have given on page 188 the letter that Saheb wrote to Bhaurao Gaikwad on 14 May 1952. There is the letter of 6 August 1953 that he wrote to Ghanshyam Talvatkar.

Actually, when he had his mild heart attack in 1953, he recovered only on account of his willpower, thus avoiding a major catastrophe. He had to be kept on oxygen for several hours at a stretch. Saheb had himself doubted his chances of recovery. He had written to Vitthal Kadam on 19 April 1954, which has been reproduced on page 195. Also, in the preface to *The Buddha and His Dhamma* given on page 263, which he modified barely a few hours before his death, he referred to himself as a dying flame.

Let's now look at examples of what some of his colleagues and intimate friends said about his health.

I have already mentioned earlier that on 14 April 1956, S.S. Gaikwad, Talvatkar and Kardak got together to publish a booklet titled *Parimal*, which contains remembrances of Dr Ambedkar. What Dr S.G. Malshe writes about his memory of 1947 gives a good idea of Saheb's physical state before he got married to me. He writes[70] [translated from Marathi]:

> 'In the year '47 I was doing my B.A. in Siddharth College. We would hang around in the college in the evening too on account of rehearsals for our play. But one evening I saw a scene that has left an impact on my personality. It has left a deep, deep mark on my mind.
>
> 'I was standing alone in the verandah waiting for one of the characters. Just then a car arrived and stopped in the college compound. A few persons rushed up to the car and helped a person step out of the car. Wondering who the unwell person was, I looked a little more carefully. It turned out to be Dr Babasaheb Ambedkar. He was not being able to handle that well-built body of his. The room where Babasaheb sat was a good twenty or twenty-five steps away. That impressive looking personality had placed his arms round the shoulders of two men and was moving with labored feet at a slow pace. His head was kind of leaning forward. I went forward with curiosity. My flippant temperament took a big jolt. Even during that time, in a near-crippled state, he had an open book in his hand and he was absolutely lost in it! He seemed to be utterly unconscious of the surroundings and the people around him! I shall never ever be able to forget this Ambedkar. What study can mean, what the hunger for knowledge can mean, here was a personification of it!'

1. Naval Bhathena

Dr Ambedkar's fellow student from 1917, intimate, sacrificing friend Naval Bhathena had come visiting Saheb in Mumbai [October 1956] two months before he passed away. Two close friends met. Bhathena writes in his memoirs:

'. . . Our longest meeting was at his [Dr Ambedkar's] house two months before he died. We were together from three o'clock in the afternoon till six in the evening, and no other person was allowed in the room. That day Ambedkar spoke from his heart. He criticized his son and also his nephew, and I left the house such [sic] saddened, and with the feeling that my friend was at [his] journey's end. Even now I can hardly believe that he lived a couple of months more.'

2. Sohanlal Shastri

Sohanlal Shastri writes in his memoirs [translated from Hindi]:

'It would be unethical to conceal this fact that Babasaheb's ailment was worsening every day because of diabetes, but even so, his lustrous, contented face always created the illusion of happiness and health . . .

'Although he was losing his health every day, he was not in the habit of lying stretched out on a cot twenty-four hours. Despite possessing a weak and ailing body, he never slackened the manner in which he carried himself around, particularly in the matter of reading and writing.'

3. K.V. Sawaadkar

Doctor Saheb's faithful colleague had come with us in 1954 for the Buddhist Conference in Rangoon. He writes about the memories of that visit in *Parimal*, which was published in 1956 when Saheb was alive. He says [translated from Marathi]:[71]

'On December 6, 1954, we went to see the temple of Lord Buddha atop Mandalay Hill, Mandalay. Babasaheb and Maisaheb were with us. This temple has 750 steps. Even people like us found it difficult to climb up all those steps. Babasaheb's health was delicate. Even in his bungalow, he would need the help of someone to walk a couple of steps. A Maharashtrian doctor friend of his (who had settled there) offered to make arrangement for a palanquin or a dooly, but Baba rejected it outright. He climbed up all those stairs by himself and climbed down the same number of steps. What faith he had in the Buddha! This was true self-dependence, this was true faith.'

4. B.H. Varale

Saheb's intimate associate had come for the Kathmandu Conference in 1956. He has described his Nepal journey in his memoirs in which he has referred to Saheb's state of health in many places. Here are a few references [translated from Marathi]:

'As decided, we presented ourselves at the Patna airport at around 12 noon. Babasaheb landed at around two o'clock in the company of Maisaheb and Dr Malvankar. Babasaheb's health looked extremely debilitated. He was finding it impossible to walk. Two or three of us helped him alight from the aircraft . . . Babasaheb's health was in a very bad state . . . Because of being in such a bad state of health, he would be lying on the cot most of the time. He wouldn't walk because that made his legs ache. He couldn't walk on his own feet. Because of extreme weakness, he could not get up and sit either. Babasaheb was fully aware of the state he was in . . . It was impossible for Babasaheb to come walking . . . Babasaheb's health had really plummeted. There were barely three or four steps to climb for getting into the temple, but he couldn't manage that either, forcing us to leave him behind . . . The debilitation was starkly visible. Anybody would feel anxious looking at the state of his health. A trace of pathos would sometimes flash across his face. Tears were flowing down his eyes incessantly in remembrance of Lord Buddha, which was deeply suggestive. They could have been suggestive of the adverse event that was soon to happen. Babasaheb's heart had got a whiff of what the future was holding, it seemed.'

It may be noted that this description of Varale's was of a period barely five or six days before Saheb passed away.

5. Prabodhankar K.S. Thackeray

Prabodhankar K.S. Thackeray had written an article[72] in 1958 on Dr Ambedkar's death anniversary, in which he had written about Saheb's health and passing away. I consider it important to present a relevant excerpt here. He writes [translated from Marathi]:

'. . . Before he passed away, while he was in Mumbai, he had phoned me three or four times, asking me to visit him.

'But because I had some health issues, I could not meet him. His last stay was in Barrister Samarth's house at Churchgate, and that was where I went to him. Doctor had gone to meet the Governor, leaving a message that I should wait.

'He came after a little time. Dr Malvankar on one side and Mrs. Ambedkar on the other helped him in and had him seated on the sofa. My heart missed a beat at this scenario. A good three or four minutes passed since he sat and yet he wouldn't speak. Just kept looking at me. After he had got his breath back, we exchanged greetings.

'I said, "Doctor, how has your health slumped so much?"

'Looking at me with wide-open eyes, he said, "Slumped? What slumped? It's gone, all of it! It's long since I've been dead in body. Try and understand, it's only in terms of mind that I am alive, alive by willpower. There are lots of things left to do, and finish fast. *Aho*, however strong the willpower, there are limits, *na*! When it is going to give out, who knows? . . ."

'Dr Ambedkar had arrived at Famous Studio with his wife for launching Acharya Atre's talkie 'Mahatma Phule'. His health then (1954) was in very bad shape. I saw that he couldn't even speak properly. What he had said about his health earlier in Barrister Samarth's house has already been mentioned above. Such being the state of affairs, as soon as the doctor passed away, some mischief-monger started a newspaper to circulate the grapevine that he had been poisoned. That not one single person among the doctor's intimates should have raised an objection or slapped the mischief-monger and shut him up is in my opinion deplorable.'

6. Dhananjay Keer's interview

Madhukar Bele of Thane had interviewed the famous biographer Dhananjay Keer on 30 April 1984. This [Marathi] interview was published in *Navakal*:

> 'When he was asked, "What do you think about Maisaheb?" he responded, "Well, actually, I feel extremely bad for her. For eighteen years since Babasaheb died, she was thrown into total anonymity, and now in her old age these *dalit* leaders want to make use of her?"
>
> 'He was then asked, "Keer Saheb, can you please clarify why you feel this sympathy for Maisaheb?"
>
> 'He replied, "You would surely know that after Babasaheb's passing away, some selfish leaders propagated that Babasaheb's death was not a natural death; there was something extremely suspicious about it and the person behind the mischief was Maisaheb Ambedkar."

> 'The interviewer said, "It is still said in the villages that Babasaheb's wife poisoned him to death."
>
> 'Keer responded, "This event is an excellent example of how caste runs so deep in our blood. I had almost 175 letters of Babasaheb. In one of those letters, written to his friend Mr. Nair [of *Free Press Journal*], Babasaheb had clearly stated that the woman had added eight or ten years to his life."'

This interview with Dhananjay Keer took place barely fifteen days before he passed away. But for two years before he died, he had been asking for a meeting with me through his literary assistant and my associate Vijay Surwade so that he could write a book on me (and particularly on Saheb's death). But my tours and other social activities simply did not allow me the time. Hence, he could not fulfil his desire to write a book on me.

Dhananjay Keer had seen Saheb being given oxygen in 1953 and had seen his state of health at that time. Later, he had visited our house once or twice in Mumbai to hold discussions on the biography. He had also seen the handwritten copy of his preface to *The Buddha and His Dhamma.* Which is why he even marked his protest in Ambedkar's biography on the non-inclusion of the gratitude-carrying preface.

Also, since he had personally seen Saheb's letters written to Nair as well as a number of other letters, he was well aware of the facts and was therefore quite clearly keen on writing a book on me. But the opportunity never arrived. Otherwise, Keer would certainly have written a detailed, fully corroborated book on Saheb's passing away.

Investigation Committee

*Nineteen members of the Parliament of those times sent a letter and demanded from Prime Minister Nehru and the home minister an investigation into Dr Ambedkar's death. Honouring the request of those members, the government appointed Deputy Inspector General of Police Mr Saxena to conduct the investigation. Saxena conducted the investigation and submitted his report. Also, the special medical board appointed by the director general, health services, Government of India, examined five electrocardiograms and gave its opinion. After making a careful and detailed study of all the evidence, the doctors' reports, and the opinion of the special medical board, Deputy Inspector General Saxena arrived at the conclusion that without any scope for doubt, Dr Ambedkar's death had occurred because of natural circumstances and there was no evidence available to suspect any kind of foul play.

Despite the DIG's report, the political leaders continued to keep the atmosphere poisoned; for the sake of their political future, they really had no alternative but to continue with this stance. Actually, the police investigation report is always confidential; but in the interest of leaving no scope for doubt, the home minister presented before the Lok Sabha the report of the deputy inspector general, which included the conclusions of cardiologists Dr Tulpule and Dr Tirodkar and of the medical board. But it was impossible for the Dalit leaders who were driven by their own political goals to be satisfied; they kept the storm raging.

The Death Report—Lok Sabha Questions and Answers

The then member of Parliament B.C. Kamble had asked a question on 9 December 1957, related to the report of the investigation of Dr Ambedkar's death. Home Minister Govind Ballabh Pant responded to that question as given below:[73]

> 'G.B. Pant: I believe that it will not be appropriate to place the Confidential Report submitted by the Dy Police Commissioner,

Delhi, before the House. However, I wish to tell the Hon'ble members that the Police Officer who carefully conducted the Inquiry and admitted the medical evidence has arrived at the conclusion that it has been proved without any scope for doubt that Dr Ambedkar's death occurred because of natural circumstances. Hence there is no evidence available to suspect any kind of foul-play. The Deputy Inspector General of Police has also recorded the evidence of the Bombay cardiologists Dr Tirodkar and Dr Tulpule.'

Dr Tirodkar

Dr Tirodkar had examined Dr Ambedkar's health a number of times between 1946 and 1956. His statement was as given below:[74]

> 'Last time in 1956, when I saw him [Dr Ambedkar] he was definitely showing signs of congestive cardiac failure. In view of the long history of his illness and the state of his health in which I saw him, I am surprised how he could have lived such a long time as he did.'

Dr Tulpule

Dr Tulpule's evidence is given below:[75]

> 'I examined Dr Ambedkar several times during [the] past 3-4 years. He was suffering, when in 1953 or thereabout, from congestive cardiac failure following bronchopneumonia. His cardiograms showed progressive deterioration and when last seen a few months before his death, he was suffering from a [sic] attacks of cardiac asthma. Considering his age, long standing diabetes and

continued weakness of heart, accompanied by occasional period [sic] of cardiac failure, his general health could be regarded as serious [sic] damaged.'

Member of Special Medical Board

The special medical board appointed by the director general, health services, Government of India, examined the electro-cardiograms of Dr Ambedkar and this is what they had to say:[76]

'We are of unanimous opinion that Dr Ambedkar had an attack of coronary thrombosis in April, 1953. Thereafter, the electro-cardiogram shows cardiac changes of another attack in 1954. In view of the fact that he was a diabetic and had myocardial degeneration, it is possible that he could have had a fatal attack of coronary thrombosis before his death.'

Lok Sabha Questions–Answers

At the request of the home minister, a question and answer session happened as given below[77] [translated from Marathi]:

B.C. Kamble: Can the Hon'ble Minister tell this House whether the statements of other doctors besides the ones mentioned just now have been taken? If yes, can he tell us their names and addresses and place their statements before the House?

Home Minister G.B. Pant: The small doubt about the second doctor regarding whom the Hon'ble Member who has asked the question and some others seem to carry is Dr Eddington. His evidence is of no use. And since I believe that the evidence is not acceptable to the Hon'ble Member who has asked the questions and others in agreement with him, I have not mentioned it.

B.K. Gaikwad: Will you tell me how many witnesses the concerned officer examined and admitted their statements?

Pandit G.B. Pant: A number of Members and a few other persons besides.

Nausher Bharucha: What is the objection to placing the entire report before the House?

Pandit G.B. Pant: Because police reports are not made public.

Nausher Bharucha: There can be an exception in this matter.

Pandit G.B. Pant: It will not be proper to do so because there are Members of this House here and other witnesses. When the Police Officer presents his report, he uses his own language regarding the evidence presented. I have placed before you the basic things. Anybody who looks at it with a realistic and nonpartisan perspective will be convinced that there is no doubt at all about the real reasons that caused the death.

Dr Sushila Nayyar: Dr Ambedkar had been ill since a long time. His death was natural and was in normal circumstances, then why was there an enquiry of his death?

Pandit G.B. Pant: It was not necessary that the government should entertain the request for enquiry. But nineteen Hon'ble members of the Lok Sabha requested [in writing] for the enquiry and we felt to go into [sic] the enquiry to honour the request of those Hon'ble Members of the House.

A question was then asked that if correspondence had taken place between the government and the investigating officer between the time that the order for investigation was passed and the final report was submitted, whether the government would place the correspondence before the House. In response, Home Minister G.B. Pant said:[78]

'I don't think any kind of correspondence has taken place. They were simply told to investigate. Whatever relevant matter came to us, it was forwarded to them. The correspondence that takes place between the government and its officers is never made public.'

Despite the Government of India clearly stating its argument and presenting excerpts from the report in the Lok Sabha, the Dalit leaders squeezed some capital out of the report and misguided the ignorant Dalit masses to bolster their leadership. But when a young, educated and critical generation arrived in a later period and refused to fall prey to their fabrications, this bunch of leaders was discarded on the rubbish heap and got politically annihilated.

I'm Still an Ambedkar

After Saheb's passing away, Prime Minister Pandit Jawaharlal Nehru offered me the job of a medical officer in a government hospital. In fact, he even showed readiness to take me into the Rajya Sabha, but I turned down the offers. The reason was that Doctor Saheb had made me give up my job after marriage, and I didn't think it proper to go against his wishes after he had passed away. Similarly, if I had shown readiness to get into the Rajya Sabha, that would have been walking into the protection of the Congress camp, and that would have been going against Dr Ambedkar's principles. Later, President Sarvepalli Radhakrishnan and Prime Minister Indira Gandhi also showed readiness to get me into the Rajya Sabha, but I humbly declined. I told them clearly, 'Joining the Congress against whom my husband fought all his life can never appeal to me, and I can never be a traitor to my husband's principles.'

I live as an Ambedkar, and I shall die an Ambedkar.

Companionship with Dr Ambedkar in Every Sense

I gave companionship to Dr Ambedkar in every sense; I gave him sincere company at every level: personal, domestic, social, political, religious, academic as well as medical.

At the domestic level, I would serve him the food that he loved at regular hours and according to the prescribed regimen. I conducted myself in line with his desires, stifling my own likings if the occasion demanded. My saris, their colours, ornaments and such other things I always wore to suit his taste. I shared his joys and sorrows in equal measure. As his conjugal companion, I stood firmly behind him in every one of his activities.

I stood shoulder to shoulder with Dr Ambedkar in his social work too. I participated enthusiastically in meetings, gatherings and conferences related to social reformation. When it was not possible for Saheb to be present, I would attend meetings and give counsel. In particular, the Hindu Code Bill that Saheb had drafted and tabled in the Lok Sabha for the upliftment of women—I had helped him in its writing, in preparing excerpts, in making some suggestions during our discussions.

I gave valuable help to him in political matters. When Saheb stood from Mumbai for the 1952 elections, I addressed many election meetings and took care of his health needs, food needs and emotional needs through the heat and dust of the election rallies. When Saheb lost, I was there to help him absorb the jolt. When the picture of the results of the Bhandara by-election [1954] started becoming clearer, I persuaded him to attend the Buddhist Conference in Rangoon so that he could get the election out of his mind.

In the matter of religion, I was with him too. With the intention of nursing him back to good health after his electoral defeats, I diverted him towards religious work. The historic religious conversion was an outcome of this. I would sing the hymns to him every day, read out the Buddhist lore. I would also copy down the Pali lore for his book *The Buddha and His Dhamma*. We had also taken on the work of preparing a Pali dictionary to help people understand the Pali books. I did the writing of that dictionary.

In Saheb's work related to education, particularly in the establishing of the college in Aurangabad, I was with him all the way during its construction and supervision.

Saheb remained a student all through his life. His reading, writing and contemplation would carry on day and night. I would help him by searching out references, writing down excerpts, searching out books, buying books and a whole lot of other things. During discussions, I would also make suggestions. Great books like *The Buddha and His Dhamma*, *Revolution and Counter-Revolution in India*, *Riddles in Hinduism*, *The Philosophy of Hinduism*, *Essays on the Gita*, *Essays on Untouchability* were composed during my time.

I entered into Saheb's life in 1948 and he passed away in 1956; we thus lived together for almost nine years. This has to be considered an extremely important period of his life. It was during this period that he performed one deed after another that was important nationally and internationally. It was during our life together that he did his nationally critical work on the Constitution. It was during my time with him again that he did the humongous task of writing the Hindu Code Bill and tabling it in the Lok Sabha.

We went as representatives of the country to international conferences on Buddhism, and Saheb was assigned a position of honour in the world of Buddhism at an international level in those conferences. During my period he acquired the reputation of a 'Bodhisattva' who revived Buddhism in India.

After that happened the greatest deed of his life: his public religious conversion in Nagpur. That was the moment of the greatest satisfaction in both our lives, and it occurred during my period.

Life after Ambedkar

Terms like women's liberation, women's rights and women's freedom have become highfalutin words today. A number of organizations have arrived today that fight against atrocities on women and defend their rights; but Dr Ambedkar was fighting for women's rights and for their protection at a time when she counted for nothing, and she had no place in society. It was through the Hindu Code Bill that he gave women constitutional protection of their legal rights and brought for them a status equal to that of men. The credit of creating the constitutional equality of 'one person, one value' belongs exclusively to Dr Ambedkar. It was on account of this equality that Indira Gandhi, in spite of being a woman, became the prime minister of India.

Dr Ambedkar expended his entire life for equality, justice and for women's freedom; hence it is unfortunate that such an ordeal should have fallen to the lot of his own wife. But this bunch of leaders that called themselves the heirs to Dr Ambedkar's political legacy could not have gone on fooling people for ever and ever. With their political existence annihilated, a new educated, critical and a tad rebellious generation has arrived that has its own mind. It is as a consequence of Dr Ambedkar's work and his movement that this generation has come into existence. It was not possible for the now politically cold bunch of post-Ambedkar leaders to mislead these alert and independent-minded youngsters. Because of the work done by the Dalit Panthers, a new power, a new inspiration has been breathed into the Dalit movement. A special mention needs to be made of Raja Dhale, Ramdas Athawale, Namdeo Dhasal, J. V. Pawar, Waman Nimbalkar, Suresh Savant, Gangadhar Gade, Rameshchandra Parmar and a number of others. Mention also has to be made of the Ambedkarites across the country.

Summing Up

Dr Ambedkar lavished every moment of his life and every grain of his self on the upliftment of the Dalits and of women. The personal experience that I gained from having been his wife has lit up my entire life. It's quite natural for me to feel individually proud of having been the wife of an epochal personality, a great and supremely reverential leader. That was the reason why I decided to write this book—I was fired by the desire to bare my heart to the people and tell them of the raw pain that throbs inside me. Through this book, I have made a sincere, honest effort to present every word of mine, every event of my life with corroborative evidence, through Doctor Saheb's words wherever possible.

After Saheb, when his followers took the decision of joint leadership in 1957, I was delighted. I had believed that this great vehicle that my husband had created with such labour would keep moving efficiently, and therefore I tried to spend the rest of my life in solitary contemplation, meditating peacefully and with undivided attention on my great, venerable husband. But from 1960 onwards, every single institution that my husband had fashioned with such toil began to splinter. One group became two and two became four. When these exemplary organizations that were regarded as among the strongest in the history of India began falling to pieces, the heart ached. The political, religious, educational and social organizations into which Saheb had poured his lifeblood, every one of these organizations has been infected by the termite of disintegration.

It's now getting to be forty-two years since we became independent; yet, atrocities of the worst kind continue to be perpetrated upon the Dalits and the Buddhists. The facilities and the rights mandated by the Constitution are being denied. Every day one gets to read in the newspapers about the barbaric persecution of the Dalits and the Buddhists in every nook and corner of the country. Blindings, beatings, murders, the disrobing and parading of women, raping a girl in the presence of her parents, putting mother and son in the same bed and compelling them to copulate, setting a person on fire, burning down entire localities, snatching away land, imposing forced labour, committing inhuman brutalities, such and many such barbarities continue to happen. The only reason why these atrocities continue is the split among the leaders. Actually, the determination among all the Dalits to stake their lives for the principles of Doctor Saheb does exist. Otherwise, hundreds of thousands of brothers and sisters would not continue to gather from all over the country at the

Deeksha Bhoomi at Nagpur on the Dhammachakra Pravartan Day and at the Chaitya Bhoomi on the death anniversary every single year to pay homage to their leader. But this prodigious power lies dispersed.

Doctor Saheb's associate N. Shivraj had once said that a dead Dr Ambedkar is more dangerous than a live Dr Ambedkar. The country has taken a sampling of this observation during the 'Riddles' episode. This episode gave evidence of the fact that the thoughts of Dr Ambedkar can shake up the entire nation even thirty-three years after his death. This episode also gave the entire country a glimpse of the identity of the Dalit Buddhists of India. The historic unity that this episode brought about among the Buddhists, the nomadic Dalits, the adivasis and the minorities handed a crushing defeat to the opponents and the regressive forces. The occasion showed for sure that their identity is very much alive in the followers of Dr Ambedkar; it also proved that the Dalits can come together for the principles of Dr Ambedkar. Unfortunately, however, this unity did not last after the 'Riddles' episode.

My reliance is entirely on the young generation. They should set about awakening their brothers and sisters in the villages and create awareness in them. So many of our Buddhist brothers and sisters in the villages, on account of their ignorance, continue observing the rituals of Hinduism, make pledges against wish-fulfilment, attend religious fairs. They need to be galvanized through the message of their great leader. The entire burden of the community, in every sense, rests on the educated and the young generation. Under the circumstances prevailing today, this educated and young generation should understand the direction in which the world is moving and match its steps accordingly. Like a lighthouse, the philosophy of Dr Ambedkar shall ever be the guiding light of the community.

It is the inevitable need of the hour for all the Dalits and the exploited people to come together. That is why it is necessary to put the social, political, religious and educational institutions that

Dr Ambedkar built strongly on their feet and bring to fulfilment the dream of their great leader of making his India Buddha-inclined. As Tathagat Gautam Buddha has said, 'Be your own light.' You may rest assured that I stand firmly behind you with all my mother's love, tenderness and determination.

Sabbe satta sukhi hontu *sabbe hontu ch khemino*
Sabbe bhadraani passantu *maakachi dukkhmaagama*

May all life-forms be happy, may there be welfare of all
May all find their path to progress, may no one be unhappy

Epilogue[79]

(Pieced together from Vijay Surwade's introductions to the second and fourth editions)

The first edition of this autobiography was published on 24 March 1990 when Savita Ambedkar was alive, but by the time the second revised edition was published in 2010, seven years had gone by since her death on 29 May 2003. While the third edition of 2013 was a reprint of the second edition, the fourth edition of 2020 carried further revisions. The passing away of the author had obviously rendered the main book (along with the preface) beyond the reach of any emendation. But, meanwhile, much had happened between the publication of the first and the second edition, and again between the second and the fourth one that needed incorporating because they dealt with the central theme of the autobiography. For one, the author had continued to work fervidly in the areas so dear to her husband: upliftment of the Dalits, gender equality and the propagation of Buddhism. For another, a few more important letters and photographs had been discovered that had not been available for the earlier editions. For a third, Vijay Surwade had established communication with some of Savita Ambedkar's erstwhile detractors that brought their involvement into sharper relief.

Surwade found three ways of making available to readers what could not find place in the autobiography: (a) he wrote an independent biography of Mrs Savita Ambedkar titled *Dr Ambedkarnaanchya*

Saavalicha Sangharsh (*The Struggles of Dr Ambedkar's Shadow*) to be read as a companion-piece with the autobiography; (b) he accommodated many of the later events in the introductions he wrote for the second and fourth editions; and (c) he published as appendices the letters that had surfaced later.

Some of the important things that Surwade mentions are given below:

1. Dr Savita Ambedkar was a member of the delegation led by Yeshwant Ambedkar that met the then prime minister of India, Morarji Desai, on 17 August 1977 to discuss the issue of providing for the Buddhists the facilities that were available to the Scheduled Castes.
2. After the passing away of Yeshwant Ambedkar on 17 September 1977, she chaired a conference held in the Dr Babasaheb Ambedkar Sanskritik Bhavan and got a resolution passed demanding reservation for the Buddhists. Copies of the resolution were submitted to the state and the Central governments.
3. She founded the Babasaheb Ambedkar Foundation in 1984.
4. She received the Bharat Ratna award posthumously conferred upon Dr Ambedkar on 14 April 1990, at the hands of President R. Venkataraman.
5. She filed a petition in 1990 claiming that the property disputed as Babri Masjid–Ram Janmabhoomi was actually a Buddhist vihara. When her case was dismissed in 1995, she challenged the decision in the Supreme Court, submitting ancient documents as well as the descriptions of the Chinese travellers to substantiate her claim. The place was known then as Saket. She wrote a letter in 1991 to the King of Thailand, as the king of a Buddhist country, and requested him to support her claim regarding the vihara.
6. She presided over the function held on 26 November 1996 to inaugurate the Dr Ambedkar Museum constructed by the Symbiosis Institute at the hands of Vice President K.R. Narayanan.

In his introduction to the fourth edition, Surwade writes [translated from Marathi]:

'As a result of the vicious propaganda that had been launched against her, Maisaheb was compelled to live a life of anonymity from 1956 to 1970. Though she had withdrawn from public life, she had continued to participate to the best of her abilities in other activities set in motion by Babasaheb and in religious activities too. She shifted in 1970 from Delhi to Mumbai. Within a short time, D.D. Bawiskar of Dadar got wind of Mai; he reached out to her and won her confidence. Little by little, her visits to Bawiskar's house began. By a stroke of coincidence, my first meeting with Mai happened in Bawiskar's house when I was still a student (1971). Like me, there were other Panther leaders and workers who would visit Bawiskar's house to meet Mai and sit there having discussions. It was my good fortune that the acquaintance that I had made with Maisaheb as a student went on gaining strength with the passing of time. It was on account of my sincerity that I became her trusted and intimate associate. From 1984 to 2000, she would often come to stay at my house with affection and as a matter of right. From 2000 onwards her physical and mental health began slipping steadily. Finally, on 29 May 2003, she breathed her last in J.J. Hospital, Mumbai.'

Dilating on Mrs Ambedkar's denigrators, Surwade writes:

'Prominent among those who had spread poison against Mai were B.C. Kamble, Sohanlal Shastri, Shankaranand Shastri, Nanak Chand Rattu, Bhagwan Das, D.T. Rupvate, C.B. Khairmode, R.D. Bhandare and a few others, with some of whom I later developed good relations. It is interesting that all of these detractors of Mai knew very well that I was very close to her and enjoyed her fullest confidence.[80] However, my intimacy with Mai never stood between me and Mai's detractors. I would often talk with them about Mai in a convivial atmosphere. I still have in my possession the correspondence I had with Shankaranand Shastri, Nanak Chand Rattu and Bhagwan Das for years together.'

Given below in Surwade's own words [translated from Marathi] are the interactions, the communication, the discussions and the arguments that Surwade had with four of Mrs Ambedkar's opponents.

1. B.C. alias Bapusaheb Kamble (1919–2006)

Bapusaheb got to hear about my collection and phoned me, expressing his desire to come over to my house to see the collection. Responding to my delighted welcome message, he came to my house on 8 February 1985. I was then living in a chawl called Tathagat Nivas, Jagtap Wadi, Tisgaon Naka Road, Kalyan (East). It had been decided that we would meet on the railway bridge between ten and half past ten in the morning. Although I did reach on time, I found Bapusaheb waiting for me, which made me feel quite guilty. There were no rickshaws plying in Kalyan during those times and we were required to carefully pick our way through the railway tunnel and step over the tracks for shunting the rakes of the goods trains. An important leader of the Ambedkar movement, handpicked as the editor of the newspaper *Janata* by Babasaheb himself, elected twice to the Lok Sabha, member of the Legislative Assembly and the Legislative Council, privileged with having spent time in Babasaheb's company—this was the person who was hopping across these obstacles to give me a visit. He spent the entire day going through my collection of photographs, reference works and files of Babasaheb's correspondence; he wrote out references behind some photographs that he wanted and marked some of the letters out with a pencil. I later arranged for photocopies of those photographs and letters to be delivered at my expense to his residence at Adarsh Nagar, Worli.

The cover page of every one of the volumes carries a photograph that came from my collection.

During our conversation I asked him point-blank: 'Saheb, do you accuse Maisaheb of having poisoned Babasaheb to death?' I had shot the question, all right, but I did carry the fear that I might have offended him. As was his wont, he waved his palms criss-crossing them against each other and calmly responded, 'Not at all. Our one single demand was that a team of expert doctors should investigate the appropriateness of the treatment being administered to Babasaheb and the dosage of the medicines and publish its report.'

As we sat for our dinner, I casually asked him, 'Saheb, you would surely have sat for dinner with Babasaheb a number of times?'

To which he instantly answered, 'Not even once. I was the junior-most among the leaders of those times and had the least interaction with Babasaheb.'

During this conversation, I also said, 'Saheb, you were handpicked by Babasaheb in 1948 to be the editor of the *Janata*. That would mean that you had frequent interaction with him, either personally or on the phone.'

His response was, 'I certainly was the editor, but he neither placed constraints upon my independence nor did he interfere in any manner. That ruled out the possibility of much interaction with him. His one single insistence was that I should show him the proof of his speeches before they went to print.'

'So, this would surely have brought about a few meetings with him?'

'Well, the occasions were extremely rare, because I would not carry the proofs personally. Anybody going to Rajgraha would carry them along, but that was only when he was in Mumbai. For the rest of the time, they would be sent by post to Delhi. Thus, my personal interaction with him was rare.'

This is probity of a very high order. The great socialist leader S.M. Joshi has often praised Bapusaheb for his sincerity, his commitment to Ambedkar's philosophy and for his rectitude. On the strength of my experience I have often said that I have had the good fortune of meeting a number of leaders, colleagues and workers who spent considerable time in the company of Babasaheb. Three honourables among them I found to be persons of great integrity:

Maisaheb Ambedkar, Bapusaheb Kamble and S.S. Rege. They never said a single untruthful thing and they never tried to gather undeserved credit. I can say with certainty that whatever they said was endorsed by some reference or evidence that I encountered later.

2. Shankaranand Shastri (1915–2000)

Sometime in 1977, I had read an article by Shankaranand Shastri on Dr Ambedkar that was published in the English monthly *Dalit Voice*. Knowing that he had spent a very long time in the company of Babasaheb in Delhi, I had written a letter to him. He was then working as director in the employment office of the Government of India at New Delhi. He sent a reply to my letter and thus began a regular correspondence with him. I then got to know that there were some original photographs of Babasaheb in the possession of the photographs division of the Ministry of Information and Broadcasting of the Government of India and these photographs could be obtained on the payment of some fee. I requested him to procure for me Babasaheb's photographs as well as some photographs that were a part of his collection. He happily gave in to my request and got eight or ten photographs sent over to me by registered post at his own expense. These included two historically important pictures of Babasaheb going over for a last darshan of Gandhiji after Nathuram Godse had assassinated him on 30 January 1948.

After that, whenever he came visiting his son-in-law Satpute who worked for Air India and lived in Mazgaon, Mumbai, he would occasionally come over to the IDBI bank to meet me. He was a trustee of the Buddhist Society of India founded by Babasaheb, as also an office bearer in the governing body of the People's Education Society, which would bring him to Mumbai quite regularly. Every time he was in Mumbai, he would make it a point to meet me. Although he was a bitter opponent of Mai, he was always affectionate to me and spoke quite candidly with me in Hindi and English. During my frequent meetings with him, he spoke to me on his own on the following issues:

i. The opinion of his entire group [including Sohanlal Shastri, Rattu and Yeshwant (Bhaiyyasaheb)] was that Mai had secreted away a lot of money and they had wanted to rifle her steel cupboard (which is now in the Dr Ambedkar Memorial Museum of Symbiosis at Pune), but could not find the opportunity. Babasaheb passed away on 6 December 1956 and his body was placed for public viewing on 7 December at Rajgraha in Mumbai. That was when Mai gave her purse to Sudama Gangawane for safekeeping and the opportunity came walking in because Sudama had already been inducted into this mission.

   Mai has written about this episode in her autobiography.

   My interaction with Shankaranand Shastri continued for a number of years, during which we exchanged correspondence as also telephone calls. Once, in the flow of conversation, I asked him, 'If you were suspicious about the manner of Babasaheb's death, why didn't you ask for a post-mortem investigation?' His response was that, however close he was to Babasaheb, a post-mortem investigation could be conducted only on the request of a close blood relative. When I asked him why he couldn't file such a request through Bhaiyyasaheb, he replied, 'We had asked Yeshwantrao to go for a post-mortem investigation, but he said there was no need for it.'

ii. Mai had once told me that after Babasaheb's passing away, a plot had been hatched to exterminate her. She had told me that B.K. Kelkar of Delhi had alerted her about it. When I asked Shankaranand about this in one of our conversations, he confessed, 'I had the devil sitting in my head at that time. Yes, I had wanted to murder her. But Sohanlal, Rattu and others persuaded me out of it by saying that Babasaheb's body was resting at that time in the bungalow. If I were to commit something untoward, all kinds of problems would crop up. What would happen to my wife and children?'

Despite knowing that I was very close to Mai, Shankaranand always interacted with me with extreme courtesy and expressed himself without any effort at concealment. Each time that we met, I would talk to him about Mai's contribution, about the preface to *The Buddha and His Dhamma*, her recitation of trisharana and panchsheel with Babasaheb on 2 May 1950, the historic conversion at Nagpur, her dedication and her work after the passing away of Babasaheb. This began to have some effect on him. Towards the later days he would say, 'Whatever had to happen has happened, but from here onwards I shall not write anything against Mai.'

3. Nanak Chand Rattu (1922–2002)

During the last few years of Babasaheb's life (1950–56), Nanak Chand Rattu would do the typing work for his books, speeches and correspondence. I had developed an acquaintance with him and exchanged letters with him for many years. I've even had telephonic conversations with him. I met him in person at his Delhi residence only once when I spent the entire day with him. That was when I said to him, 'If you had doubts about the manner of Babasaheb's death, you should have gone for a post-mortem.' He replied, 'Post-mortem would have been of no use. Mai would give him an overdose of insulin and it was this slow poisoning that caused his death. The post-mortem would not have revealed this.'

Rattu had told me that when Mai's effects had been thrown out of 26, Alipore Road and the bungalow had been sealed under court orders, he had given her shelter in his house. Rattu's complaint was that whenever she gave him money for buying something, she would immediately ask him to return the balance.

It appears to me that Rattu's behaviour was duplicitous. If he had really suspected Mai of having committed murder, why did he, then, shelter her in his house for many months? Why did he step forward to help her whenever the occasion demanded? Why did he help her sell the Mehrauli house once she had decided to shift to Mumbai? Why did he continue with his correspondence with her once she had settled down? (I have the entire correspondence in my possession.) Why did he place her in the dock of suspicion when he gave typewritten statements to both the biographers Dhananjay Keer and C.B. Khairmode of his memories and recollection of events? On the one hand, he would stretch himself out at her feet in reverence and on the other he joined the adversaries and pointed fingers at her.

When Shankaranand Shastri was once in conversation with me in Mumbai, he said, 'Nanak Chand is Mai's stooge.' To which I responded, 'He is her opponent.' At that, he said, 'It was Nanak Chand who looked after her in Delhi. Mai had his support. He was the one who sold the Mehrauli house for her.' I had always considered Rattu to be in the opponents' camp on the basis of the information he had supplied to Dhananjay Keer and Khairmode, which I have in my collection. The information that Shankaranand was now giving me on Rattu ran contrary to what I had believed all along.

When I queried Mai, she said that Rattu had helped her during her stay in Delhi. Every time he visited Mumbai, he would pay her a visit and spread himself out at her feet in reverence. I then informed her that Rattu had given typed and signed statements of his memories and recollection of events to both Dhananjay Keer and Khairmode that indirectly brought her under suspicion. The writings of these biographers only strengthened the misgivings against her. Mai was completely dumbfounded. I then got photocopies made of Rattu's statements, put them in a file and took them over to her. (The file still exists in my collection.) It was only after reading those statements that Mai realized the duplicitous nature of Rattu.

She would call me up at my office three or four times every day. One day she called me up at around four or half past four and said, 'Something very interesting happened today.' On my asking her what it was, she said, 'That Rattu had come to see me today. I asked him point-blank what statement he had given to Dhananjay Keer and Khairmode about me. When he started making denials, I threw at him the file you had given me. When he glanced through them, he was completely nonplussed. I then drove him away and told him never ever to darken my door.'

This event happened in 1994 or 1995. Rattu never returned to Mai after that.

Meanwhile, Mai had gifted to Rattu a number of things that she and Babasaheb had used: clothes, neckties, vessels, typewriter, cutlery, gift items, as also a few documents. All these things Rattu had turned over to Wamanrao Godbole for his museum at Chincholi near Nagpur. But in the first half of 2001, some clashes happened among the committee members and Rattu got to know that Godbole himself was being ousted. He now wanted all those things back. Since they had been given to him by Mai, he needed a certificate from her by using which he could claim back those things. He obviously couldn't gather the courage to write directly to Mai, hence he wanted to use me as mediator. He therefore called me and requested me to help him procure Mai's signature on the document of certification. As discussed on the phone, he sent me a draft of the letter that he wanted from Mai. This letter reads as follows:

Phone: 5586855

NANAK CHAND RATTU

A – 1/88, Paschim Vihar, New Delhi – 110 063

Ref. No____________ Dated 13-7-2001

My dear Surwade,

Jai Bheem: I draw your kind attention to the telephonic conversation that I had with you in connection with the affairs of

Ambedkar Museum at Nagpur. I am enclosing the declaration to be signed by Dr Mrs. S. Ambedkar. The same speak for itself [sic].

I constructed DR [sic] Ambedkar Museum with the generous donations I had got from U. K. Now [a] few persons at Nagpur are bent upon to create [sic] mischief to do away with the personal belongings and relics which I preserved for more than 35 years at my place in New Delhi. Part of these had been taken to Pune, about which you are already aware.

There is [a] lot to be said and written. I request you kindly to take the trouble to meet her immediately on receipt of this letter and return the enclosed one duly signed by her. Some mischievous elements are bent upon to sell [sic] out and destroy all these which I preserved all these years. I have told you enough and need hardly to write more. You are so near to her and this may not be difficult for you to get this signed. The services that I rendered to her will never be repaid for generations to come. Infact [sic] I did my best to build up her image and protect her from the fury of the masses.

With best wishes:
Yours sincerely,
(Signature)

(N. C. Rattu)
13. 7. 2001
Shri Vijay Surwade,
C-8 Usha Apartments,
Usha Nagar, Murbad Road,
Kalyan (W), Distt. Thane,
421304

Mai's health had been failing day by day from 2000 onwards. She would occasionally slip into amnesia. At other times she would not be able to recognize anyone. She would sometimes babble disconnectedly. I had got my friend Ashok Gajbhiye of the IDBI to type out the draft sent by Rattu on the Dr Ambedkar Foundation letterhead. But Mai was in a state in which she could not understand things. I therefore didn't think it proper to get her signature during her unbalanced state of mind. Thus, considering it morally improper, I did not get her signature. Nanak Chand Rattu later died in 2002, making the subject of Mai's letter altogether redundant. It appears incongruous that although Mai had driven Rattu away from her house, he still expected Mai to sign a letter that would help him retrieve the things he had given over to Chincholi, Nagpur.

4. Bhagwan Das (1927–2010)

Bhagwan Das was another of Mai's opponents in Delhi, but unlike Shankaranand, Sohanlal, Rattu or Khairmode, he did not get into talking against her publicly. My first meeting with him happened in quite an unexpected manner. My wife and I had gone to Delhi in 1980 along with our daughter, Vaishali. After having done the round of the tourist places in Delhi, Simla, Kulu-Manali, Agra, etc., we were returning by train from Delhi to Nagpur. Right opposite our seat I found a gentleman checking out the proofs of Babasaheb's speeches. Noticing those proofs, I introduced myself to him. He gave his name as B. Das. After this first meeting, our intimacy increased with the passing of time. We continued having correspondence and exchanging documents/references till the day of his passing away. He had wanted the entire set of booklets of Santram B.A. (1887–1988), which I had in my collection. I promptly got them photocopied and sent them over to him. We would continue with this exchange of books and documents. Whenever a book of his or mine got published, we would dispatch a copy to each other without fail. I met him four or five times at his house in the DDA Flats, Munirka, New Delhi.

Instead of calling him Mai's opponent, it would be better to say that he was not one of Mai's supporters. It was likely that there were some things about Mai that he didn't approve of; or, perhaps, he might have felt offended on some occasion during his visits to Dr Ambedkar. But it does appear that he didn't carry a good opinion of Mai. Whatever it may be, it has to be admitted that he was a researcher, a scholar and an eminent lawyer at the Supreme Court. In September 1980, he published a small book titled *Rare Prefaces Written by Dr Ambedkar* (Bhim-Patrika Publication, Jullunder, Punjab). In this booklet, he made available to the readers and scholars of those times five prefaces of Dr Ambedkar's unpublished books. Bhagwan Das writes in this booklet, 'A copy of this preface [meaning the preface of *The Buddha and His Dhamma*], included in this collection, is available with Nanak Chand Rattu. I saw a copy of this preface also in the library of Milind Arts College. Aurangabad.' (Page 10.) The preface that Bhagwan Das published was of 5 December 1956. Babasaheb had handwritten the original preface on 15 March 1956. He had then made corrections to it on 6 April 1956, and had gone on modifying it right up to the night of 5 December 1956. These corrections can be seen done sometimes with an ordinary pencil, some other times with red and blue pencils and at yet other times with a fountain pen. Some lines were scored out while other lines were added. Nanak Chand Rattu was not merely a witness to these changes, but also a participant. But after all this, Rattu showed the shrewdness of getting that preface printed which mentioned his name and the name of Parkash Chand, but ensured that the preface that acknowledged gratitude for Maisaheb and Dr Malvankar did not go for publication. He was involved in the plot that had been hatched by the nefarious gang of Shankaranand, Sohanlal Shastri and Khairmode to defame Mai. The lines in the preface that acknowledged indebtedness to Mai and Dr Malvankar would have exposed the conspiracy of these intriguers in the eyes of the public. One thing that stands out clearly against this background is this: Bhagwan Das had come in possession of the 5 December preface through Rattu; but despite the fact that he was not a supporter of Mai, he showed the researcher's probity of publishing the preface that acknowledged Babasaheb's gratitude to Mai and Dr Malvankar.

Appendix 1

Four unpublished letters written by Dr Ambedkar to his fiancée Dr Sharada Kabir

During the occasion of the publication of the first edition of Mai's autobiography (1987–88), I had studied the entire correspondence of Dr Ambedkar from 1947 to 1952 that was in Mai's possession. Of them, the letters that Babasaheb wrote to Mai have been used in her autobiography. But in 1995, Falcon Books, Delhi, published an English book written by Babasaheb's typist Nanak Chand Rattu, titled *Reminiscences and Remembrances of Dr Ambedkar* for the Babasaheb Ambedkar Memorial Committee of Great Britain. Nanak Chand Rattu has published ten letters that Babasaheb wrote to Mai (pages 59 to 75). I noticed that since four of those ten letters were not in Mai's collection, they could not be published in the first edition. Babasaheb had written those four letters to his fiancée Dr Sharada Kabir (Mai) on 25 January 1948, 1 February 1948, 6 February 1948 and 13 March 1948. Six of those ten letters were in Mai's collection, but how did the four above-mentioned letters land in Rattu's possession? The opinion I have arrived at is this: As per the court's order, the bungalow on 26, Alipore Road was evacuated on 31 August 1967. Since Mai had nobody to lean on, she took shelter in Rattu's house for a few months. Rattu kept this matter of sheltering Mai a secret.[81]

During the period that she was staying with him, since he knew of the existence of those letters, he would, perhaps, have taken them from Mai for getting them typed out. While typing out Babasaheb's letters, Rattu might have kept these four letters for himself or Mai might have misplaced them. But because these letters are of historical importance, I am making all these four letters available for the readers.

—*Vijay Surwade*

Letter No. 1: Letter dated 25/1/1948 of Babasaheb from Delhi to his fiancée Dr Sharada Kabir, Bombay

25.1.48

[Dearest Sharu,]

I got your letter. You have undoubtedly stolen a march on me. I had hoped to be the first to write. But since my arrival I have been so much overburdened with work that I had not had a minute's time to attend to my personal affairs.

With regard to my illness I wish your sentiments were also a fact. Unfortunately my pain in the leg has come with me to Delhi and I don't know how long it will remain with me. I find its rhythm has changed. As before it starts between 3/4 in the morning but instead of stopping at about 2 in the morning [sic] as it did before it now continues for the whole day. Generally I feel that I have come back with less health than what I had when I came to Bombay. This feeling is probably one [sic] to the general sense of depression which has overcome [sic]. Somehow it has become a conviction with me that I shall never regain the health I once possessed. Only those who have seen me in the bloom of health—nay, even such health as I possessed only two years ago—can realize my sorrow regarding my health.

Of course, neither you nor Dr Malvankar should think that the cause of the delay in my recovery has anything to do with the treatment in the clinic. On the contrary I am grateful to both of you for the care and attention you have bestowed on me.

As to the bill, if my friends have said that it is heavy, they had more in mind my purse than the value of the service. I have no desire to raise any contention regarding the bill. All that may be necessary is to ask Dr Malvankar to ask [sic] for some time.

I now turn to the other matters to which you have referred. There was no particular purpose in sending you the stationery or the ruled card. The ruled card goes with the pad. The only thing that made me think of it was the fact that last time when you wrote you wrote on what is called a scribbling paper. As to replenishing the stationery I should be very glad to do it if it is available in Delhi. Unfortunately, it is not. It is available only in Bombay that too at Thacker & Company. It is not very costly. The pad costs only rupees 1/8. If you cannot afford it you can buy it at Thacker & Company and have it charged to me.

Your thoughts on my having a woman as a companion to look after me, I am sorry to say, were not quite welcome to me. There could not be much seriousness behind them. I have been brought up in a terribly moral and religious atmosphere. I could never entertain such a thought, much less a proposal, which would give rise to a public comment as being a misalliance. My wife died fourteen years ago. Since then I have remained unmarried—and have resolved to remain [so]. My friends who think I must live as long as possible have not been very happy about my resolution. But I have not listened to them altho [sic] they not only love me but worship me. I have been very much afraid of marriage. It is very difficult to say what sort of wife the woman would turn out to be. Intelligence is not the only qualification to be sought in selecting a woman nor beauty. Moral virtue is the chief criterion. I am also afraid of children. I am overwhelmed by the mere sense of responsibility of bringing them up. I am also overwhelmed by the fear that they may turn out to be bad children and disgrace their parents. Notwithstanding this I have been beginning to feel that in the interest of my health I may have to revise my resolution and that my own people will not forgive me if I refuse the aid of a woman, assuming [that] such aid is absolutely essential for the restoration of my health. If at all it comes to this, such a woman can only be [a] lawfully wedded wife and not a nurse or a companion.

You were perhaps disappointed when I declined to accept your services as a nurse to accompany me to Delhi and stay there for a month. But my whole position in public life is built up on [sic] my reputation as a man of character and unsullied morals. If my enemies are afraid of me and respect me, it is because of this. I can never be a party to damage it in any way. If it is damaged, the whole purpose of my life would not only vanish but my people for whom I have lived and sacrificed and who rightly or wrongly think I am their God would be destroyed.

The long and short of it is that if circumstances compell [sic] me to depart from my resolution I may marry but will not agree to keep a nurse or a companion especially when there is no other woman in the house. I am sure you will agree with these sentiments of mine.

It may be a long search for a woman who could be a satisfactory wife to me. But I am prepared to start my search with you if you on your own part are ready and are willing to explore the field. Are you?

My official correspondence is of course opened by my secretaries but not my personal correspondence. I should however advise you to take double precaution –

(1) to write Personal on the cover
and (2) to use double covers (one inside the other) both marked personal.

Write as and when you feel like writing.

Sincerely yours
B

Mai would tell me, and she has said this in the autobiography too, that on 26 January 1948, Shankaranand Shastri personally brought Dr Ambedkar's letter over from Delhi to give to her. This is that letter of 25 January 1948.

—*Vijay Surwade*

Letter No. 2: Letter of 1 February 1948 of Babasaheb from Delhi to his fiancée Dr Sharada Kabir, Bombay. This is the only letter in which he addresses her as 'Savita'.

Dear Savita,

Replies to two of your letters are in arrears. I wanted to clear up the arrears earlier but I could not. Friday, Saturday and Sunday have been used up in the Gandhi episode. It is now 11 at night and I am really feeling tired. My first thought was to postpone writing to you till tomorrow. It was also supported by my feeling that you deserved punishment for having put into the head of Dr Malvankar the idea of coming over to Delhi, which has put me in a great dilemma. It was a most thoughtless act and hysterical in the extreme, but my native kindness, which is a great weakness in me, has asserted itself—and I have been moved to sit up and write because I am sure you must be like the Pauranic Chatak bird waiting for my reply.

So you have accepted me and accepted my reasoning. As the proverb says a woman is like a flax, man is fire, the devil comes and blows the bellows. The best thing therefore is not to take a chance. I however thought that you would ask some questions about me and my past. But you haven't. I could see this time when I came to the clinic that you had already become a casualty. In such matters where one is [unclear word] down to life inquiries are necessary. Better be sure than sorry. I am a difficult man. Ordinarily, I am quiet as water and humble as grass. But when I get into [a] temper I am ungovernable and unmanageable. I am a man of silence. There is a charge against me that I don't speak to women—i.e. other women. But I don't even speak to men, unless they are my intimates. I am a man of moods. At times I can talk endlessly: at other times I shall not utter a word. At times, I am very serious. At times I am full of humour. I am no gay person—pleasures of life do not attract me. My companions have to bear the burden of my austerity and asceticism. My books have been my companions, they are dearer to me than wife and children. Morally I am intractable and I do not tolerate any lapses from strict rules of morals. I have recounted these facts about myself to give you some idea of what a difficult customer you have to deal with. Evidently you are not worried about all this. You perhaps think that, as by scratching and biting cats and dogs come together, so in the same [way] we too by scratching and biting shall come together. I wish you all success. You have not cared to inquire into my past. But it will be available to you at any time in the pages of many a Marathi magazine. But your personal history is not available to me. I would like you to give me some idea about it. It is not for decision, that is already made. It is out of curiosity. There is no hurry you may do it at your leisure. How we were [sic] brought together? What decision have we come to? It is all very strange!! The path of destiny is very strange. [I] accept it and will try to deserve you.

I have been wondering whether you have communicated to Dr Malvankar the great and grave decision you have come to. I have also been wondering what he would think of it. Would he be able to run his clinic without you? We must give him sufficient time to find a substitute. This is the least bit we can do for him.

I entirely agree with you in what you have said about Dr Malvankar. He resembles me very much. I have the greatest regard and respect for him. I would be prepared to do anything for him which lay [sic] within my power. If he wants my help I would like him to give me some concrete proposals. I shall certainly consider them.

I have sent you a small gift in a separate parcel which will reach you on Wednesday. Let me know if you like it. I am glad you are pleased with the stationery. I like art and have a great sense of asthetics [sic]. I do not like ugly things. How do you like the name I have given you? It is a great name. It means as shining as the sun.

With fondest love
from B

Letter No. 3: Extract from the letter of 6 February 1948 of Babasaheb from Delhi to his fiancée Dr Sharada Kabir, Bombay

. . . I entirely agree with you that Gandhi should [not] have met his death at the hands of a Maharashtrian. Nay! I go further and say that it would have been wrong for anybody to have committed such a foul deed. You know that I owe nothing to Mr. Gandhi and he has contributed nothing to my spiritual, moral and social make up. The only person to whom I owe my being is Gautam [Buddha]. Notwithstanding his antipathy to me, I went to the Birla House on Saturday morning and was shown his dead body. I could see the wounds. They were right in the heart. I was very much moved on seeing his dead body. I went with the funeral procession for a short distance as I was unable to walk and then returned home and again went to the Rajghat on the Jamuna but could not get to the Burning Place being unable to break the ring formed by the crowd.

You rightly say that we are passing through a very critical time and don't know the future. My own view is that great men are of great service to their country, but they are also, after a certain time, a great hindrance to the progress of their country. There is one incidence [sic] in Roman history which comes to my mind on this occasion. When Caesar was done to death and the matter was reported to Cicero, Cicero said to the messengers, 'Tell the Romans, your hour of liberty has come.' While one regrets the assassination of Mr. Gandhi, one can't help finding in his [sic] heart the echo of [the] sentiments expressed by Cicero on the assassination of Caesar. Mr. Gandhi had become a positive danger to this country. He had choked all free thoughts. He was holding together the Congress—which is a combination of all the bad and self-seeking elements in the society, who were agreed on no social or moral principle governing the life of society, except the one of praising and flattering Mr. Gandhi. Such a body is unfit to govern a country. As the Bible says, something good cometh out of evil, so also I think that good will come out of the death of Mr. Gandhi. It will release people from [the] bondage of a Superman, it will make them to think for themselves and it will compel them to stand on their own merits.

The deed having been done by a Maharashtrian, it is likely that the Maharashtrians might incur the odium of the wrath of Indians. I heard that in Delhi Cloth Mills, some Maharashtrians were molested by the Delhi workmen. You need not, however, be worried about it. I shall survive all these fearful occasions. People's wrath is a passing mood. What is surprising is that those who feel wrath or those who feel grief for the assassination of Mr. Gandhi seem to be so few. Indeed one of the most surprising thing[s] I noticed about the funeral procession—which no doubt was very large—a majority of them were in [a] holiday mood, as [if] they were going for [an] Urus and Jatra . . .[82]

Letter No. 4: Letter of 12 March 1948 of Babasaheb from Delhi to his fiancée Dr Sharada Kabir, Bombay

B

New Delhi
12/3/48

My dear Sharu,

Last night I promised you over the phone that I would sit down to write to you. Curiously enough the moment I left the phone I was overcome by a terrible feeling of exhaustion, so much so [that] I fell into my bed with my clothes on and could not get up till the morning. Even when I got up and went to the Assembly, I was still feeling exhausted. I recovered just this evening. I suppose it must be [due] to the train journey, which always brings about fatigue. [Today] I am better so sitting down to write a few lines to relieve you of anxiety.

I am glad you did not come to the station. I could not have controlled myself. I am wondering how you managed to control yourself. I am too weak, too tender and terribly subject to emotion. People have a very wrong notion about me. They think I am a [sic] hard-hearted, brutal, frank, cold, logical, all head and no heart. There is a tenderness and softness in me, which makes me weak and yield [sic]. I hope you won't regard me as a weakling for the tears I shed.

I am [sic] glad to see your father at the station. I don't know what impression he formed of me. I hope it was not unfavourable. He is at the close of his life and [I would] be very unhappy to find him feeling that his beloved daughter made a mistake in choosing her husband.

I don't know if you are satisfied with the things which I have selected as part of your bridal attire. If there is anything else you wish to have, you have only to write to me and although I am not a rich man I will do my level best to procure it for my Sharu if she will be happy to have it. Of course, you will admit that you could not choose the right thing without my help and guidance and I am, therefore, not certain of the wisdom of letting you choose things for yourself. But you[r] happiness is to me more important than the fitness of the thing chosen. Don't hesitate to let me know if you desire to have any other article. I several times reminded you [of] the necessity of having a wrist watch. Somehow, you never took kindly to the suggestion. I don't know why. While in the train I remembered that you had mentioned a dressing gown. I forgot about it. I give you the liberty to buy one. But can you assure me that you can choose a good one in point of colour and material? Better you wait till you come here.

I am feeling very lonely. It is very funny for a man like me to say that I feel lonely. I have lived a lonely life at least for the past fifteen years. I have had no companion but I had learned to live a happy life without there being anyone to bestow personal affection on me. Why then do I suddenly begin to feel lonely now? The answer is that there is Sharu. When there was no Sharu then I was alone and not lonely. Now, there is Sharu and I am lonely because I am alone, without her company. I wonder if you feel lonely just as I do at this end.

I am anxiously waiting for your letter, which I hope to get tomorrow.

With fondest and deepest love to dearest Sharu.

From
Raja

Appendix 2

Three unpublished letters written from Delhi by Mai: two to Kamalakant Chitre and one to Balwant Varale, both close associates of Dr Ambedkar

Letter No. 1

Dear Mr. Chitre,

Dr Saheb tells me to inform you that we will be arriving there on Sunday, the 14th, by morning air-service, reaching Bombay at 12 noon. We would be staying at Rajgruha [sic] and request you to get the place cleaned etc. through Tipnis. I would like to have a cot and mattresses, as we had last time, from the college. Rest of the other things are already there and on our arrival I could look to that. You will also have to arrange for our food, as Sudama is staying back. It will be nice if we could get a cook boy to look after the things during our short stay.

Barring [a] little lack of energy (which is entirely his doing, for he is so much after reduction that no laxity in food is permissible), Dr Saheb is much better in his legs and everyday feeling more confident about movements.

Delhi gives him much rest, besides giving full scope and time for his literary pursuits, which he must be after in right earnest.

The weather here is specially suitable for him, as he feels much comfortable and at ease [in] colder climate.

With kind regards,
Yours sincerely,
Savita Ambedkar.

Letter No. 2

Dear Mr. Chitre,

It is nearly a week [since] we left Bombay and as yet there are no signs of Sawatkar's [Kashinath Savaadkar] coming here. As you know, we wanted him for more than one reason. Besides other things, the boxes he was to have brought with him contained, besides books, some other articles which are badly needed here. You told at the airport that Sawatkar would leave in 3/4 days time, hence I didn't say anything though Dr Saheb didn't believe it. Now, his typing work [is] almost finished and we will have to plan [a] date for Aurangabad. If it [is] not possible to release Sawatkar, Dr Saheb suggests Mane—our driver. Somehow the boxes must be sent with either of the two—to that [is] added [the] recent water scarcity. We have purchased [an] air-cooler for Dr Saheb's study-cum-bedroom, but it doesn't work satisfactorily. He is very uncomfortable and restless. Hence, we must run away from here as early as we can. Heat, besides causing general disturbance, leads to a peculiar type of body-aching, which is relieved by oil-massage. Here, there is nobody who can attend to such needs of the Doctor. Here, an attendant who could do every personal service for Doctor Saheb is necessary. His new book—Riddles in Hinduism—will definitely jeopardize his personal safety, hence it is absolutely essential to have an honest, intelligent and devoted man to be with him constantly.

We hope Bombay has had a change in temperature for the better and that you are also keeping well.

With kind regards,
Yours sincerely,
Savita Ambedkar.

Letter No. 3

Dear Mr. Varale,

Mr. Chitnis must have informed you about our correspondence with Alegason. We haven't received any reply from [him] yet. Dr Shrimali's visit may turn out to be of some help to our school. Mr. Shrikant is asking for details about [the] technical school, which Chitnis has to supply to us, then Dr Saheb means to discuss personally with Mr. Shrikant. Then he will explore the possibility of getting some building grants for our hostel.

Damu has proved very useful. We must have some such person always with Dr Saheb. What happened to your search? Bhaurao [Gaikwad], who accompanied us from Bombay, has offered to be here at least during next Parliament Session, for it's then that I require some companion like person for him. Last time, Chitnis was here and this time I don't know what arrangements to make. When there is no Parliament, I go about with him, but it doesn't look nice for me to go like that in the Parliament. Bhaurao is such a busy person and I don't like him to be tied down here for over a month, though he has very willingly offered his service during the coming Parliament Session. If you can think of some other person, it may do. We need a faithful and intelligent, strong person. My father was wondering if you could spare Bhalu [Bhalchandra] for a month or so—but that depends on his college and studies. From all these points of view, I think it's better we get a constant and trustworthy fellow as companion for Doctor. Somebody like you is very much desirable, for even if he is able to move about alone, we must have somebody like a bodyguard, for his activities are such that many people get offended and naturally are waiting for a chance to vindicate [sic]. He is much better than what [sic] you saw him last time in Bombay. When I say better, it is his legs—he is inclined to walk without [a] stick and with confidence.

I have procured for our garden [Milind College garden] some very beautiful saru sapling [sic]. They are sent with Damu and Dada (who is specially detained here sometimes about a week)—you must receive them personally for they are very delicate things. They must be carried from Manmad by you very carefully and preserved in shade near a well till their site for planting is decided. There are some tall ones and some short (मयुरपंखी) colour is like peacock feathers. Nathu, our Delhi gardener is not accompanying Damu, his fare money will be utilized for purchasing these seedlings. In all I have asked for hundred plants, the cost we shall know by Monday.

Delhi is warmed up because of monsoon. I hope everybody at home is well so also your shoulders and yourself.

With kind regards,
Yours sincerely,
S. Ambedkar

Appendix 3

The following are the twenty-two vows administered by Ambedkar to his followers.

Omvedt version 1

1. I shall have no faith in Brahma, Vishnu and Maheshwara, nor shall I worship them.
2. I shall have no faith in Rama and Krishna, who are believed to be incarnations of God, nor shall I worship them.
3. I shall have no faith in Gauri, Ganapati and other gods and goddesses of Hindus, nor shall I worship them.
4. I do not believe in the incarnation of God.
5. I do not and shall not believe that Lord Buddha was the incarnation of Vishnu. I believe this to be sheer madness and false propaganda.
6. I shall not perform *shraddha* nor shall I give *pind*.
7. I shall not act in a manner violating the principles and teachings of the Buddha.
8. I shall not allow any ceremonies to be performed by Brahmins.
9. I shall believe in the equality of man.
10. I shall endeavour to establish equality.
11. I shall follow the Noble Eightfold Path of the Buddha.
12. I shall follow the ten *paramitas* prescribed by the Buddha.

13. I shall have compassion and loving kindness for all living beings and protect them.
14. I shall not steal.
15. I shall not tell lies.
16. I shall not commit carnal sins.
17. I shall not take intoxicants like liquor, drugs, etc.
18. I shall endeavour to follow the Noble Eightfold Path and practise compassion and loving kindness in everyday life.
19. I renounce Hinduism, which disfavours humanity and impedes the advancement and development of humanity because it is based on inequality, and adopt Buddhism as my religion.
20. I firmly believe the Dhamma of the Buddha is the only true religion.
21. I consider that I have taken a new birth. (Alternatively, 'I believe that by adopting Buddhism I am having a rebirth.')
22. I solemnly declare and affirm that I shall hereafter lead my life according to the teachings of Buddha's Dhamma.

—Omvedt (2003, *pp. 261–62)*

Glossary of Sanskrit, Pali and Marathi Terms

Aarti (aa-ra-tee)	The swirling of a platter before a person's face or an idol, with a lighted lamp placed on it for worshipping or expressing devotion.
Aga	An interjection addressed to an intimate lady; the equivalent of a 'hey'. Used mostly to address one's wife.
Aho	A more respectful form of 'aga' above. Used mostly by a wife to address her husband.
Akashvani (aa-kaash-vaa-nee)	State-run radio station offering service in Indian languages.
Bahishkrut Bharat	Ostracized India: Marathi fortnightly launched by Dr Ambedkar in 1927.
Bai (baa-ee)	Lady
Bhakari (bhaa-ka-ree)	Unleavened bread made of sorghum (jowar); the staple food of the poor, often eaten with chutney and raw onions.
Bhiksha	Alms
Bhikshu	1. A mendicant; 2. A fully ordained Buddhist monk. Such a monk is required to own no possessions and live by the alms that he receives by begging.
Bhikku	The Pali word for bhikshu.
Bodhisattva	In Buddhist doctrine, a person intent on becoming the Buddha.

	Also, a person who can reach the state of enlightenment, but does not do so out of a desire to help living beings.
Brahmanetar (brah-ma-ney-tar)	Literally, other than Brahmins.
Chaitya Bhoomi	'Chaitya' is a temple or a shrine; 'bhoomi' is land. Here, Chaitya Bhoomi is the place on Dadar beach, Mumbai, where Dr Ambedkar was cremated. It has become a pilgrimage site for his followers.
Chamar (cha-maar)	A community of Dalits now classified among the scheduled castes. The community has traditionally been associated with the profession of tanning.
Chapatees (cha-paa-teez)	Anglicized pluralization of chapatee: unleavened bread made from wheat flour.
Dak bungalow	Here, government rest house.
Dalit	Literally, 'oppressed'. The word is now adopted by and for the communities that were formerly regarded as falling outside the four-tier caste system of the Hindus. They were considered untouchables.
Darshan	Literally, special sighting. Going to a temple to view the idol of a deity, or visiting a holy man or a great person or even looking at any heavenly body on special occasions is called 'taking a darshan'.
Deeksha (deek-shaa)	The symbolic ritual of being initiated into a religion. When a person receives deeksha from an authorized person, that person is regarded as having accepted and officially been admitted into the religion.
Deeksha Bhoomi	The name given to the fourteen-acre plot of land in Nagpur where Dr Ambedkar received his initiation into Buddhism on 14 October 1956. After embracing Buddhism, he gave the deeksha to about 5 lakh of his followers who had assembled for the purpose. It is an important pilgrimage site for Ambedkar's followers.
Dharma	1. Creed, religion; 2. Duty; 3. Quality. As used in this book, it means religious creed.

Dhamma	The Pali word for 'dharma'. The teachings of the Buddha.
Dhamma prachar (pra-chaar)	The propagation of religion.
Dhammachakra	Literally, the wheel of dhamma; it is a symbol widely used in Buddhism.
Dhammapada	A collection of the preachings of the Buddha put in verse.
Dhotar/dhoti	A length of cloth wound at the waist to cover the body from the waist down. One end is often passed between the legs to create a fork for the two legs.
Harijan	Literally meaning the 'children of god', this term was coined by the Gujarati poet-saint Narsinh Mehta for all devotees of Krishna. Gandhiji later gave this name to the Dalits. Mrs Ambedkar uses this term here to refer to the Dalits who stayed with the Congress Party.
Jai/Jaya	Victory. The word 'jaya' is attached to the name of a person/place, wishing that person or place victory.
Janata	Literally, the common people. Here it is the name of a newspaper started by Dr Ambedkar in 1930.
Jayanti	Birth anniversary.
Karma	1. Deed; 2. In Indian philosophy, a law of cause and effect by which good and bad deeds determine a person's existence in the next life.
Kurta (koortaa)	A loose tunic worn mostly by men.
Lungi	A single sheet of cloth wrapped round the waist and the lower limbs. It is used most commonly in eastern and southern India as daily wear by men.
Mang (maang)	A community of Dalits now classified among the scheduled castes. Their profession by tradition was the playing of drums, rope-making, broom-making, castration of cattle, leather curing, etc.
Mahar (ma-haar)	A community of Dalits now classified among the scheduled castes. They were responsible for maintaining law and order in the village. Some

	authorities say that they were also required to carry messages from one village to another and also to remove the carcasses of dead cattle from the village.
Mandal	Loosely, an association formed for some specific purpose.
Mangalsutra (mangal-sootra)	A necklace worn by a Hindu woman once she is married. In its commonest form, it is made of small black beads strung together and interspersed with a few gold beads.
Manu Smriti	'The Laws of Manu'. It is commonly believed to be the first legal text and code of conduct for Hindu society. It explicates the four-varna system or the caste system, which is generally traced to the Purusha Sukta verse of the Rig Veda.
Mook Nayak (Mook Naayak)	Literally, 'mute hero'. It was the name of a fortnightly newspaper started by Dr Ambedkar in 1920.
Mook samaj (mook samaaj)	Mute (voiceless) community
Panchsheel	The five precepts that form the minimal standard of ethics in Buddhism. These precepts are often recited as an act of worship.
Peeth	1. Spiritual and religious headquarters; 2. centres of religious learning.
Pooran poli	A popular Maharashtrian sweet dish. It is a pie made from gram flour, sugar and ghee (clarified butter).
Puranas	Literally, ancient. It is a vast genre of literature that ranges across genealogies and stories of gods and goddesses, demons, kings, heroes, sages, folk tales and legends on every conceivable subject.
Sanatana	Literally, 'eternal', it is an alternative name of Hinduism. In this book it is used to represent the ultra-orthodox strain of Hinduism.
Sapinda	Term used in the context of consanguinity in marriage among the Hindus. As per the Hindu Marriage Act of 1955, a man and a woman are

	regarded as 'sapinda' if they fall within the third ascending generation through the mother and fifth ascending generation through the father and hence are prohibited from marrying each other.
Satyagraha (sat-yaa-gruha)	'Satya' means truth and 'aagraha' means 'insistence'; Gandhiji initiated, developed and popularized this non-violent form of protest. It advocates non-violent resistance to injustice. This form of protest went international when both Martin Luther King (Jr) and Nelson Mandela adopted it for their struggles.
Satyanarayana	Satyanarayana is a manifestation of Lord Vishnu. People organize Satyanarayana pooja (prayers) at their homes or workplaces, often after marriage or at the launching of a new initiative.
Savarna	The word initially referred to people belonging to the four varnas, or the Hindu caste system. However, it now means people belonging to the upper castes.
Shastra (shaastra)	A Sanskrit word that means a book, a treatise, a manual, a set of instructions on any subject, including religion. It is used as a suffix for knowledge in any specific area of study.
Shloka	A piece of verse or stanza in most Indian languages composed in a specific metrical structure.
Shubh din	Auspicious day
Smriti	Sacred Hindu literature based on memory; as different from *shruti*, which is heard literature (such as divine revelation), as the Vedas are.
Trisharana	The three-fold refuge of the Buddha, the dhamma and the sangha
Vihara (vi-haa-ra)	Commonly means a monastery for Buddhist monks. In ancient Sanskrit and Pali texts, it meant any arrangement made for dwelling.

Notes

1. See Glossary.
2. See Glossary.
3. See Glossary.
4. 1. Gandhi quote: '[T]he [Satyagraha] Ashram has a firm belief in the varnashrama dharma. The discipline of caste seems to have done no harm to the country.' *Collected Works of Mahatma Gandhi,* Vol. XIII, p. 94. New Delhi: Publications Division, 1958–94. 2. 'I believe that caste has saved Hinduism from disintegration.' Ramchandra Guha quoting Gandhi in *Gandhi: The Years that Changed the World*; p. 123; Penguin Random House India, 2018.
5. Translator's note: This seems to be an error on the author's part. Dr Ambedkar was not appointed but elected as the chairman of the Drafting Committee on 30 August 1947.
6. Dr B. R. Ambedkar, *Dr Babasaheb Ambedkar Writings and Speeches* (Dr BAWS), Vol. 21, p. 25. It is undated in the original.
7. *Letters by Dr Babasaheb Ambedkar to Dadasaheb Gaikwad*, ed. Waman Nimbalkar, Prabodhan Publication, Nagpur, February 2011, p. 493.
8. Dr BAWS, Vol. 21, p. 54.
9. Ibid., Vol. 1, p. 35.
10. Ibid., Vol. 21, p. 132.
11. Ibid., Vol. 21, p. 93.
12. Actually, A.V. Alexander came to India in 1942.
13. The author would most likely have meant the Vice-Regal Lodge.

14. In Hindi and Marathi, the suffix '-in' changes the gender of the word to feminine. Thus, a minister's wife would be a 'ministerin' and a woman doctor or a doctor's wife would become 'doctorin'.
15. Dr BAWS, Vol. 21, pp. 260–63.
16. Letter dated 15 April 1948 from Vallabhbhai Patel to Nehru, *Sardar Patel's Correspondence*, Vol. 6 (1945 to 1950), ed. Durga Das, Navjivan Trust, Ahmedabad, 1973, p. 303.
17. 'Hindu Brahmin Weds Untouchable Leader Forfeiting Her Caste Right to Enter Heaven', *New York Times*, 16 April 1948.
18. Translator's note: The author clearly means Mehr Chand Mahajan, the third chief justice of the Supreme Court of India.
19. *B.R. Ambedkar: Selected Speeches*; Vol. XI (14 November to 26 November 1949); Prasar Bharati, https://prasarbharati.gov.in/whatsnew/whatsnew_653363.pdf, p. 34.
20. Ibid., p. 42.
21. 'Dr Rajendra Prasad' in *Eminent Parliamentarians Monograph Series*, Lok Sabha Secretariat, New Delhi, 1990, available at: https://eparlib.nic.in/bitstream/123456789/58684/1/Eminent_Parliamentarians_Series_Rajendra_Prasad.pdf – p. 170.
22. Dr BAWS, Vol. 21, p. 291.
23. Ibid., Vol. 21, p. 300.
24. Ibid., Vol. 21, pp. 301–02.
25. Actually, it is Article 17 that relates to untouchability, not Article 11.
26. *B.R. Ambedkar: Selected Speeches*; Vol. XI (14 November to 26 November 1949); Publisher: Prasar Bharati, https://prasarbharati.gov.in/whatsnew/whatsnew_653363.pdf, p. 45.
27. Dr BAWS, Vol. 17/III, pp. 404–05.
28. Dr BAWS dates it as 6 June 1950. See p. 406.
29. Dhananjay Keer, *Dr Babasaheb Ambedkar: Life and Mission*, Popular Prakashan, Mumbai, first published: 1954, fifth edition: 2016, p. 422.
30. Dr BAWS, Vol. 17/III, p. 406.
31. Ibid., Vol. 17/III, p. 409.
32. Ibid.
33. Translator's note: Translated from the original Marathi book. However, Dr BAWS, Vol. 17/III, p. 408, quotes Dr B.R. Ambedkar on this matter as follows: '[The Muslims] destroyed the Buddhist idols

and killed the *bhikkus*. They mistook the great Nalanda University as the fort of [the] Buddhists and killed a large number of monks thinking they were soldiers. The few *bhikkus* who escaped an [sic] onslaught fled away to the neighbouring countries like Nepal, Tibet and China.'

34. *Dr Babasaheb Ambedkar: Writings and Speeches*, Vol. 18, Part 3, Govt. of Maharashtra, 2002.
35. Dr BAWS, Vol. 14, p. 283.
36. Ibid., Vol. 14, p. 270: 'The question that I want to ask of honourable Members is this: are you going to have the law of the 90% of the people as the general law of this country, or are you going to have the law of the 10% of the people being imposed upon the 90%?'
37. Ibid., Vol. 14, p. 270: '. . . [W]hat has happened in this country is that somehow, unfortunately, unnoticed, unconsciously, custom has been allowed to trample upon the text of the *shastras* which were all in favour of the right sort of marital relations.'
38. Ibid., Vol. 14, p. 255: 'There is never any obligation cast upon this House for circulating any bill for publication before the House can take the matter into consideration.'
39. Ibid., Vol. 14, p. 255: 'My second submission is . . . this that we have deliberately confined the operation of this Bill to the provinces of India, and so far as the provinces are concerned, the opinion has been canvassed three times, and I do not think any more purpose would be served by canvassing public opinion for the fourth time. When the occasion comes for the extension of the Bill to the Indian States, no doubt, this Legislature . . . will take care that the wishes and the intentions of the States which have come into the Indian Union will be consulted.'
40. Ibid., Vol. 14, p. 260: 'When a father is disqualified by reason of the fact that he had changed his religion and ceased to be a Hindu, the mother has been given the right to give a boy in adoption.'
41. Ibid., Vol. 14, p. 261: 'A disability has been introduced to the effect that if the widow ceased to be a Hindu, she would also lose the right of giving the boy in adoption.'
42. Ibid., Vol. 14, p. 260: 'Hitherto, there are various forms of adoption . . . Therefore, the Select Committee decided that . . . nobody can make any adoption except in accordance with the provision of this code.'

43. Ibid., Vol. 14, p. 262: 'The power of the Hindu father as a natural guardian of his minor son has been taken away if he renounces the world or ceases to be a Hindu . . . The Committee felt that as this was a Code intended to consolidate the Hindu society . . . it was desirable to impose this condition.'
44. Ibid., Vol. 14, p. 264: 'The original Bill said that the daughter shall get a share equal to half the share of the son . . . The Select Committee . . . increased . . . the share of the daughter in the father's property from one half to one full share.'
45. Ibid., Vol. 14, Part Two, p. 1326.
46. Initials not mentioned in the Marathi original.
47. A social organization established by Dr Ambedkar on 24 September 1924 for safeguarding the interests of the oppressed classes. It is headquartered in Nagpur.
48. Personal collection of Vijay Surwade.
49. Dr BAWS, Vol. 21, p. 372. Letter of 1 May 1952.
50. Ibid., Vol. 21, p. 378. Letter of 14 May 1952.
51. Besides being Dr B.R. Ambedkar's favourite colour, blue was also the colour of the flag of the party floated by Dr Ambedkar's Scheduled Castes Federation of India in 1942.
52. Translator's note: Mentioned in the Marathi original as 'Kambaoora Palace' (transliterated).
53. Translator's note: Spelling uncertain. Transliterated from the original Marathi script.
54. Translator's note: The English original could not be located.
55. See Appendix 3.
56. Translator's note: *The Buddha and His Dhamma: A Critical Edition*, published by Oxford University Press, 2011, carries the revised preface Mrs Ambedkar refers to. Page xxvii: 'The successful rekindling of this dying flame is due to the medical skill of my wife and Dr Malvankar. They alone have helped me to complete the work.'
57. *Dr. Babasaheb Ambedkar: Writings and Speeches*; Vol. 21, Govt. of Maharashtra, 2006, p. 434.
58. *Prabuddha Bharat*, Year 1, Issue 15, 2 June 1956.
59. Translator's note: Upwards of forty volumes have been published till date.
60. Translator's note: As part of the project to publish Dr B.R. Ambedkar's complete works, the Government of Maharashtra brought out his yet

unpublished work *Riddles in Hinduism* in 1987. This triggered a clash between those who wanted the book to be banned because it hurt Hindu sentiment and those who supported its publication. Around 5 lakh followers of Ambedkar took to the streets of Mumbai on 5 February 1988 in support of the book.

61. See Appendix 3.
62. Ranganath Divakar.
63. One among the Saptarshi, the seven sages, who form the Great Bear Constellation. Notorious for his short temper.
64. Saint and mystic poet of the fifteenth century.
65. See note 56.
66. Translator's note: Compare with the preface published in *The Buddha and His Dhamma*: A Critical Edition; OUP, 2011, pp. xxv to xxviii. They are not altogether identical.
67. A copy of this document is in the personal collection of Vijay Surwade.
68. Dhananjay Keer, *Dr Babasaheb Ambedkar*, Popular Prakashan, Mumbai, first edition 1966, fourth improved edition 2006, p. 576.
69. Ibid., p. 570.
70. *Parimal*, pp. 19–20.
71. Ibid., p. 51.
72. *Dr Ambedkar Jeevan Katha*, Dr Ambedkar Dvitiya Punyatithi ('Dr Ambedkar's Life Story', Dr Ambedkar's Second Anniversary); T.M. Salve, pp. 72–74.
73. *Prabuddha Bharat*, 28 December 1957
74. Ibid.
75. Ibid.
76. Ibid.
77. Ibid.
78. Ibid.
79. Based on Mr Surwade's personal experiences and conversations.
80. Introduction, *Dr Ambedkaranchya Sahavaasaat*, Savita Ambedkar.
81. Nanak Chand Rattu, *Last Few Years of Dr. Ambedkar*, Amrit Publishing House, New Delhi, 1997, p. 201.
82. Nanak Chand Rattu, *Reminiscences of Dr. Ambedkar*, Falcon Books, New Delhi, pp. 63–64.